PRAISE FOR *1941: THE GREATEST YEAR IN SPORTS*

"Outstanding . . . I loved the book."

—Michael Rosenberg, *Detroit Free Press*

"For sports buffs of all stripes."

—*Morning News*

"A masterful recreation [of 1941]."

—FoxSports.com

"Strong writing and diligent research . . . a worthwhile read."

—*Newsday*

"The best sports moments usually occur while the time clock is clicking inexorably toward zero. Bottom of the ninth. The fifteenth round. The eighteenth hole. Five . . . four . . . three . . . two . . . one . . . In 1941, all of the fun and all of the games were played out with the sounds of jackboots marching across Europe in the background, louder and louder, an inevitable sad end on the horizon. The frenzy to finish, do, accomplish before World War II arrived brought out magic in stadiums, arenas, and racetracks across America. There never has been another sports year like 1941. There never will be. Mike Vaccaro lets us see, feel, touch it all. He recreates an extraordinary period, with extraordinary drama. Very nice work."

—Leigh Montville, *New York Times*
bestselling author of *The Big Bam* and *Ted Williams*

"Vaccaro recreates the excitement surrounding each of these sporting milestones as he places them in the ever-more-dangerous world of 1941. Carefully researched and entertainingly written sports history."

—*Booklist*

1941

THE GREATEST YEAR IN SPORTS

Also by Mike Vaccaro

EMPERORS AND IDIOTS

1941

THE GREATEST YEAR IN SPORTS

*Two Baseball Legends, Two Boxing Champs, and the Unstoppable
Thoroughbred Who Made History in the Shadow of War*

MIKE VACCARO

BROADWAY BOOKS

New York

Copyright © 2007 by Mike Vaccaro

All Rights Reserved

A hardcover edition of this book was originally published in 2007
by Doubleday.

Published in the United States by Broadway Books,
an imprint of The Doubleday Publishing Group,
a division of Random House, Inc., New York.
www.broadwaybooks.com

BROADWAY BOOKS and its logo, a letter B bisected on the diagonal, are
trademarks of Random House, Inc.

Library of Congress Cataloging-in-Publication Data
Vaccaro, Mike.
1941—the greatest year in sports : two baseball legends, two boxing
champs, and the unstoppable thoroughbred who made history in the
shadow of war / Mike Vaccaro.
    p.   cm.
Includes index.
1. Sports—United States—Sociological aspects. 2. Baseball—United
States—History. 3. Boxing—United States—History. 4. Horse racing—
United States—History. 5. Nationalism and sports—United States—
History. I. Title.
GV706.5.V33 2007
796.0973'09044—dc22
             2006102417

ISBN 978-0-7679-2416-0

PRINTED IN THE UNITED STATES OF AMERICA

1 3 5 7 9 10 8 6 4 2

First Paperback Edition

For Leigh Hursey Vaccaro, the why and wherefore I'm alive. Of all the news joints in all the towns in all the world, she walked into mine. Thank goodness.

CONTENTS

1941

THE GREATEST YEAR IN SPORTS

INTRODUCTION

Joe Louis, left, wears his customary dead pan, as he and Billy Conn prepare to leave the ring after their fight at the Polo Grounds June 18. In the center is Johnny Ray, Conn's manager.

He was a young man in a hurry in those first weeks of 1941, twenty-three years old, ambitious, obsessed with chasing the American dream in the most American way possible, by playing the blissfully democratic game of baseball.

"You could be a regular guy like me," Phil Rizzuto would explain, "and you could still make a living at it, if you were good enough, if you worked hard enough."

Rizzuto stood only five feet, five inches tall, weighed but 155 pounds, and he'd grown up a Dodgers fan in Ridgewood, Brooklyn. For years he'd dreamed of playing in his home borough until the day in 1936 when he showed up at Ebbets Field for a tryout and was crushed by a dour, disapproving Dodgers manager who couldn't believe this runt of a shortstop had dared to fancy himself a would-be, could-be big-leaguer.

"Son," the manager said, "you can stay and watch the game, but after that you'd better run home and get a shoeshine box."

There was a small part of Phil Rizzuto that never forgave Casey Stengel for that dismissal, but a more important piece never forgot it, either. Hunger was a powerful motivator, and even as economic forecasts grew brighter as the 1930s melded into the 1940s, young men everywhere shared a common fuel: the eagerness, the *necessity*, to find a better place for themselves, and for their families. For Rizzuto, that meant trying to add to the twenty-dollar weekly salary that his father took home each week as a waterfront watchman. For his future teammate with the Yankees, Joe

DiMaggio, and a future rival, Ted Williams, it meant evading the erratic prospects of day-work employment in the fishing basins of Northern California and the dull gray warehouses of Southern California. For a truculent pug from Pittsburgh named Billy Conn, it meant fleeing the backbreaking death sentence of forty inevitable years in a steel mill, and for the most famous athlete in the world in 1941, Joe Louis, it meant staying exactly where he was, lest the pull of poverty ever suck him back into the vile vortex from which he'd already escaped once.

"All you cared about," Rizzuto said, "was getting ahead. It was all you thought about."

In 1941, however, the world at large eventually caught up to everyone. It reached Rizzuto on the morning of March 6, when he walked into the Yankee clubhouse and discovered a letter in his locker from Public School 68 back home in Ridgewood, where Draft Board Number 284 was headquartered.

"Please advise us," the dispatch began, *"of the address of the local board nearest your home in St. Petersburg in order that we may send them the order of transfer for physical examination."*

Suddenly a curtain had been opened on the world beyond Al Lang Field, the Yankees' spring training headquarters. There was no such thing as hiding your head in the sand in 1941, not if you were an able-bodied male, not with the nation's first-ever peacetime draft going on, and not with the world seemingly crumbling bit by bit, piece by piece, day by day. This was true for Rizzuto, hoping to earn his first promotion to the big leagues. It was true for Hank Greenberg of the Detroit Tigers, the most decorated and highly paid team sports player in the country, whose two Most Valuable Player trophies and hefty salary helped make him the Alex Rodriguez of his baseball generation, but whose low draft number made him just as vulnerable to military service as a Kansas farmer or a Brooklyn apprentice plumber or an aspiring California actor.

The morning papers didn't simply report the news in 1941, they screamed it, and whatever they missed the afternoon papers shouted even louder a few hours later. The same day Rizzuto received his letter, the dailies were stuffed with stories speculating about Yugoslavia's immediate future.

Hitler's army had encircled it, and it seemed the country was only hours away from capitulating, one more trophy for the Fuehrer's mantel. Every day brought something new, something worse, something unspeakable.

"You read the sports section a lot," Rizzuto would say years later, "because you were afraid of what you'd see in the other parts of the paper."

To appreciate how much sports meant in 1941, you must first understand what its landscape looked like. Basketball was a minor-league curiosity, its professionals confined to barnstorming tours and chilly armories, many of its games still contested behind chicken-wire netting, earning its practitioners the derisive nickname of "cagers." Football was king on college campuses, but since the majority of Americans in 1941 had never set foot in a university lecture hall, it was a pastime that thrived detached from most of the nation's urban centers. And pro football was still a nascent phenomenon, played before sporadic pockets of fans, still searching for its niche just fifteen years after boasting such hub cities as Racine, Hammond, and Duluth as members. It didn't pay very well; for much of 1941, Tommy Harmon, who'd won the 1940 Heisman Trophy at Michigan, insisted he wasn't going to play pro ball, opting instead for a more lucrative radio gig in Detroit. Auto racing was mostly a once-a-year carnival act contained at the Indianapolis Motor Speedway. The National Hockey League existed in only four U.S. cities. Golf was a pastime mostly pursued by the fortunate segment of well-to-do citizens who hadn't been decimated by the Depression.

No, in 1941, only three sports truly mattered in the American consciousness. There was baseball, the undisputed king, the game still favored by an overwhelming number of children, one that filled every sandlot and every playground in one incarnation or another. There was boxing, dominated in 1941 by Joe Louis, entering his fourth year as the undisputed heavyweight champion, an African American whose appeal crossed racial and cultural boundaries of every kind—no small feat in a nation where Jim Crow laws dominated the lower half of its geography, where a "gentleman's agreement" barring men of color from organized baseball still thrived, where even in the army races weren't yet mixed. And there was horse racing, the self-styled "sport of kings," which offered Americans almost everything they could have desired in 1941: wide-open outdoor spaces, cheap admission prices, and the opportunity to leave with their pockets a little fuller than when they'd arrived, thanks to the recent advent of pari-mutuel betting.

People embraced all sports that year in ways they never had before. In March the National Invitation Tournament drew 70,825 college basketball fans over four nights at Madison Square Garden, easily a record. New attendance records were broken at the Kentucky Derby and at the Indianapolis 500. Boxing nights in Philadelphia, Washington, D.C., St. Louis, Denver, and Baltimore all drew record single-night crowds. In the spring, over 155,000 people flocked to St. Paul, Minnesota, to watch the American Bowling Congress tournament. A brash young Californian named Bobby Riggs electrified Forest Hills by winning the U.S. Open, the only one of tennis's four Grand Slam events held in 1941 because of more strident matters occupying the sites of Wimbledon, the French Open, and the Australian Open. Even though tennis was still mostly a country-club game, unprecedented crowds made their way to the West Side Tennis Club.

Still, 1941 was defined, and will always be defined, by four sporting achievements that energized a nervous nation on the brink, that provided sustenance to the American need to seek and worship secular idols. Soon enough, that void would be filled by soldiers fighting the bloodiest conflict the world had yet seen, and sports would once again seem hopelessly trivial by comparison. But that was for another day. For now, for 1941, the nation would hand itself over to sports, and to four very different entities that would carry it through.

There was DiMaggio, who even in 1941, as a twenty-six-year-old, carried himself regally, who was married to the beautiful actress Dorothy Arnold and lived the life of a millionaire, even though he would pull down barely $35,000 that year (about $200,000 in 2006 dollars). At the start of 1941, DiMaggio was the logical heir to the grand Yankee legacy started by Babe Ruth and continued through Lou Gehrig, despite whispers that he didn't always devote himself as much as he should to his craft.

There was Williams, an impatient twenty-two-year-old third-year player, who, like DiMaggio, didn't report to the early part of spring training, a ploy that was frowned upon in those years (there was still a Depression afflicting most of the country, after all), but was especially discouraged since so many boys making so much less than baseball players were starting to make twenty-one dollars a month as army privates. If Williams heard the scorn, he never let on, probably because he was used to it. He'd welcomed ridicule the previous year by suggesting that he might chuck baseball entirely sooner rather than later and head home to San Diego to become a fireman. Bench jockeys across the American League immediately brought fire helmets to their dugouts in derision, but there wasn't a soul anywhere who could deny the kid's talent for hitting a baseball.

There were two prizefighters, both hailing from hardscrabble backgrounds out of two of America's great industrial cities, one black, one white, headed on a collision course for one night in New York City that people would still be talking about sixty-five years later. Joe Louis was the most famous athlete in the world, heavyweight champion, conqueror of Max Schmeling and patron saint of millions of African Americans who still believed, despite overwhelming evidence to the contrary, that they could be party to the same American Dream to which white folks aspired.

Louis was quiet, even-tempered, mild-mannered, and as 1941 began he was fully engaged in an exhausting tour of monthly bouts against challengers who didn't belong in the same city as he did, much less the same ring. Boxing fans longed for something better than this "bum-of-the-month club," and they thought they had it when Billy Conn was matched with Louis for a June 18 bout at the Polo Grounds in Upper Manhattan.

Conn was then the reigning light-heavyweight champion but had grown bored by the belt, knowing that this division would always be considered the junior varsity to the heavyweights. Of Irish descent, from the East Liberty section of Pittsburgh, Conn never stopped yapping. He weighed at least twenty-five pounds less than Louis, and that would've been if they'd tipped the scales after Conn pushed himself away from Thanksgiving dinner and Louis emerged from a two-hour steam bath, but he believed with every ounce of his Gaelic soul that he knew how to fight Louis. And he said so. Neither man could know just what lay in store for him on the night of June 18; when it was over, neither man would ever be allowed to forget what had happened. And neither would ever want to.

And there was maybe the grandest pure athlete of all of these, one who'd not yet reached his third birthday when 1941 dawned, but one whose feats would be seen by more people, in more places, with more mouths set agape and more hearts set racing, and who would earn more American dollars, not incidentally, than all the others combined. This was Whirlaway, the Thoroughbred racehorse who in early spring was considered one of 1941's greatest disappointments, yet by late summer would be one of its lasting icons. In 1941, if you'd asked almost any American what athlete they would pay to see on any given day, the near-unanimous answer would come quickly and easily: I want to see the horse.

In June, Whirlaway would run in the Belmont Stakes, and the Louis-Conn bout would be fought, and DiMaggio's hitting streak would continue to mount, and Williams's quest to become the first man in eleven years to hit .400 would quietly build momentum. And Kaiser Wilhelm II would die in exile in the Netherlands at age eighty-two. And Lou Gehrig, baseball's beloved Iron Horse, would die of amyotrophic lateral sclerosis at age thirty-seven. And Japanese ambassador Kichisaburo Nomura would express a "firm conviction" that war would never break out between his country and the United States, even as high-ranking members of his nation's government and military were plotting to shatter that tenuous peace within six months' time. And word would reach the States that survivors of the sunken American freighter *Robin Moor*—attacked in cold blood by a German U-boat the month before—had been wandering around the Atlantic Ocean for weeks on life boats, the first tangible evidence that the United States was involved in the war, even if it hadn't yet declared as such. And the Nazis would storm across Russian borders, millions of them, in a strategy called Operation Barbarossa that was intended to alter the war's course irrevocably—and wound up doing just that, although not the way Hitler anticipated.

That was just one month. But in truth, they were all like that—the real mingling with the surreal, triumph framed by tragedy, exhilaration tinged with anxiety. One of the war's most significant characters, Gen. Douglas MacArthur, began the year in obscurity, in retirement; by the end, his name would be known by every citizen in every state in the union. Once, while describing the exploits of the beloved football team at his alma mater, West Point, MacArthur tried to explain why sports not only mattered to him, but why they should matter to all men in some small way.

"Upon the fields of friendly strife," he said, "are sown the seeds that on other fields, on other days, will bear the fruits of victory."

Never were MacArthur's words more apparent, or more relevant, than in 1941. This is why.

1

"GOOD-BYE, DEAR, I'LL BE BACK IN A YEAR."

THE DRAFT HOVERS OVER EVERYBODY, EVEN A SLUGGER NAMED HAMMERIN' HANK

———•———

Hank Greenberg enters the Tiger dugout before his final game in 1941, on May 6 against the Yankees. He would hit a pair of home runs in a 7-4 Tigers victory. He was sworn into the Army the next day.

———————●———————

The cops knew early on that they were in for a long night. There were 1,489 of them on duty, most of them in uniform, most of them drawing overtime, all of them startled at the steady stream of humanity pouring into the ten square blocks bracketing Forty-second and Forty-ninth Streets, Fifth and Eighth Avenues. This was Times Square, New York City, and on this thirty-first day of December, 1940, it was suddenly home to over a million temporary citizens, as many human beings as had ever seen fit to gather at one place in the city's history. It had been a gray Tuesday afternoon, unseasonably warm, and now the day had given way to a clear, starless night, 35 degrees, perfect for revelry, perfect for noisemaking, perfect for stealing sips from pocket-sized flasks, perfect for a grand old party. Perfect for a New Year's Eve celebration that many sensed they would need to keep with them for a long, long time, for who knew when they would be allowed to be this happy, this carefree, this uninhibited, ever again?

"It's bigger, better, and more joyful than ever," Louis F. Costuma, the New York Police Department's chief inspector, said as he watched the swelling crowds grow from makeshift police headquarters on Forty-sixth Street and Duffy Square.

Standing next to Costuma, cupping a Camel cigarette, Deputy Inspector John J. DeMartino nodded and pointed at the eclectic array of faces. People had been coming to Times Square to ring in the New Year since 1904. Only once, on December 31, 1918, less than two months after Armistice Day, had there ever been a turnout that approached what was happening now. "Over a million," he said. "Definitely."

"It's bigger than ever before," Costuma said, checking his watch, marveling that it was still over two hours before midnight, wondering how many more tens of thousands might still be on their way, and where they'd possibly find room to stand—or breathe. "We never had to shut down the streets so early before."

New York, like the rest of America, was in the mood to celebrate on this last night of 1940. And why not? After a desperate decade of bleak times and bleaker prospects, the economy was finally picking up, and though 9 million people remained out of work, more and more regular folks finally had spending money in their pockets again. To commemorate this promising prosperity, the nation had just delivered Franklin Delano Roosevelt back to the White House for an unprecedented third term, sweeping him home with 55 percent of the popular vote. Just a week earlier, a Gallup poll had listed the president's approval rating at a robust 79 percent. Eight years earlier, Roosevelt's favorite song on his path to Washington had been "Happy Days Are Here Again," and finally they truly seemed to be. Employment was up. Breadlines were vanishing. Best of all, in his Christmas address Roosevelt had restated a pledge that had become his campaign cornerstone: At all reasonable cost, the United States would refrain from joining the fighting that had already begun to ruin the European continent for the second time in as many generations.

But even Roosevelt couldn't completely ignore one gnawing reality.

"It is clear," he said, "that Nazi Germany will not stop until it achieves complete world domination, or until they are destroyed in that pursuit. We pray to Almighty God for the latter."

In New York City, these truths were only slightly tempered by the joy of the season. Millions of its citizens were fully aware of just how grave the situation had become across the Atlantic, because so many of them still had close ties to relatives living through the growing, stultifying nightmare. They may have come to Times Square this night to celebrate, yes, but they also arrived understanding that all the laughter and buoyancy of another Auld Lang Syne couldn't possibly halt the miserable momentum advancing elsewhere on the planet. The president could pledge peace and promise pacifism, but what man could truly guarantee tranquility? Too many wars had been fought, too many war memorials built, too many cemeteries filled, and too many lessons forgotten to forge a peace of permanent penitence in too many souls.

All you had to do was see how other nations were greeting the dawning of 1941 if you wanted a cold shot of perspective with a chaser of gloom. In Berlin and in Rome, cornerstones of the Axis, blackouts curtailed whatever festivities might otherwise have been planned, and mandatory curfews with shoot-on-sight consequences discouraged anyone from breaking these solemn codes. In France—which had entered 1940 a free nation and exited it a divided state, with most of its landmass occupied by German invaders and over 2 million of its citizens rotting in prison and detainment camps—there was no place for celebrating and even less cause for it. Early on New Year's morning, in Vichy, capital of the unoccupied country, Marshal Henri Philippe Pétain would issue a somber forecast for the coming year: "We will go hungry in 1941."

In London, hundreds of smoldering buildings offered silent testimony to months of German air raids. Smoke still filtered into the streets. Thousands of families mourned loved ones who'd been unfortunate enough to be in the wrong place when the bombs had fallen. Still, at midnight, Big Ben defiantly rang out twelve times, echoing through a deserted Parliament Square, and on the final peal a voice cried out "Hooray!" followed by another, in a distinctly Cockney accent, that bellowed: "An' London's still 'ere!" Underneath Piccadilly Circus, some Londoners had gathered in a "tube" stop to toast the New Year and say good riddance to the old one, forcing a joyful, if halfhearted, respite from their daily melancholy.

The source of so much of this dimness had wasted little time delivering his first message of the New Year, addressing his troops at dawn while much of Europe was still engaged in fitful spasms of sleep.

"This year, 1941, will bring consummation of the greatest victory in our history," Adolf Hitler told his soldiers. "This war must be continued as a result of the democratic warmongers and the Jewish capitalists. The representatives of a broken world believe they may achieve in 1941 what they were unable to do in 1940. We are ready and armed as never before."

Then, in a none-too-subtle swipe at his declared *and* undeclared enemies, the Reichsfuehrer offered a sinister New Year's wish for the world's remaining free peoples: "The stupidity of rulers in the plutocratic democracies rejected all methods and measures that could put brakes on the limitless egoism of the individual in front of the life of all. Every person that dines off the democracies will die with them. When Churchill and his international democratic comrades declare that they are defending their world, and that their world cannot exist beside ours, then that is their own misfortune."

Less heralded, but just as ominous, was this cheery salutation from Yosuke Matsuoka, foreign minister of Japan, a nation just starting to flex its international muscle thanks to a recently signed Tripartite Pact with Germany and Italy and its emerging dominance in the Asiatic sphere: "I pray that God and all godfearing people will cooperate with me in saving 1941 from being the first year of the decline and fall of modern civilization. It's my fervent desire that 1941 be the first year of a world revival containing a new order. This is the dream of the Japanese nation, and it is the spirit with which the alliance with Germany and Italy was conceived."

The world was a much larger place in those final hours of 1940 than it would be within even a few short years, but not so vast that these snapshots couldn't touch the American cousins sitting on the opposite shores of two oceans. Still, if for only one night, folks tried to set aside the echoing madness surrounding them in order to usher in the New Year in the traditional manner—even though the supply of champagne was terribly short, limited by the German invasion of France which, in the words of one restaurateur, "gave domestic wines a great break." Scotch, however, was still coming into American ports in barrel quantities, defying Nazi submarines, proof that some vices were worth dying for. Those who were able to toast the New Year with bubbly did so with bottles ordered in bulk shortly after the Nazis crossed France's borders, but before they seized the vineyards and started sending all the remaining champagne to Germany.

By midnight, Times Square was a twitching tinderbox of color and light. An electrician named Thomas Ward engineered the sixty-foot drop of the luminous three-hundred-pound ball that would descend from the top of the Times Tower, a task he had fulfilled for twenty-seven consecutive years, one that never failed to energize him.

"For a minute every year," Ward said, "I'm the most popular man in New York."

This year was no different. In a noisy eyeblink, 1940 morphed into 1941, and in a flash the square was covered with millions of slivers of paper, lit up with thousands of crackling flashbulbs, filled with a million voices wistfully wishing, in song, that old acquaintances never be forgotten.

Prominent among the partyers were thousands of soldiers and sailors, in town on leave, most of them greeted by civilians with handshakes and backslaps. This was an increasingly common sight throughout the country, as thousands of young men between the ages of 21 and 35 had been thrust into military service thanks to the nation's first-ever peacetime draft. In New York City alone there was a quota of 66,651 men, a sizable segment of the 789,000 who would be called up before this first phase of the draft was completed.

One of the men who filled both rations was Ben Kish, a former All-American football player at the University of Pittsburgh and presently a member of the Brooklyn Dodgers of the National Football League, who'd received word earlier on New Year's Eve that the army expected him to report for duty no later than January 16.

"I'm used to taking orders from the coach, so I guess I will be able to bear up under army discipline," Kish said. The news item went little-noted at the time, especially in a crush of New Year's stories focusing on the Rose Bowl, the Sugar Bowl, the Cotton Bowl, and the Orange Bowl, but Kish thus became one of the first professional athletes summoned to active duty, even if his name wasn't terribly well known outside the borough of Brooklyn.

He wouldn't be alone on that list for long.

———————— • ————————

Years later, Hank Greenberg would rue his carelessness and shake his head at how haphazardly he'd allowed his life to be folded inside out. In the fall of 1940, Greenberg stood alone at the top of the American sporting pantheon, the highest-paid baseball player in the game, pulling down $50,000, the most money ever earned by anyone not named Babe Ruth. He was coming off a splendid season in which he'd hit .340 with 41 home runs and 150 runs batted in, would soon earn his second American League Most Valuable Player plaque, and had just led the Detroit Tigers to within one win of a championship before losing the World Series to the Cincinnati Reds. He was also an unrivaled hero to millions of youths, particularly Jewish kids who'd marveled at his resolve in sitting out High Holy Days during much of his career. What's more, Greenberg was just entering his prime. He wouldn't turn thirty until New Year's Day, and he'd already hit 247 career home runs, giving him at least a reasonable chance to surpass Babe Ruth's career record of 714 lifetime.

He was the Alex Rodriguez of his time, a two-time MVP by age twenty-nine, a fearsome slugger who still maintained a hefty batting average, an above-average fielder, drawing the sport's fattest paycheck.

"I was sitting on top of the world," Greenberg recalled some forty years later.

Yet he was about to make a terribly foolish decision, though he had no way of knowing it. On October 8 the Tigers dropped a devastating 2-1 decision to the Reds in the seventh game of the World Series at Cincinnati's Crosley Field. Afterward, Greenberg spent a few days settling his affairs before meeting his younger brother Joe, himself a minor league ballplayer. Together, the brothers Greenberg would set out in Hank's car for their parents' modest home in the Bronx, which both still listed as their primary residence. They left Michigan early in the morning of Wednesday, October 16, and knew that before they reached their final destination they'd have to make an important pit stop. For October 16 had been looming for weeks as an unofficial national holiday, replete with capital letters:

National Registration Day.

For the first time, the United States was about to conduct a peacetime military conscription. President Roosevelt had quietly set the groundwork for this the previous May, when he'd asked Congress to appropriate $2.5 billion to rebuild the nation's sagging military infrastructure as global events began turning darker and gloomier by the day. By late summer the war in Europe had grown increasingly dreary, and the logic in maintaining an all-volunteer army with the world going to seed no longer appealed, or applied. So on September 6, the Burke-Wadsworth Bill became the Selective Training and Service Act of 1940, and October 16 was designated as the day that each of the nation's 16 million men between the ages of 21 and 35 would be required to formally enter his name in a draft lottery. Failure to do so would incur five years in prison and a $10,000 fine, and there were no exemptions: married men, fathers of nine, even aliens who weren't yet American citizens had to register. Everyone.

That included the most feared slugger on the planet.

The Greenbergs were about eight hours into their trip when they pulled off the road to find a registration center. They had just reached Geneva, a small town in western New York, near Rochester, so they pulled off U.S. 20 and found a small schoolhouse where men had been lining up all day to sign in. Greenberg's appearance caused a brief ripple. Hank and Joe were both handed the necessary forms.

For his address, Joe wrote in "663 Crotona Park North, Bronx, New York," the Greenberg family homestead.

For his, Hank wrote in "400 Bagley, Detroit, Michigan." That was the location of the Detroit Leland Hotel, which is where Greenberg stayed during the baseball season.

"I don't know what prevailed upon me to list my residence as Detroit," Greenberg would lament, years later, in his autobiography. "Maybe somehow I thought it would keep me from being drafted too soon."

If so, the strategy backfired because the exact opposite happened. When Henry L. Stimson, Roosevelt's secretary of war, wrapped a blindfold around his eyes on October 29 and plucked the first capsule from a fishbowl, 16 million men around the country waited to see when their serial number would emerge, and where they would stand on the list of imminent inductees. As each pod was opened, and each slip of light cardboard was posted on a blackboard and photographed for the National Archives, another few thousand men saw their lives instantly—and in some cases, irretrievably—altered. Greenberg drew a reasonably low number of 621 (thanks to deferments and geographic quotas, though there were some 8,500 serial numbers selected, only those with numbers under 500 were likely to be immediately called) and if he'd been registered in New York City, with its dense population, he would almost certainly have avoided an early call-up even though, as a single man with no dependents, he was all but certain to be classified 1-A. But not only had he registered in Michigan, which had fewer men than New York overall to fill its quotas, he'd picked an especially unfortunate precinct in Detroit, packed mostly with transients and hotel visitors and very few actual residents. Instead of getting a pass until 1942 at the earliest, it soon became very clear that Hank Greenberg might not even make it out of 1941 spring training before having to trade his $50,000 annual salary for the $21 monthly stipend provided a buck private.

"There was no arguing with the law," Greenberg said. "When you were called, you went, and it didn't matter how famous you were. In fact, the more famous you were, the more attention was paid to you. Even if you'd had a good reason to seek a deferment, people didn't want to hear about it. They wanted you to serve, the same as their sons and brothers and cousins. No exceptions."

The actor Jimmy Stewart was the first to experience the whispers and the rumors that would instantly surround a famous name that didn't immediately fall in and eagerly swap wingtips for dog tags, no matter the circumstances. Stewart had become a superstar in 1939 thanks to *Mr. Smith Goes to Washington*, and his acting legacy would be forever solidified early in 1941 when he earned an Academy Award for best actor for his work in *The Philadelphia Story*, the number-one movie of 1940. Still, on February 1, when it was announced that Stewart would be granted a six-month occupational deferment, the snickering began at once.

Stewart was helped neither by his $1,500-a-week studio salary, which incurred instant resentment, nor by Maj. E. J. Plato, the draft coordinator for Southern California, who said Stewart's work in pictures "justifies postponement of his being called into a year of training." In truth, Stewart was initially turned down for service because he weighed only 143 pounds, five fewer than the army minimum, and it was a ruling Stewart fought to overturn from the start, even as cynics had begun besmirching his name, and even as Stewart began religiously guzzling milkshakes to try and add the necessary weight. The furor wouldn't cease until March 22, when a slightly beefed-up Stewart boarded a Hollywood streetcar bound for Fort MacArthur and was greeted by a Col. John Robinson, who said for the cameras: "We're glad to have you in the army." Stewart replied, rather bashfully, "Thanks. I'm glad to be here. I expect to get a lot out of it."

As Greenberg would soon discover, people were keeping score as 1940 gave way to 1941. The draft was still far more of an inconvenience than a frightening threat to anyone's health, and the public faithfully subscribed to the belief that if their own anonymous existences could be upended, so could lives whose every detail was preserved on the pages of *Variety* or

The Sporting News. If your number came up, you weren't concerned that someone would be shooting at you as much as that your life would be disturbed, your career interrupted, your entire subsistence placed on hold for the 365 days of service required by the Service Act. Soon, Tin Pan Alley songwriter Mack Kay penned a ditty that kept people humming for most of the year:

> *Good bye dear, I'll be back in a year*
> *'Cause I'm in the Army now.*
> *They took my number right out of a hat*
> *And there's nothing a guy can do about that.*

There was nothing Greenberg could do now but shrug his shoulders, accept the inevitable, and fire off a series of quotes that all said essentially the same thing: "I'm ready to go when I'm called." Such was life in the early days of 1941. He kept in shape by playing handball and squash near his parents' home in the Bronx. He looked forward to spending a long vacation in Honolulu. On January 15 a selective service official named W. H. Wells, chief clerk of Detroit Draft Board Number 23, was quoted in newspapers around the country saying, "Greenberg will get a draft questionnaire within two or three weeks. If the number of draftees into the army continues at the present rate, he probably will be called sometime in May and hardly later than June 1."

Greenberg was not alone. In fact, if the draft asserted one thing, it was its impartial blind eye to reputation, income, or surname. On January 22, Winthrop Rockefeller, scion of one of America's most celebrated clans, stepped out of his apartment at 24 West Fifty-fifth Street and into a taxicab waiting to ferry him uptown, to 125th Street, where he was quickly processed, transformed into Private Rockefeller, serial number 32-002-756, and sent off to Fort Dix. On April 16, William McChesney Martin, thirty-four-year-old president of the New York Stock Exchange, dubbed the "Boy Wonder of Wall Street" and one of the nation's leading economic minds, left his $48,000-a-year job to join Company B of the 39th Training Battalion at Camp Craft, South Carolina, departing with an observation that was music to the public's ears: "Naturally, all of us who are subject to this law must expect inconveniences, but I am sure many others have been more adversely affected than I."

It wasn't long before sports started feeling the draining impact of the draft's detached sword, too. On January 9, professional golfer Ed "Porky" Oliver was getting set to plant his tee in the ground on the tenth hole at Sequoyah Country Club in Northern California, where he was competing in the first round of the $5,000 Oakland Open. Oliver was one of the sport's most popular figures, garrulous and gabby, 240 pounds and twenty-four years old. A year earlier he had nearly won the U.S. Open, finishing in a three-way tie for the lead before being disqualified for the playoff for starting his round fifteen minutes early. Oliver had just completed his front nine by carding a birdie 3 on the ninth hole and was feeling splendid about his chances when a messenger boy clutching a telegram elbowed his way through the gallery and onto a tee box, informing Oliver he had six days to report to his local draft board in Wilmington, Delaware.

"I thought I was below par on that one," Oliver quipped, referring to his draft number, drawing gales of laughter from the spectators. He'd have to drive home immediately to beat the deadline, so he removed his tee from the ground, shook hands with playing partners Johnny Revolta and Earl Fry, and told them, "I'll see you fellows later. I've got to be going." After driving nonstop for three thousand miles and showing up bleary-eyed at the draft board as ordered on the fifteenth, Oliver discovered there had been a miscommunication: He hadn't been called, just placed on the reserve list. "Guess I'll go back to work now," he announced, and two weeks later he won the Western Open in Phoenix and the thousand-dollar first prize that went along with it.

Oliver hoped to put off his draft call until fall, so he could sock away his golf earnings for his parents, but his luck finally ran out on March 3 when, after he had already qualified for the semifinals of the big-money Four-Ball Championship in Coral Gables, Florida, another messenger appeared bearing another telegram, and this time there was no mistake. One more time Oliver withdrew his name (and forfeited the chance to win another couple of grand), piled into his Chevrolet, and declared, "I'm the fittest two-forty anyone's ever been. Tell Uncle Sam he can write me an IOU for the tournament winnings I'm leaving on the table."

Professional baseball wore the largest target because of its status as the nation's unofficial pastime and its employment of thousands of draft-eligible men. Whenever a feature story was prepared about a ballplayer as they turned up in spring training in 1941, that player's draft status was mentioned before anything else, whether he was Bob Feller (likely to last until fall) or Phil Rizzuto (deferred thanks to his family's dependence on his baseball income) or Joe DiMaggio (deferred due to his pending fatherhood) or Ted Williams (single, low number, good health, fifty-fifty to make it through the summer).

Every ballplayer with a vulnerable draft number crossed cautiously through the same gauntlet. There was Morrie Arnovich, a serviceable player with the New York Giants who was reclassified from 1-A to 1-B thanks to a "dental deficiency," which he explained thusly: "I have been wearing partial upper and lower dental plates for the last fifteen years as the result of losing several teeth in basketball." For the rest of the season, bench jockeys up and down the National League rode him relentlessly for that.

There was Johnny Rigney, a fine right-handed pitcher for the Chicago White Sox who, on June 10, was granted his sixty-day deferment just ten days before his scheduled induction. The next day, Paul Armstrong, Illinois director of the Selective Service Act, protested that the deferment showed favoritism for "high-salaried people" (as Rigney pulled in the princely sum of eight thousand dollars per year) and demanded an appeal, suggesting that President Roosevelt himself should issue the ruling. But a perforated eardrum made the issue moot, and he was reclassified 4-F. "Frankly," Rigney said, "I'm disappointed. I was looking forward to serving in the army."

Hugh Mulcahy wasn't so fortunate but, then, Mulcahy was used to bad luck. It was Mulcahy's fate that he should play with the Philadelphia Phillies, the most woeful team in the major leagues, and so not only would he become an incongruous oddity in 1940—earning a spot on the National League All-Star team during a season in which he would lead the league in losses with twenty-two—but he would also earn one of the most unfortunate nicknames in baseball history: "Losing Pitcher." In the spring of 1941, though, nobody much cared that Mulcahy's career record sat at an unsightly 42-82. No, baseball was searching for its current generation's version of Hank Gowdy, who twenty-four years earlier was a fairly pedestrian catcher and first baseman for the Boston Braves but gained instant and lasting fame when, on June 1, 1917, he became the first active ballplayer to enlist in the service for the Great War, where he carried the colors for the Fighting 42nd, the famed "Rainbow Division," and endured some of the most vicious trench fighting of the war.

Gowdy's name hovered over every ballplayer who pondered deferment until March 10, when Mulcahy reported to Camp Edwards, on Cape Cod, and became the first major leaguer to officially swap flannels for khakis. Before reporting, Mulcahy wired Phillies president Gerald Nugent with these philosophical parting words: "I'll do my pitching for Uncle Sam this year but I wish I could be with you and wish you the best of luck."

Losing Pitcher had earned his nation's gratitude.

It wouldn't be quite so easy for the reigning MVP.

———————●———————

The newspaper photograph captures what was probably the last completely carefree moment of Henry Benjamin Greenberg's life. The image of the slugger at rest, at ease in paradise, had been taken only the day before, on the beach at Waikiki. He is smiling, with a drink in one hand, flanked by friends both male and female. He is clearly enjoying the spoils of a young, wealthy, successful life and doesn't seem to have a worry in the world, probably because he had yet to be told of the furor brewing six thousand miles to the east.

On the same day the picture appeared in hundreds of newspapers across America, a very different kind of story broke on the front page of the February 21 edition of the *Detroit Free Press,* replete with blaring headline: GREENBERG ASKS FOR DEFERMENT OF DRAFT CALL.

According to the newspaper, in Greenberg's draft questionnaire received by Board 23, there was a request made for deferment as a "necessary man." This, under the Selective Service Act, was defined as one who either "cannot be replaced satisfactorily because of a shortage of persons with his qualifications or skill in a particular activity" or one whose civilian activities "are contributing to the national health, safety and interest" and whose removal from civilian activity "would cause a material loss of effectiveness in such activity." This provision was supposed to cover small-town doctors, for instance, without whom entire rural counties would suffer, or certain business leaders whose companies provided small communities with most of their employment opportunities. While most would agree that there was a shortage of civilians who had the skill to hit forty home runs against big-league pitching, this situation didn't necessarily reflect the spirit of the law.

Still, Greenberg had done nothing wrong. Each of the 16 million men

who filled out a draft questionnaire in 1941 was encouraged to list potential reasons for deferment or reclassification. Such opinions were supposed
to be kept in strict confidence. So Greenberg was completely unprepared
for what he was about to walk into. When his ship, the *Mariposa,* docked
in California, a fleet of news reporters boarded, descended on his cabin,
knocked on his door, and awakened him. Greenberg, leaning against the
door frame in a bathrobe and wearing a sleepy, awkward smile (dutifully
captured by an Associated Press photographer), provided a stark contrast
to the beaming beach bum. Then the writers started asking how it felt to
be called a draft dodger and a slacker. A VFW post had already condemned
Greenberg, calling for a resolution to boycott Tigers games since Greenberg "turned us from boosters to booers."

"I'm in Class One, ready to be called and I'll go when they call me, and
I will not seek a deferment," he insisted, his fury growing. "I'll go when they
collar me."

When Greenberg arrived at the Tigers' spring headquarters in Lakeland,
Florida, a few weeks later, the question of deferment *still* stalked him, and
he finally snapped with exasperation: "Jesus, you would think I was the
only guy going into the army." Each day brought an unwelcome adventure.
On March 11 he visited Dr. Grover C. Freeman, who administered a physical, and when the doctor asked Greenberg, "Do you know you have flat
feet?" Greenberg quipped, "Of course I do. I've had them my whole life."

The army hadn't known. When it found out, it granted Greenberg precisely the same thing it would give more than 8,000 other would-be
draftees in 1941 who suffered from the same affliction: a 1-B classification
and automatic deferment. But those other 8,000 men didn't have their
names in the papers every day, and didn't earn $50,000 as an athlete who
managed to hit towering home runs in spite of his flat feet. Back home,
Greenberg's draft board overruled Dr. Freeman and arranged another
physical for April 18, the same day as the Tigers' home opener. By now
there was little doubt that Greenberg could show up with both feet ampu-
tated and be classified 1-A. It all moved very quickly after that. Greenberg's
draft order came. His induction ceremony would be held the morning of
May 7.

And his last game for at least a year would be May 6, in Tiger Stadium,
with his hometown team, the Yankees, in attendance. The night before, in
a spirited send-off, Greenberg's teammates and a few guest Yankees had

gathered at Franklin Hills Country Club for a private dinner. Del Baker, the Tigers manager, bid his star an emotional farewell: "Pal, I hope those flat feet of yours are flat enough to send you back to us in a few days." When it was Greenberg's time to talk, he did so dry-eyed and clear-voiced without a whiff of sentiment. He was tired, he was angry, he was hitting .258, and his drop-off had reminded him that turning thirty was sometimes all a ballplayer needed to start heading south—even without the obsessive glare of a nattering nation.

"There's no chance for a reprieve," he said. "Even now, I can hardly realize that I'm about to leave baseball. It's a pretty tough thing to give up. It's almost the only thing I've thought about my whole life."

He would savor every second of his last day on the job, every otherwise mundane rite of a baseball workday: batting practice, infield practice, bullshitting in the clubhouse, jabbering in the dugout. His teammates, who'd presented him with a gold watch the night before, inscribed with all their names, voted him captain for the day and so he took the lineups out to home plate before the game, drawing a warm rain of cheers from the 7,850 in attendance. *Damn,* he said more than once. *I'm going to miss this bad.* Soon enough, he'd remember what he *really* was going to miss. In the second inning, sitting on a 2-and-0 count, he drilled an Ernie Bonham fastball deep into the overhanging upper deck in left field, his first home run of the year. An inning later he crushed another one to almost the exact same spot. The two blasts gave him 249 for his career, and when he strode to the plate for the last time that afternoon, in the bottom of the eighth inning with the Tigers leading 7-4, he found himself craving one last moment.

"Two-fifty would be a nice, round number, wouldn't it?" he joked at the plate, turning to Yankee catcher Bill Dickey.

"Well, we're gonna give you nothing but fastballs here, Hank," Dickey replied in his Arkansas twang. Twice fastballs came straight down the pike. Twice Greenberg missed them. One last time, Dickey said, "Look fastball, Hank." Greenberg said nothing, swung viciously, and popped out meekly. "I don't know if Hank believed me," Dickey said, sadly, years later.

That was it. By early the next morning Greenberg would raise his right hand and take the soldier's oath alongside 301 other recruits and officially become a serial number in the eyes of Uncle Sam, 36-114-611. "I don't want the papers to think I'm a good guy, because I'm not. I think the papers are full of shit," Greenberg railed. "I'll be glad when this day is over. I'll be glad to get in the army. This has been an awful strain." And with that he was off, to Fort Custer in rural Michigan, to basic training with the 5th Division's Anti-Tank Unit, to occasional KP duty and early reveille and softball practice and hours of dull, endless toil.

———————————●———————————

On that very morning of May 7, German air raiders bombed the British port city of Liverpool for the seventh straight day, the House of Commons gave Winston Churchill a vote of confidence by a 447-3 count, American immigration officials began to quietly identify and round up some two hundred German soldiers living illegally within U.S. borders, and from the largest city in Greece, the ancient cradle of civilization, came the wistful news that a street formerly known as Franklin Roosevelt Boulevard was to be renamed Adolf Hitler Boulevard, an item accompanied by this fawning message from Ambrosius Plitas, the mayor of newly conquered Athens, to Hitler: "Expressing the feelings of all the citizens of Athens, I wish to assure you of my deepest gratitude for the irreproachable conduct of the German troops and for the solicitude shown by the German authorities in dealing with the city."

And Hank Greenberg's baseball career came to a grinding halt. While his contemporaries would fill the coming months of 1941 with an astonishing array of accomplishment, Greenberg would be peeling potatoes in military kitchens, learning how to clean his rifle, and killing time in barracks with his fellow draftees, most of whom were ten or eleven years younger than him. In his stead, the call was out for a new national sporting hero, which would soon be answered from a most unlikely place.

2

"GOD GAVE HORSES TAILS FOR A REASON."

THE RISE, FALL, AND REBIRTH OF A HORSE CALLED "MR. LONGTAIL"

Jockey Eddie Arcaro is shown whispering into the ear of Whirlaway during one of their training runs together in May 1941.

Hoofs that beat in record time
Racing rhythm, racing rhyme
Speed that won the crown of crowns
On the course of Churchill Downs
Speed with not a need for thrift
(Eddie, don't let Whirly drift!)

—Tim Cohane, *New York World-Telegram,*
May 9, 1941

———————●———————

It wouldn't have occurred to Ben Jones that people might look askance at what he was about to do. After all, the muck beneath his feet was considered holy ground to just about anyone who might be able to see him, especially on this day, May 3, 1941. In a few hours, eleven Thoroughbred racehorses would be led into starting gates on this very dirt, the most hallowed oval in American racing. A few seconds after that, the stalls would fling open, the sixty-seventh running of the Kentucky Derby would be under way, and the world would officially hear for the first time what the crush of a hundred thousand racing fans gathered in one place at one time sounded like. It was a grand moment for this sport to which fifty-eight-year-old Benjamin Allyn Jones, "Plain Ben" to his friends, had devoted his life as a horse trainer, and it was an even grander opportunity for Jones himself, because he had one hell of a horse running in the race, the kind of colt a trainer sometimes spends his entire life chasing and never finding, not just a once-in-a-lifetime horse but a once-in-everyone's-lifetime horse.

Jones had started out on the bullring tracks of Kansas, Missouri, and Oklahoma more than thirty years earlier, and on the county fair loop, and he'd spent some hard time running third-rate horses in Mexico, too. On those early circuits a trainer had a difficult time even dreaming about winning a race like the Derby; that would be like a slo-pitch beer league softball player fancying himself roaming centerfield for the Yankees then actually winning the batting title to boot. You had to be a tough guy to emerge standing and walking from that life, a hard guy, and you'd better be prepared to settle the occasional negotiation with your fists, if the occasion called for it, as it often did.

"Sometimes," Jones recalled, years later, "we walked the horses twenty miles from one track to the other. It was a tough way to make a living. You had to take broken-down horses and patch them up some way or other and make them win. Two hundred bucks was a juicy purse then, and you seldom got a crack at that kind of money. You had to be crazy about horses, or maybe just crazy, to stick with it."

Now, as Jones blinked away the first sharp rays of morning sunshine, pleased that the storm clouds threatening to imperil the day had vanished, he approached this horse about whom he'd been dreaming his entire adult life. His name was Whirlaway, and he was the product of pristine bloodlines, his sire the former English champion Blenheim II and his dame a sharp filly named Dustwhirl. Whirlaway was a tad on the smallish side, but he had a rich chestnut coat and a tail that Jones purposely kept long and flowing. He'd done this for strategic purposes—the tail regularly distracted other horses, sometimes literally flying in their faces—but hadn't minded a bit when the newspapermen had dubbed the horse "Mr. Longtail" during his wildly successful two-year-old campaign. Jones wasn't one to court attention, and he never went chasing spotlights, but he never ran away from them, either. He was an unmistakable sight at the track, always turned out in coat and tie, always wearing a white Stetson hat. He was bedecked in this very uniform as he hopped off his white pony and walked over to Whirlaway, grabbed his reins, and led him slowly along the Churchill Downs backstretch.

There they stopped. Alone. Together.

And it was there that Ben Jones began speaking softly into Whirlaway's ear. Maybe this would have seemed odd anywhere else in the world, but not at a racetrack, certainly not at Churchill Downs on the first Saturday in May, a holy day of obligation throughout the Commonwealth. The stable-boys ignored them, as did the exercise riders, and the custodians, and the early-arriving concessionaires. Plain Ben talked to all of his horses all of the time. But it was Whirlaway who actually seemed to listen, who actually seemed to *understand*. In later decades Jones might be referred to as a "horse whisperer," a term he probably wouldn't have liked very much, for it implies a mystical relationship when, in truth, the bond this trainer and this horse shared was quite visceral.

"Now look here, old fellow, that's the rail, see?" Jones said, retracting his head a few inches to see if he had his star pupil's attention, his left forefin-ger pointing at the white fence that bordered the track's infield. "Every-body's been talking about how you bear out at the turns and that's why you haven't been winning. Well, you don't want them saying things like that about you, do you? Now take a good look at this. And when you're out there this afternoon keep as close to it as you can."

Jones stepped back. He studied Whirlaway's expression, saw him brush his huge tail slowly, left to right, right to left, left to right.

"Okay, Whirly," he said. "I think we're ready."

Jones really said that. He may even have believed it. But the truth was, he didn't know, and he couldn't know, and it was killing him not to know, because the next few hours would determine not only what kind of year Whirlaway was going to have, but what kind of career, what kind of retire-ment in stud, what kind of legacy, what kind of *life*. A lifetime reduced to two minutes and change on a track. And Jones had filled so many hours, spilled so much blood and toil in training this horse, proffered so much hope and hype and hyperbole, that it was also *his* reputation sitting squarely on the line this day. He had long believed that this undersized, overachieving animal had the talent and the track sense to accomplish some extraordinary things, and if he did, then Ben Jones would ride shot-gun the whole way. It was a marvelous blueprint.

With only one potentially fatal flaw.

Whirlaway was dead in the eyes of most experts. His future was a flat line at best, his present even less encouraging. In the weeks leading up to the Derby, Whirlaway's stock had plummeted to nothing, to worse than

nothing in some sectors. Though he'd been as much as a two-to-one favorite on the day Derby entries were accepted the previous January, this
morning most of the racing cognoscenti had failed to even include Whirlaway in their predictions for win, place, or show. It was true that the early
wagering had been a different story, with many of the railbirds selecting
Whirlaway, but even this was dismissed as sentimental pap. Whirlaway was
a Kentucky horse. His owner, Warren Wright, was a Kentucky gentleman
whose Lexington stable, Calumet Farms, was slowly growing in status and
in reputation. Whirly was also the most famous of all the listed three-year-
olds, and status still counted for something, especially on Derby Day. But
reputation wouldn't win the blanket of roses. Skill would. Savvy would.
Discipline would. Luck would. And in the run-up to the Derby, Whirlaway
had been conspicuously lacking in all four.

The year had started so promisingly. Whirlaway raced sixteen times as a
two-year-old in 1940, an extraordinarily large workload, but he'd handled
it well and was doing his best running toward the end of the season, winning three of his last four starts and banking $77,275, easily the highest to-
tal of his age group. His seven overall wins had included victories in the
Saratoga Special, the Hopeful Stakes, the Breeders Futurity at Keeneland
Park, and the Walden Stakes at Pimlico. He'd already developed a signature
style and a fetching personality; both would make him one of the most
crowd-pleasing Thoroughbreds ever, and both would provide Ben Jones
with a ceaseless supply of sleepless nights thanks to Whirlaway's scatterbrained reluctance to focus, a maddening tendency to bear out on straight-
aways, and an almost incredible ability to make up ground at the very last
instant. None of these traits is terribly surprising in young horses, few of
whom emerge as ready-to-race prodigies. But Whirlaway had displayed
such early aptitude, capturing the attention of the sport's speculators, that
when his three-year-old season got off to a less-than-rousing start, he
quickly fell out of favor.

"Maybe he's a half-wit," someone suggested to Jones sometime in the
winter.

"Maybe so," Jones replied. "But if that's the case, what does that make
me?"

On January 15, Whirlaway officially became the horse to watch for 1941
when John B. Campbell, veteran secretary of the New York Metropolitan
Racetracks, released his annual tabulation, ranking the previous year's

juvenile standouts and providing them with experimental handicap weights. Whirlaway was allotted a "top weight" of 126 pounds, meaning that if a handicap race should be run at that specific moment, the recommendation would be to force Whirlaway to carry between three and twenty more pounds than any other three-year-old horse alive. These rankings were mostly for amusement, since in the Triple Crown races that would ultimately determine the sport's best three-year-old that spring, every colt would carry the same poundage. But they were enough to get the people talking, which was good for the sport, if not necessarily the horse.

When Whirlaway made his 1941 debut in victorious—and typical—fashion, storming back from far off the pace to capture the Coconut Grove Purse at Miami's Hialeah Park Racetrack on February 8, the racing community was instantly electric with expectation, and so were general-interest sports fans. Every day brought word of a fresh batch of baseball players, football players, tennis players, and golfers scooped up by the draft, taken from sports pages that suddenly seemed shriveled and barren. Whirlaway wasn't eligible for the draft, so this was one burgeoning superstar upon whose shoulders a nation could rest its own athletic aspirations without worry.

Ben Jones welcomed the attention, but he also had a nagging sense, and instinctive fear, that something wasn't quite right with his horse. He wouldn't dare share those opinions with the world, of course, because if he was right, the world would find out soon enough. For now, his job was to figure out a way to fix whatever was ailing Whirlaway, because it wasn't just Ben Jones's dreams that would die if he couldn't.

———————————●———————————

His whole life, Warren Wright had admired his father's tenacity, his wisdom, his stubborn belief in right and wrong, and he'd been lucky enough to inherit all of those qualities in addition to the vast fortune the old man had left behind. William Monroe Wright had struck it rich by seizing on a brand-new turn-of-the-century invention, double-acting baking powder, just as it made its way across the sea from Germany, at the very moment it became a must-have product in every American kitchen. Thanks mainly to an inherent knack for marketing (the company slogan, "Baker's Best and Always Pleases," was the "Where's the Beef?" of its day), Wright turned an initial $3,500 investment in Calumet Baking Powder (produced at first in a 400-square-foot office space on Chicago's West Side) into a booming $32 million juggernaut whose centerpiece was a massive 160,000-square-foot factory. Warren Wright studied at his father's knee and was ceded the old man's cunning, his ambition, and his supreme self-confidence.

One of the few areas where father and son differed was in their choice of leisurely avocation. William Wright had fallen in love with Standardbred horses, and with his business thriving, he'd purchased a small patch of land in Libertyville, Illinois, christened it Calumet Farms, chosen "devil red and blue" as its favored colors, and begun breeding and training trotters and pacers. In 1924 he purchased a 407-acre slice of heavenly bluegrass on Versailles Road near Lexington, Kentucky, and moved his operation into the heart of American horse country. Harness racing captured William Wright's imagination even as it puzzled Warren, who enjoyed spending time around the Standardbreds but whose true passion lay in the higher-profile, more stylish, more potentially lucrative—and expensive—Thoroughbred side of the racing game.

But Warren was a dutiful son. Not only had he shrewdly sold the family's entire interest in Calumet Baking Powder to General Foods in March 1929—six months before the stock market crash wrecked so many of their well-heeled contemporaries—but he put aside his own hobbies, devoting himself to helping his father reach the one goal in his life that remained unfulfilled: winning the Hambletonian Classic, the most prestigious race in all of harness racing. So it was that on August 14, 1931, at Good Time Park in upstate Goshen, New York, Calumet Butler, cloaked in devil red and blue and driven by William's friend Dick McMahon, beat five other horses and captured the Hambletonian. But William Wright never knew of his grandest triumph. He'd died earlier that same morning.

On his own now, Warren Wright decided to do exactly what his father would have wanted him to do: follow his own path, chase his own dreams, create his own legacy. He quickly liquidated Calumet's entire stock of 550 trotters with the exception of one horse, Zombrewer, the granddam of Greyhound, maybe the greatest trotter ever born. As Wright filled his sprawling farm with Thoroughbreds, Zombrewer would remain the lone link to Calumet's past life (and in 1941 she lived there still, at age thirty-five), a reminder of simpler times and smaller stakes. Wright, though he still had other business interests, decided to throw himself into Calumet's daily operations, a hands-on boss in a traditionally hands-off business. And just as his father had chased a championship, quite literally to his dying day, Warren Wright, too, became singularly obsessed with one thing: He wanted to win the Kentucky Derby.

He believed he knew the secret to making that dream come true, too. Wright had seen how successful his father's business had become by developing and adhering to a strict formula for production, for distribution, for marketing. The company's excellence had been in its efficiency, and once that was mastered, storekeepers couldn't keep enough product on their shelves. If it could work for baking powder, Wright reasoned, why couldn't it work for Thoroughbred racehorses?

Wright soon discovered the hard answer to that question: A business owner could control every aspect of his company. Micromanagers like the Wrights could expect that the more fingerprints they had on their operation, the more they could guarantee its success. You just couldn't do that with horses, who are far more unpredictable than human employees, and far less concerned with the potential consequences of irritating their employers. Twice in his first years in the game, Warren Wright brought highly regarded horses to Churchill Downs and twice he saw them crash and burn: a filly named Nellie Flag placing fourth in 1935, and a colt named Bull Lea tumbling to eighth in 1938.

"After a while," Wright would say a few years later, "you do start to wonder if maybe things just aren't in the cards for you. In business, there are some companies that make it and some that don't, and sometimes it's hard to distinguish what separates a success from a failure. Only one horse can win the Kentucky Derby every year. A lot of people want to own that horse. Not all of them get to."

As bitter as Bull Lea's failure had been, though, a fateful confluence of serendipity and smarts was about to restore Wright's belief in his mission. A month before Derby Day, on April 2, 1938, Calumet Farms had welcomed a new foal, progeny of the farm's star stud, Blenheim II, and a bay mare named Dustwhirl. Blenheim II had won the 1930 English Derby when he was owned by the Aga Khan, the Muslim spiritual leader and one of the planet's richest men, but with the breezes of war beginning to blow, he'd first withdrawn to France, and then decided to liquidate his stables altogether. Over the howling protests of the British racing establishment, the Aga Khan agreed to sell Blenheim to an American racing syndicate of seven men, with Wright putting up the largest stake, a quarter share of $62,500 that secured him the horse's breeding rights. That was a fortuitous decision. So was his choice to include one of his well-to-do friends, New York philanthropist John Hay Whitney, in the syndicate, a decision that would one day yield extraordinary good fortune.

The new foal was named Whirlaway after his mother, though around the farm he quickly became known as "Whirly," and he was, indeed, a whirling dervish, equal parts mischievous, clumsy, stubborn, and willful. In what would turn out to be a poor crop of Calumet yearlings, this was clearly the colt Calumet would have to count on, but it was immediately evident that it would take a special hand and a special eye to control him.

Wright had precisely the man for the job, too.

Even as he was lamenting Bull Lea's poor showing on Derby Day, Wright couldn't help but notice how splendid the winning horse that day, Lawrin, had looked. His jockey, a Kentucky kid named Eddie Arcaro, had ridden a perfect race, but as Arcaro would later admit, "A horse that's trained this well doesn't need any help, he can do it all by himself if he has to." That was all the endorsement Wright needed to hear about the training skills of Ben Jones. A few weeks later Wright offered to double Jones's salary if he'd move to Kentucky, agreed to hire the trainer's son as an assistant, and promised to stay the hell out of Plain Ben's way—which proved to be the hardest part of the contract for Wright to fulfill. But he would. He'd have to. Warren Wright was on a mission, sitting in the owner's box.

And so was Benjamin Allyn Jones, after all those years of training all of those fifth-rate horses, charged now with the simple task of winning the most famous horse race of all.

———————●———————

From the start of the 1941 racing season, it was clear that Whirlaway possessed an unmistakable charisma that would draw even casual fans to the racetracks of Florida and Kentucky and New York and New England, a prospect that thrilled the sport's governors. Jones sometimes muttered that it might eventually kill him to keep watching Whirly swing out wide in turns—sometimes it would take Whirlaway two hundred yards to cover a hundred-yard straightaway, yet he was *still* more likely than not to overpower the field—but it was precisely that swashbuckling flair that lifted fans out of their seats as he galloped toward a finish line. He looked the part of a star, too. When Whirlaway was at top speed, his tail seemed to wave farewell to the other competitors in the field, and his mane was left unclipped, and while it looked dazzling, it had the added effect of spooking away any horse that might wish to approach Whirly from behind.

"Some plait the tail and braid the mane," Warren Wright explained. "We think Whirlaway has a nice mane and tail and that they look best whipping in the breeze."

Reasoned Ben Jones: "God gave horses tails for a reason. I'm leaving 'em there."

By February 1941, with his three-year-old campaign off to a smashing start, with the Derby now less than three months away, Jones knew he needed to figure out a way to keep Whirlaway from bearing out wide as he'd been doing his whole life, and he needed to solve that puzzle in a hurry. Jones was never shy about chatting with his horses, cajoling them, reprimanding them, but the one power he didn't possess was forcing them to listen to him. Only time, and trust, could make that happen, and with Jones and Whirlaway now entering their third year of partnership, the seeds of such patience would need to bear fruit soon, if it was ever going to happen. The trainer knew it might ultimately take a little humbling to break Whirlaway of these bad habits. Jones had been around the track long enough to know that when a horse gets whipped, he either learns from that mistake or he withdraws forever into the thick list of would-be champions that never quite learned how to win. Whirlaway had yet to suffer such a failure.

On February 18 he finally did, and it nearly sent all of Calumet's carefully laid plans and rapidly expanding ambitions into an irrevocable tailspin. Whirlaway was a three-to-ten favorite to walk over the field at the Arcadia Purse at Hialeah Park, a tune-up for the Flamingo Stakes four days later, the signature event of the entire Florida racing calendar. But Whirlaway didn't simply lose the Arcadia, he was thrashed, staggering home in third place even though he hadn't really veered outside at all. He was just beaten, and by a couple of no-name horses, too.

This was your Derby favorite?

This was the horse that would carry racing in 1941?

"Maybe he just had a bad day," Jones said. "Horses can have those, you know."

The trainer was far more concerned than he let on. The clock was ticking down toward the Derby—seventy-four days and counting—and Whirlaway needed to be broken down and built back up, and that was going to be a full-time job. The horse also wasn't looking like himself just yet. Always undersized, Whirlaway had lost weight since the end of his two-year-old campaign, and his coat didn't look quite right. All of these issues were addressable, and Jones had no doubt in his ability to pull this off in just under three skinny months, but he was about to enter virgin territory in his relationship with his boss. Wright had pledged to stay out of Jones's business when the two men had shaken hands on their deal three years earlier (mere weeks after Whirlaway was born); now Jones needed to see if the man who wrote the checks would be equal to his word.

The first blow Jones delivered was informing Wright that Whirlaway would have to be scratched from the Flamingo, a crushing development for Wright, who'd eased into a comfortably prominent place in South Florida society. The Flamingo was a socialite's delight, a highlight of the winter season, and if having a favorite in the Flamingo wasn't necessarily the same as owning a Derby winner, it wasn't a terrible place to be, either. Wright tried talking Jones out of withdrawing the horse, but Jones was inflexible, and Wright, looking at the bigger picture, relented. Jones breathed a sigh of relief. The boss had passed his first test.

The next few weeks were like boot camp for Whirlaway, with Jones throwing every trick in his vast manual at the horse, nursing him back to health, and developing a relationship that Arcaro would in later years describe as "the kind of love and trust that a father has with a wayward son, where they argue with each other and love each other, often at the same time." It was working. Whirlaway would be shipped to Kentucky in less than two weeks and the endgame would be on, but before then Ben Jones had one last surprise for everybody. An obscure sprint race, the Silver Springs Purse, five and a half furlongs, was scheduled for March 28 at Tropical Park, a little rockpile of a track on the outskirts of Miami. Jones thought it would be a delightful place to give Whirlaway his first true test in nearly six weeks, since the meltdown at Arcadia.

There was only one problem: Jones never informed Wright of his intentions. Instead, the owner, relaxing at his home in the Keys, nearly split a vein when he snapped open his copy of the *Miami Herald* and the headline slapped him in the face: DERBY FAVE WHIRLY TO GO IN SPRINT RACE.

Wright was beside himself. He was beyond furious. He ran to his car and started speeding toward Coral Gables, muttering to himself. *This son of a bitch keeps my horse out of the Flamingo and he runs him in this two-bit race? Is he crazy? He must be crazy! I have to stop this!*

"I do *not* want this horse to run today," Wright screamed at his trainer a few seconds after breathlessly arriving at Tropical Park.

"No, sir," Jones replied. "He's running."

"He is my horse," Wright fumed. "He belongs to me. And so, may I remind you, do you. If you want to continue that partnership, I suggest you change your mind at once."

"No, sir," Jones replied. "And if you force me on this one, you won't have to worry about firing me, because I'll sooner quit than have someone force me to ignore what I know is right. I don't tell you how to run your businesses. Never, ever tell me what's in the best interest of the horses I train."

"You wouldn't quit me."

"Yes, sir, I would."

Jones was too old to play games, and he wasn't the kind to bluff; Wright knew that much about him. He'd come from nothing, and the prospect of returning to nothing didn't frighten him as it did other men. Wright was at a serious crossroads here: let Jones have his way, and face the razzing of his society friends; or risk something else, maybe something worse, in entrusting another trainer at this late date with the horse that was supposed to finally win him a Kentucky Derby, now only thirty-six days away.

"Okay," Wright said. "You win. But you'd better be right."

Half an hour later Whirlaway zoomed home, winning easily, looking strong and free and healthy. Wright once again sought Jones out.

"I'll never second-guess you," he said, "ever again."

The rest of the sport wasn't as easily converted, however. While Whirlaway had been wasting away in Florida, several of his three-year-old classmates had turned in strong winters and passed Whirlaway as smart-money favorites. This fact remained unchanged even after Whirlaway returned to Kentucky and won the six-furlong A. J. Joyner Handicap at Keeneland Park on April 11. Ten days later the first Derby betting lines were installed, and they were telling: Our Boots—Whirlaway's chief rival as a juvenile, named Horse of the Year among two-year-olds in 1940—was listed as the favorite at three-to-one; Whirlaway wasn't even a clear second choice, sitting at four-to-one along with the relatively unheralded King Cole.

And it was about to get even worse.

On April 24, closing day at Keeneland, Jones entered Whirlaway in the $10,000 Blue Grass Stakes, the last chance any of the entered colts would have to shift public perception before the Derby nine days later. It was an enormous challenge for Whirlaway, but a wonderful opportunity, too. The race would be a mile and an eighth, the longest distance he or any of the other horses had ever run before, an eighth of a mile shorter than the Derby. And Our Boots, the new darling of the handicappers, would be there.

The two horses already knew each other well, having squared off four times as two-year-olds. Our Boots had actually beaten Whirlaway in three of those races, but each of those times he'd carried less weight. The only time they'd run with equal imposts, the previous October at the Breeders' Futurity at this same track, Whirlaway had won going away. This time both horses would carry 123 pounds, only three less than they'd bear at the Derby. By any measure this would determine who the better horse was heading into the most important race of their lives.

Whirlaway actually held the lead at the head of the stretch, and that threw the heavily partial crowd of 7,500 into a rabid frenzy, but then, to the horror of just about everybody, Whirlaway resorted to an old trick. Upstairs, in the owner's box, Warren Wright's wife, Lucille, let out a shriek as she saw her horse head for the outside, losing ground with every gallop. She'd seen this too many times before and knew what was about to happen. She turned to the gentleman standing to her right, Royce Martin, an old friend who also happened to be the owner of Our Boots.

"You're going to win now," Lucille said.

"I know," Martin said, trying to maintain his composure since he suffered with a bad heart, but bursting inside. Martin was staying at the Wrights' mansion in town as their houseguest, and the night before, the Martins and the Wrights had all played four-handed gin rummy, and though Martin was a cardplayer of some renown, Mrs. Wright had managed to take $26.50 off him.

"I think you'll pay for that tomorrow," Martin had said then with a laugh. Now he was laughing again, watching Our Boots pull away, gaining steam down the stretch while Whirlaway was all but heading back to the barn. The final margin was six lengths, but it might well have been sixty. Whirlaway's moment had passed, his reputation was shattered, and his owners' hearts lay in tatters.

"Well," Lucille told Warren, "at least our friends should have a good chance at winning the Derby. That ought to make you feel good."

"It doesn't," Warren muttered.

Lucille realized he was right. Her husband had put so much of himself into this horse that those dreams had become her own dreams, and now they'd all but vanished.

"Ah, sure, it makes you sick to lose with a colt like Whirlaway," she said a day after the Blue Grass Stakes, on a morning when newspapers across America officially pronounced her horse's Derby dreams dead. "You think you can't possibly smile again. But what I do is close my eyes and think hard enough of the things I've got. I think of my health and the health of my family and my kids. But sometimes it's hard. It's even hard to remember the Hopeful at Saratoga, and the other grand races Whirlaway has won. But you've got to remember them, and forget what's happened here. And if you can't, there's always tomorrow. Tomorrow, I guess, is the only real remedy horse owners have."

Trainers, too. Ben Jones was crestfallen, but he was also furious. Before the Blue Grass, he'd given Wendell Eads, Whirlaway's rider, implicit instructions on how he wanted the race run, that he wanted Eads to keep Whirlaway as close to the rail as possible, at all costs. Eads wasn't the kind of jockey to openly defy a trainer, so it wasn't that he wouldn't. At 102 pounds, he *couldn't*. Jones had feared this very thing from the moment Eads became Whirlaway's primary mount in Florida. Eads was a good jockey, attentive and workable. He was just too weak, and when Whirlaway challenged him he simply lacked the physical presence to change the horse's mind. Jones's frustrations were now bubbling, and they were now there for the world to see, and read.

"The colt's all right and will prove it," Jones vowed. "This was his first race this year longer than seven furlongs and he just naturally tired at the end, that's all. He needs a strong boy to keep him straight and hard work to keep him fit."

The hard work Jones was certain he could provide. But the strong boy? Nine days before the Run for the Roses, nine days before this once-in-a-lifetime colt would run the only race he'd ever really been trained for, where was Ben Jones going to find a jockey strong enough to keep Whirlaway in line, skilled enough to harness all that energy properly, arrogant enough to believe not only that the horse should win, but that he couldn't possibly be beaten?

Whirlaway desperately needed a hero to rescue his flagging spirit.

In those closing days of April 1941, he wasn't the only one.

———————•———————

To understand the point of prominence that Charles A. Lindbergh had once commanded in the American sphere, you must remember the time in which he emerged as one of the nation's first international superstars. When he'd flown the single-engine *Spirit of St. Louis* from Long Island's Roosevelt Field nonstop to Paris across thirty-three and a half hours of May 20 and 21, 1927, he was hailed a hero on two continents. After receiving the French Legion of Honor from the president of France, he'd been escorted home by a fleet of American warships. President Calvin Coolidge greeted Lindbergh upon his arrival and pinned the Congressional Medal of Honor to his chest. In the final years of the 1920s, as the United States' self-confidence grew to unprecedented levels, there was no greater representative of what Americans believed themselves to be than this son of Swedish immigrants who'd never coveted such fame, but who nevertheless grew to embrace its perks.

The memory of that flight, and of the brio it represented, was especially important for Americans to hold onto once the stock market crashed in October 1929, once the nation's economy turned to dust, once the Great Depression started clutching the country by its jugular vein. The memory of what Americans could do, and the promise of what they could do again, was powerful, and it was encapsulated in the person of Charles Augustus Lindbergh. The Lone Eagle, he was called.

"You can live the rest of your life in this country and never understand the place Lindbergh held," says Howard Flanders, in 1927 a ten-year-old student who, like most of his classmates, worshiped Lindbergh and all he stood for. "Who's the most famous person you can think of in this country now, Muhammad Ali? Michael Jordan? You still might find places in this world where they've never heard of those names. But in the 1930s, you weren't going to find anyplace on the planet where they hadn't heard of Lucky Lindy."

But Lindbergh's storybook life was given a horrifying and permanent jolt on March 1, 1932, when his infant son, Charles Jr., was abducted from the family home in Hopewell, New Jersey, and later found murdered. Shaken by the vicious violation, embittered by the resulting media circus that surrounded both the investigation and the trial and ultimate execution of Bruno Hauptmann, Lindbergh moved his family to England in December 1935, seeking a quieter life. Back home, he was still idolized by millions who would never have believed they'd have cause to turn so completely against him within five years' time. But that's exactly what his experiences in Europe would bring about. Lindbergh watched closely as the Continent began building toward another seminal conflict, observing the air forces of both Britain and France. And in 1938 he accepted an invitation to meet Hermann Goering, commander of the Luftwaffe—the German air force—at the American embassy in Berlin. There, he was presented with the *Verdienstkreuz Deutscher Adler,* the German medal of honor, or Order of the German Eagle, the highest honor the Nazi government could bestow on a non-German. Lindbergh accepted gladly and refused to give the medal back, even after public outrage in America was clear, saying it would be a "high insult" to Germany if he did that.

Overnight the luster was off Lindbergh's impeccable public dossier, and he didn't help matters by coming to believe, after studying the Luftwaffe, that the Nazis were mobilizing an armed force that no country on earth—the United States included—could hope to match. He believed his ominous prophecy was borne out by the way Germany overpowered France in 1940, ultimately seizing Paris and splitting the country into two precincts, the occupied zone that included the capital, and the smaller unoccupied zone, soon to be governed by a Nazi-friendly government in Vichy, led by Marshal Henri Philippe Pétain. Lindbergh returned home hoping to stem the growing inclination toward intervention that had started to swirl in the United States, and when early in 1941 a new pro-isolationist group, the America First Committee, was formed, he became its most prominent member and most active spokesman.

So it was that in April 1941, as Whirlaway's struggle became a daily part of the sporting soap opera, as baseball teams broke training camp in Florida and headed north, as Joe Louis maintained his "bum of the month" routine, and *Citizen Kane* began playing to capacity crowds everywhere,

Charles A. Lindbergh went on a speaking tour of the nation's industrial cities and its heartland outposts, hoping to spread a message that he believed was a peaceful one, but one to which a growing number of opponents attached a far uglier moniker:

Appeasement.

On April 17, not long after his formal induction into America First, Lindbergh entered the Chicago Arena, a small facility in which a crowd of 8,000 would normally have piqued the interest of the fire marshal. On this night there were 10,000 people crammed inside, and another 4,000 swarmed outside, kept orderly by some 70 members of the Chicago police force. As would be the case with most America First rallies, the assembled crowd was loud, it was enthusiastic, and it was soon eating out of Lindbergh's hands, even as he bluntly announced that the war in Europe was already lost and that President Roosevelt's efforts at aiding Britain were just a smokescreen camouflaging his true intentions.

"I call for unity among the forces and the people of America who stand against our intervention in the European war," he said, beginning a speech that would run two thousand words and be interrupted no fewer than thirty-one times by wild applause. "It would be a tragedy, even to Germany, if the British Empire collapses. But I tell you frankly that I believe this war was lost by England and France even before it was declared, and that it is not within our power in America today to win the war for England, even though we throw the entire resources of our nation into the conflict."

In Washington, Roosevelt was stunned. He understood that Lindbergh was no friend of his administration, or his policies, but he'd never before known the extent of Lindbergh's beliefs. Privately, he seethed, knowing Lindbergh's reach, worried that Lindbergh's broad popular appeal might cause people to ignore the dangerous tenor of his words which were, Roosevelt believed, doing nothing short of lending aid and comfort to hostile nations, if not out-and-out sedition. Such actions were the quickest way to fall into disfavor with the president, who on one hand truly hoped the nation could avoid spilling its sons' blood on the battlefields of Europe, but on the other understood that he needed the people to be as united and committed as possible in the event that war became inevitable. Joseph P. Kennedy, formerly Roosevelt's ambassador to the Court of St. James, discovered how vast the president's wrath could be when he'd said in a speech,

"England is not fighting our battle. This is not our war." Those words ruined Kennedy's political career, and he was hounded with the tag of "appeaser" for the rest of his life.

Lindbergh was only warming up. Six nights after roiling the crowd in Chicago, a few hours after Our Boots handed Whirlaway the most devastating defeat of his young life in the Blue Grass Stakes, he was again the featured speaker at an America First rally, this one at a mass meeting at the Manhattan Center on New York's West Thirty-fourth Street. Ten thousand more ticket holders jammed the undersized meeting hall, and this time some 35,000 others gathered outside, listening to Lindbergh's speech as it was piped into huge loudspeakers. This time, though, Lindbergh's intentions were known by everyone on both sides of the aisle, on both sides of the issue, and they were out in force. Many protesters, believing the core of Lindbergh's belief system was pure anti-Semitism, showed up with placards, though cops mostly diverted them across the street, away from the loudspeakers. One man wearing a Lindbergh button reportedly yelled in a heavy German accent, "Down with the British!" at the protesters, and a man wearing a sailor suit turned and punched him in the face, breaking his glasses.

"Land of the free, my eye," the man said.

But there *was* a strong Nazi presence at the meeting. Joe McWilliams, the self-proclaimed Jew-hating Fuehrer of the Christian Mobilizers, had announced to his members that whenever Lindbergh was speaking, they should postpone their weekly meetings and attend America First rallies instead. Still, it wasn't just the fringe elements that began to worry many middle-of-the-road Americans. It was the words Lindbergh used which, when separated from the excitement his charismatic presence gave them and planted in cold newspaper type the next morning, grew slowly but steadily more worrisome.

"A crisis is here," Lindbergh told the New York gathering. "We have been led toward war by a minority of our people; this minority has power; it has influence; it has a loud voice, but it does not represent the American people."

This time Roosevelt could not contain his anger, though he was comforted by more polls showing Americans growing increasingly resigned to the prospect of inevitable intervention, a mood pushed along by the Nazis presently rolling through Greece. By the end of the week a swastika would fly high atop the Acropolis in Athens, the very cradle of human civilization, as ominous a symbol yet of where the world was, and where it was heading.

Still, Lindbergh was unbowed. His next stop was an especially meaningful one for him: the St. Louis Arena, in the city where three prominent businessmen had financed the flight that earned him his fame, the city whose very name was stenciled on the side of the airplane that won him this platform in the first place. "In England, in France, and now in my own country I have listened to politicians and idealists calling upon the people for war without hardly a thought of how that war is to be fought and won," he said before another house packed with acolytes. "I have seen France fall. I see England falling, and now I see America being led into the same morass. . . ."

The words were powerful, and they were increasingly bitter, but on this day, outside the sold-out arena, they mostly fell on deaf ears. For earlier in the day, eleven horses had run around an oval in Louisville only 260 miles to the east, and what happened there in the land of Kentucky colonels would drown out, for the moment anyway, the observations of one erstwhile Missouri colonel.

———————●———————

The call had come from Ben Jones, and it wasn't an offer Eddie Arcaro had ever expected to receive, not in his wildest imagination. Arcaro was perhaps the most famous jockey working in American racing in 1941, only twenty-five years old but already a veteran of some eight thousand races. He was good, and knew he was good, and wasn't afraid to tell anyone who asked him how good he thought he was. He was also a tough son of a bitch who'd grown up in racing at a time when jockeys had to be part-horseman, part-wrestler.

"We made up our own rules as we went along," Arcaro would recall years later. "Besides being able to have to stay on the horse, we had to know all the tricks, like tugging on the saddlecloths of the other horses, hitting them with the whip, leg-locking the other jockeys, and everything else you could think of to win a race. It's an odd thing, about jockeys. They're the only paid athletes who, if you left them alone, would kill one another. I mean that. You could start out with twenty jocks and, at the end of three months of racing, there'd only be one left. It's just what racing does to you. I know, because racing did it to me."

Arcaro was the son of an Italian immigrant cabdriver, born in Cincinnati on February 19, 1916. He reached a height of five foot three and stopped right there, which was perfect because by then Arcaro had already decided he wanted to spend his life enjoying the view from the top of a horse, nudged in part by his father's mid-career decision to leave chauffeuring in favor of bookmaking. He dropped out of school at age thirteen and exercised horses in Florence, Kentucky, for twenty dollars a month, getting little encouragement for all his toil. His first race was at the old Maple Heights track, near Cleveland. He lost. In fact, he lost the first forty-five races of his life before getting his first winner, a claimer named Eagle Bird at Agua Caliente in Tijuana, Mexico, on January 14, 1932. It was at Caliente that Arcaro's swagger first caught people's attention. A trainer there watched him struggling to stay on a horse in his first days and sneered "You'll kill yourself" when Arcaro came back to the barn.

"If you can make a rider," the trainer said, "I can make a watch."

Not long after, Arcaro began to ride a few winners, and after he'd secured his first stable contract, he sought out that trainer.

"Okay," he said. "Now where's my fucking watch?"

Arcaro's first stable contract in the United States had been with Warren Wright and Calumet Farms, and his successes there later earned him a lucrative deal with the prestigious Greentree Stables, owned by the Whitney family in New York. Arcaro's departure angered Wright, who never much cared for jockeys with large egos and larger opinions of themselves. Still, he couldn't deny Arcaro's talent.

Neither could Ben Jones. In fact, Arcaro was largely responsible for Jones's first great brush with fame. In 1938, Jones was working for Herbert L. Woolf's Woolford Farms, based in Kansas City, and he was training Lawrin, a horse with some modest skills that was slated a nine-to-one shot in the Derby. But Jones couldn't find a jockey with whom he was comfortable to ride Lawrin. He knew Arcaro's work, and he also knew Greentree would not have an entry on Derby Day, so he asked Woolf to ask the Whitneys if they could borrow Arcaro's services for the day. It was agreed. Arcaro celebrated this wonderful career break by going out the night before the race and never coming home, proceeding straight to the track from last call. He met Jones for a predawn stroll around a mud-soaked track.

"He walked me around that track twice, pointing out the mudholes by the fence," Arcaro would remember many years later. " 'Don't run him there,' he told me."

It was a sound plan. Only, that afternoon, Arcaro couldn't run anywhere else. The rest of the field apparently had the same instructions, and since he had the No. 1 post Arcaro had nowhere to go but straight. "I never went outside a horse all day," he said. As it turns out, it was a wonderful break. His eyes may have been bloodshot, but they could still see that the 100-degree temperatures had dried the inside lane completely. All the holes had vanished. "It was the best place on the racetrack to be," Arcaro said, and so he stayed there, against orders, and because of it won the Derby by two and a half lengths, running a much shorter race than the others had in avoiding the inside lane.

"Everybody thought I was a genius," Arcaro said. "If I could have gotten out, I woulda been able to do what Ben wanted me to do. And we might not have beat a horse."

Jones understood Arcaro's decision to buck his instructions and respected Arcaro's candor in admitting the helping hand dumb luck had provided. Mostly, he was impressed by Arcaro's quick brain, by the way he'd been able to easily handle a difficult horse, and he made a mental note that he would remember Eddie Arcaro's phone number if he was ever in a similar predicament.

And now here it was.

Wright was reluctant at first, still hurt by Arcaro's defection to a rival stable, but by now Jones had mastered the perfect blueprint to getting what he wanted from his boss. "Get me Arcaro," he said, "or get yourself a new trainer." And the fact is, Warren Wright was the one man who could make that happen thanks to the cozy business arrangement he'd established years earlier with John Hay Whitney, the man who held Arcaro's contract. Greentree Stables had no entries in the Derby, but Wright still needed Whitney's permission, something that was more easily granted given the fact that if Whirlaway—son of Blenheim II—won the Derby, then so, in his own small way, would Whitney.

"He's all yours," Whitney told Wright.

On April 28, the day Charles Lindbergh's festering relationship with President Roosevelt culminated in his resignation from the Army Air Corps, five days before the Derby, Calumet signed up Eddie Arcaro for some very important temp work. Arcaro, who always coveted the biggest stages and the biggest races, said he'd walk to Kentucky if he had to, though Jones urged him to fly instead. So excited was he that on the day he left for Louisville, Arcaro first reported for work at Jamaica Racetrack in New York and rode four winners.

Now, he would face the most daunting challenge of his life. Racing fans, defying professional bookmakers and cynical touts, were wagering hard and heavy on Whirlaway, even if most would readily admit they were betting with their hearts and not their heads. Those were looking more and more like sucker bets with each passing day, especially after Whirlaway lost, again, in the Mile Derby Trial four days before the big race, when Eads again couldn't prevent the horse from sprinting out wide, and a desperate straightaway charge could secure only second place. It was good enough to officially earn Whirlaway a spot in the Derby field, and also enough to solidify in most expert minds that Whirlaway was officially yesterday's news. Jones could understand the skepticism. He knew he had only one chance to prove everyone wrong. But first, his jockey and his horse would have to get acquainted.

"Whirlaway ought to be an interesting challenge," Arcaro said before heading off to Kentucky. "I look forward to meeting him."

3

"A HELL OF A LOT OF HORSE ON YOUR HANDS"

"HERE COMES WHIRLAWAY!" ECHOES FROM LOUISVILLE TO BALTIMORE TO NEW YORK

Ben Jones shows Eddie Arcaro the blinker he devised to help Whirlaway overcome a tendency to run wide on the turns.

Open the gate at Pimlico
Let the long-tailed chestnut go
Down the backstretch, on his way
Let him run like Derby Day
First-place money? Just a gift
(Eddie, please, don't let him drift!)

Irishman could not be here
Makes no difference—never fear
You can leave them all behind
Whirlaway, if you've the mind
When to homestretch-high you shift
(Eddie, please don't let him drift!)

—Tim Cohane, *New York World-Telegram*,
May 9, 1941

———————•———————

At first the nickname of choice was a derisive one, as so many sobri-quets were in an era when "politically correct" referred to voting for the winning ticket on election day, when anything and everything was in play when you slapped a moniker on someone: ethnicity, religion, appearance, sometimes a little of all three. So Eddie Arcaro carried the name "Old

Banana Nose" with him for a good long while, whether he wanted it or not. That was part of the game, Arcaro figured, and what he'd have to do is work his ass off in order to earn a better handle. That happened to Joe DiMaggio, with whom Arcaro spent more than a few nights in the boozy exile of Toots Shor's famous gin joint on Fifty-first Street in midtown Manhattan. DiMaggio led the league in nicknames, and two of them were unforgettably poetic: Joltin' Joe and the Yankee Clipper. But when he'd first made it to New York, the newspaper guys called him "the Big Dago," and his older teammates called him "Daig." DiMaggio was never terribly fond of either one, even if he rarely complained about them.

Arcaro wasn't thrilled that his Roman schnoz was the first thing people noticed about him as he tried to make his way north along the racing food chain, but he also knew this: If he wanted to be successful, he would have to endure certain indignities in addition to enjoying all the available perks, too. And it was a trade-off he was willing to make. For one thing, he never thought of fame as a burden. "I like being a celebrity," he once said. "I'm being honest. If someone tells you he doesn't like being on top, you'd better look at his head. When I retire I'll be just another little man."

For another . . . well, the nickname *was* dead-on: He *did* have an enormous nose, and years later it would nearly kill him on a track, in the 1959 Belmont Stakes, when a colt named Black Hills fell at the five-sixteenths pole just as Arcaro had fueled him to a position near the leaders. It was a rainy day, there was standing water all over the place, and Arcaro wound up falling unconscious into a large puddle, face-first, and he might really have been in trouble had a photographer stationed right by the pole not dragged him out of the muck. "I got my big nose in that water," he would say, "and the guys wound up having to pump me for half an hour. It's a wonder I didn't drown with that damned beak sucking up all that water."

By the spring of 1941, though, the "Old Banana Nose" tag had been filed away and replaced by another, which nobody—certainly not Arcaro—could find fault with: The Master. "Eddie was a combination of strength and intelligence, and he had a sense of daring to go with it," Joe Hirsch, executive columnist for the *Daily Racing Form*, would say many years later in eulogizing Arcaro. "The nickname 'The Master' wasn't newspaper hype. That name came from his fellow riders, who tried to copy everything he did. There have been riders who've had some of Eddie's great skills, but nobody with the total package."

Arcaro would have to be equal to that new nickname now as his plane touched down at the Louisville airport less than thirty-six hours before the start of the 1941 Kentucky Derby. As soon as he walked off the ramp, Arcaro was mobbed by Whirlaway well-wishers and men with notebooks, all of them enthralled with the notion that this ninety-six-pound powerhouse could figure a way to tame the stubborn fifteen-hundred-pound steed. A Kentucky boy and a Kentucky horse, who wouldn't even meet each other until the day before Kentucky's biggest race? It was a Bluegrass Blowout Bacchanal, and it was all anyone could talk about. And Arcaro loved every second of it.

"I've never sat on the horse," he reminded everyone. "But I believe he's a good one and has as good a chance as any of them to win if ridden right. I believe I can handle him if anybody can. Of course, that habit of bearing out at the turn is a bad one, and sometimes these 'tear-outs' never get over it. But I'm going to give him the best ride I know how and let it go at that. If the stuff's in him, he'll show it when the chips are down. From all I hear, one reason Whirlaway has gone wide at the stretch turn in some of his races is that he's been out front at that stage. A horse like him has no business being in that spot at that particular point. I hope I can save him for the stretch battle. If I can, I think you'll really see him at his best."

Ben Jones read every word Arcaro uttered that day, and he loved every syllable. One of the reasons Arcaro was so good, Jones knew, was that the jockey had an enormous ego, and this was the kind of challenge that would gorge his self-esteem. If Arcaro could ever figure out how to bring Whirlaway home, it would be his second Derby win in only three Derby starts (in addition to his '38 win with Lawrin, Arcaro had been the rider on Nellie Flag, the Calumet filly who'd finished fourth in '35 behind eventual Triple Crown winner Omaha). Lots of jockeys had won one Derby; in the history of the race, held every year without interruption since 1875, only eight had ever won it twice to that point. A victory would catapult Arcaro into the elite of his profession, a fact Jones hoped would discourage Arcaro from replicating the candle-at-both-ends regimen that he'd followed the last time they'd worked together. As an added bit of motivation, Jones mentioned to Arcaro that on Thursday, while he was flying, the man he would be replacing, Wendell Eads, had ridden three winners at Churchill Downs, his quiet protest to a high-profile demotion.

It worked. Arcaro showed up for work Friday morning clear-eyed and eager to conduct business. Before they headed onto the track, there was the formal entrants' ceremony and the post-position lottery to conduct. Jones, as always the first man to the track, made certain Whirlaway's was the first name dropped in the entry box at 7:40 A.M., and he was pleased when he earned the number-four position coming out of the gate. "Whirlaway will be in front at some point in that mile and a quarter," Jones said as he walked to the barn where Whirlaway was waiting. "I'm not saying he'll win, just that he'll be in play. He'll be ready."

Quipped Arcaro: "If it's riding he's needing, he's going to be getting plenty of it."

Arcaro's lone training run on Whirlaway would be at a little over half a mile, and the one thing Jones needed to see was that Arcaro could control the uncontrollable horse, stopwatch be damned. To make things more interesting, Jones positioned his lead pony at the head of the stretch, leaving only a sliver of a gap between animal and rail, and he instructed Arcaro: "At all costs, you are to keep this horse inside that pony, understand?"

"Let's go," Arcaro said.

And off they went. Immediately Arcaro could sense the horse's sensitivities, and his reluctance to do what he was told simply because he was being told to do it. That could be a problem, sure. But it could also propel him to places few racehorses ever see. He was that good. He was that strong. "The kind of horse you have to pamper," Arcaro said a bit later. "He has a delicate mouth and you have to ride him without pulling hard on the bit. Just let him do the running."

As the pony came into sight, Jones expected Arcaro to go to his whip to provide Whirlaway an extra reminder of what needed to be done, but to the trainer's delight Arcaro never even lifted his arm. And to Jones's eternal relief, as Whirlaway made the turn, he stayed snugly inside the pony, hugging the rail, and came roaring home straighter than a preacher. He covered the whole half mile in fifty seconds flat, still slower than Jones would have preferred, but acceptable. More important, he did it without once flinching to the outside, which had Jones ecstatic. Whirlaway was still listed as the bettor's choice for third, at five-to-one, behind old friend Our Boots (nine-to-five) and Porter's Cap (two-to-one), but Jones felt especially good about that, saying, "Something tells me when the Kentucky folk get here tomorrow and they start laying their money at the window, it's gonna be hard for them to go against a couple of Kentuckians like my horse and my rider."

One thing did concern him, though: Porter's Cap would be starting in the number-nine stall and Our Boots would be in number ten, meaning Whirlaway's two chief rivals would be well to his right, on the outside. They would be natural bait for Whirlaway if he wanted to take up his old habit of leaning that way. So overnight Jones came up with a three-pronged strategy to ward off those potential demons.

First came the pep talk he delivered directly into the horse's perked-up ears early Saturday morning, although that was always a standard part of Jones's race-day routine, no matter who the horse was. Second was a final skull session with Arcaro. One of the reasons the old trainer was so enamored with the kid rider was that, for all his obvious talents, Arcaro was—to borrow a term that wouldn't be invented for at least another half century—very "coachable." He didn't act as if he'd invented the sport of horse racing, and while he was as stubborn and self-confident as any successful athlete, he was willing to take advice, especially from men he respected. And Arcaro never respected anyone the way he did Ben Jones.

"Listen," Jones said Saturday morning, pleased to see there wasn't a trace of crimson lurking in the whites of Arcaro's fun-loving eyes, "this is a horse that can beat any other horse in America. But you have to ride him the way I tell you to ride him."

Arcaro nodded, sipped his coffee, didn't say a word.

"He has one run in him," Jones continued. "If you let him, he'll go right out to where the leaders are, and then you'll never keep him for a mile and a quarter. So here's what I want you to do. When the gate opens, stop him. Get him left [behind] at the gate. Then dangle the reins so they don't grab him by the mouth, and he'll relax. Then you've got him. He'll look all over, he'll check out the stands. He'd just as soon be out in the lots, helping to park the customers' cars. He won't know he's running with competition, and he won't know that this is the biggest day of his life. And then you'll have a hell of a lot of horse on your hands."

Arcaro took another silent sip of coffee. He was on board.

Which left only one more trick, and this Jones produced in the paddock, moments before the horses would be marched to the starting gates. It wasn't unusual for a trainer to outfit his horse with a mask featuring "blinkers" flanking both eyeholes, the better to keep the animal focused on what was in front of him, to curb the reach of his peripheral vision; Whirlaway had been fitted with them most of his career. Jones certainly wanted Whirlaway to forget that the world to his right side even existed, to keep him from drifting in that direction, and a horse won't run to something he can't see.

But Jones didn't mind a bit if this horse became transfixed with the rail. In fact, he wanted Whirlaway to stay as close to that white fence as possible. Even if Whirlaway understood every letter of their conversation that morning, he could forget it in half a heartbeat once the race got under way. So Jones came up with a mask that had an extended cup of a blinker over the right eye, while keeping the left eyehole bare. He fastened it around Whirlaway's head, then bid him farewell, scooting into the grandstand where he would hold his breath the rest of the day until 5:45 P.M., local time, when the gates would fling open and none of it would be in his hands any longer.

Surrounding Jones on this first Saturday of May were more people than had ever before assembled at a sporting event in the state of Kentucky, more than had ever before watched a horse race anywhere in North America. Colonel Matt Winn, who saw the first Derby at age fourteen when his father brought him to the sparkling new Churchill Downs, and who was now the racetrack's iconoclastic president, had predicted that over 100,000 people would pass through the turnstiles, and by mid-afternoon they'd easily topped that number. Famous names like Don Ameche, Robert Young, Joe E. Brown, Bing Crosby, Lana Turner, and no fewer than fifteen U.S. senators and twelve governors mingled with anonymous faces, all of them inhaling 90,000 hot dogs, 250,000 bottles of beer and soda, 35,000 sandwiches, and enough mint juleps that concessionaires went through 50 bushels of fresh mint to keep up. By ten o'clock the three-dollar general admission seats were already filled, as were the fifty-cent temporary bleachers built around the track's upper turn. By noon, 25,000 people were swarming the infield, where there was neither seating nor shade, and nobody seemed to mind a bit.

Together, the gathered gamblers would wager a total of 1,937,111 Depression-era dollars, not quite a track record but an astonishing total nonetheless, and so many of them would cast their lots with the local favorite that by race time the odds on Whirlaway had shrunk from five-to-one to two-to-one. Thirty-six special trains kept flooding Louisville with guests from Los Angeles, New Orleans, Memphis, Fort Worth, New York, Boston, Detroit, Chicago, and Washington, who snapped up all but a handful of three-day hotel blocs. American Airlines sold out five 21-seat specials. Bowman Field, the local airstrip, reported it was overflowing with private planes. To police the grounds, 449 state militiamen and 240 ROTC students from Eastern State Teachers College were commissioned (the task normally fell to the local National Guard, a unit that had recently been called to active duty and was now serving at Camp Shelby, Mississippi). Six hundred press credentials were distributed to writers, all of them lined up sweaty cheek to sticky jowl in a press box built to house half that number, at most.

But nobody minded. As the horses eased into the starting gates, for the first time in far too long the nation's attention was riveted on something pleasurable, something fun, something other than draft numbers and V-for-victory slogans and newspaper headlines that predicted grislier and gloomier days ahead. Around the crowded grandstand in Louisville, and gathered around radio consoles in hundreds of American cities beyond, millions of men, women, and children waited for track announcer Frank Ashley and NBC broadcaster Clem McCarthy to declare, simultaneously: *"And they're off!"*

And then they were.

Dispose, the number-eleven horse, went straight to the lead of the pack, and if this would otherwise have worried Ben Jones, peering through his binoculars, he could see that this time there was no need to worry. Seven spots over to the left, Arcaro was doing exactly as he'd been told. Whirlaway settled into the middle of the pack and ran easily, and while the slow start may have concerned a hundred thousand of Jones's neighbors at Churchill Downs, so many of them screaming his horse's name, this was precisely the race Jones himself wanted to see.

Still, even Jones couldn't know if the one run that he told Arcaro Whirly had in him would be enough. And as the dusty crowd of horses made its way across the backstretch, even Jones started to wonder if this was really meant to be. At the half-mile pole, Dispose was still comfortably in front, but the favorites were starting to close in fast. Our Boots looked primed to make his move as they made the far turn. Whirlaway was barely in the picture, some fourteen lengths behind. By the three-quarters pole he'd narrowed the gap some, had moved up to sixth place, and it was here, as the horses approached the head of the stretch, that all of Jones's careful game planning bore the most satisfying fruit of his long career.

Arcaro knew he was running out of racetrack and he was running short on time, and he had to make a quick and fateful decision. In front of him he could see Staretor, a thirty-to-one longshot running over his head the whole race, loping just to the outside of Our Boots. There was enough room between them for maybe a horse and a half, and even if Arcaro could coax Whirlaway through that slit, he'd be all but inviting the horse to take the scenic route home to the finish line. It was a definite gamble. But it was one Arcaro knew he had to take.

"Your job," he would say, "is to give your horse a chance to win the damned race. And this was his chance."

As the main pack made its way around the turn then, 100,000 people saw the most remarkable thing, and at once screamed what they saw:

Here comes Whirlaway!

It was a battle cry that would soon become the sport's mantra, but on the afternoon it was born it was merely the visceral reaction of 100,000 people to the sight of a chestnut blur daring to split two horses—*Holy mackerel, did he really just DO that?!*—with a quarter of a mile left in the most important race of his life. Each of the eleven horses was entering unseen territory now, because none of them had ever run as long as a mile and a quarter before. That was the unique challenge of the Derby. How many dozens of horses had crashed into the invisible wall lurking just beyond the mile pole? How many would-be champions had simply disappeared at a mile and a sixteenth? Vanished at a mile and an eighth? Only the greatest horses would even think to find a different gear when most of his opponents were gasping for enough oxygen simply to stay upright.

Yet here came Whirlaway. Once he cleared Staretor and Our Boots, as everyone held their breath, half expecting him to bear out, he instead headed straight for home, and as he did you could see the spirit die in Porter's Cap, and in Blue Pair, and finally in Dispose, as Whirlaway roared past all three. Arcaro would say later that at this point he was no longer a jockey but a pilot, flying down the backstretch, not riding. And Whirlaway wasn't just passing the other horses, he was *dismissing* them.

On NBC, Clem McCarthy, who'd broadcast more important prizefights and more prominent horse races than any man alive, nearly lost his voice as he gasped: *"Whirlaway takes the lead by half a length!"*

And with each stride, the lead grew exponentially: Two lengths! Four! Six lengths! Seven! Churchill Downs couldn't contain the raucous glee exploding within its old wooden frame, the people wanting to run out of the stands and gallop alongside this magnificent horse, settling instead for yelling at the very top of their lungs even as Whirlaway crossed the finish line, even as Arcaro finally took a satisfying peek behind him to see where the rest of the pack was, discovering to his utter amazement it was some eight lengths back. Eight lengths! No horse had ever won this race by more than that. Then they posted the winning time: two minutes, one and two-fifth seconds—two-fifths of a second faster than the previous race record! Before long, the split times would be revealed, and these were even more astonishing. The last quarter mile—the part of the race a human marathon runner would call "heartbreak hill"? Whirlaway had covered that in twenty-three and three-fifths seconds, a mark that would last thirty-one years, until another chestnut colt named Secretariat broke it. The last eighth of a mile? Whirlaway chewed *that* up in eleven seconds flat, and to this day no horse has ever touched that.

As the men whose dreams Whirlaway had made come true gathered in the winner's circle, eager to drape him in a coverlet of roses, they were ebullient.

"I told you what Whirlaway could do when ridden the right way!" Ben Jones rejoiced. "He might be a crazy horse at times, but when they let him come from behind and save his speed for the stretch he can run over a rifle bullet. Arcaro rode a perfect race and the minute I saw them starting to move at the head of the stretch I knew the race was over. I told you he could do it! I told you he could do it! I told you he had the greatest burst of speed the racetrack knows today! All he needed was the chance to run his race in the way he likes to run it. He must have a target to shoot at."

Said Arcaro: "He's the runnin'-est horse I ever sat on. I won't say he's the best—you have to watch him too close—but he's the damned runnin'est. He wanted to run so badly today I couldn't possibly keep him down quite as long as we wanted to. I was told to hold him back until we'd finished that last turn, but Whirly saw all those horses out in front and wouldn't stand for any holding back."

And Warren Wright, who'd built himself a Thoroughbred powerhouse in less than ten years, was practically speechless. "This is the greatest thrill of my life," he whispered, his voice reduced to a hoarse rasp. "I'd rather win the Derby than any race in the world." Then, turning to Colonel Winn, Wright said, "I think I'd like to propose a toast."

To which a thirsty Arcaro quipped, "Mind if I come, too? I could really use one."

All across America, as Saturday afternoon blended into Saturday evening and then blurred into Sunday morning, people shared Arcaro's giddy sentiment. It sure was nice to be able to celebrate something for a change, to scream with delight at what came tumbling out of the radio speaker rather than recoil in horror.

———————●———————

On the other side of the Atlantic Ocean, Whirlaway's saga was greeted with considerably less enthusiasm, with barely a nod of recognition, which was as sobering a reminder of where the world lay as anything else. For England was where the sport of Thoroughbred racing had been born in the twelfth century, when English knights returned from the Crusades with teams of swift Arabian stallions. Across the next four hundred years, thousands of them were imported and bred with British mares, producing horses of unparalleled speed and endurance. Match races featuring two especially speedy horses for private wagers became a popular pastime among the ruling class (it wouldn't be dubbed "the sport of kings" for nothing).

In the early eighteenth century, horse racing as a professional sport flourished in England, where a boom of racecourse construction yielded rich purses and even more profitable stud farms. Such was the rapid, rabid interest that in 1750 the sport's elite gathered at Newmarket to establish the Jockey Club, which wrote comprehensive rules governing the sport and also founded the English Triple Crown, a distinguished racing series consisting of the Two Thousand Guineas at Newmarket Heath; the Epsom Derby at Epsom Downs, Surrey; and the St. Leger Stakes at Town Moor, Yorkshire. So regulated was the Thoroughbred industry, so inbred were the horses themselves that the pedigree of every one could be traced father-to-father to one of three English Arabian stallions, called the "foundation sires": the Byerley Turk, foaled in 1679; the Darley Arabian, foaled in 1700; and the Godolphin Arabian, foaled in 1724.

So Englishmen rightly saw Thoroughbred racing as their personal domain, and the Jockey Club, nearly two hundred years old, was still very much in existence in 1941 (as it is today). The English Triple Crown series would go off as scheduled that summer, one of the few major sporting events to survive the onset of war, and three different long shots won the races. But the moods of the crowds were distinctly subdued, and at the Derby—held in Newmarket rather than Epsom Downs, to keep large gatherings as far from bomb-weary London as possible—there was an epic traffic jam caused by thousands of racing fans trying to pass along roads clogged by thousands of soldiers. Even when they tried to get away, they couldn't get away, not really, not entirely.

London had been a regular target of German air raids for months, and over a million of its citizens were now living in shelters, their homes and businesses reduced to rubble by the Luftwaffe. Unbowed, England's Royal Air Force had begun taking its own measures of revenge, battering German targets and inflicting its own share of suffering and death, but these retributions, while necessary, hardly allayed the miseries visited upon the people of London and Leeds and Liverpool.

Winston Churchill was the man in whom England had entrusted its present, and its future, after the betrayals of Munich in 1938. There, English prime minister Neville Chamberlain, in the name of peace, in the hope of sparing a nation still weary from the Great War of a generation before further battlefield bloodshed, had agreed to allow Germany to annex the Sudetenland, a primarily German-speaking territory ceded to Czechoslovakia after the war. Chamberlain had further made a pact with Adolf Hitler stating that all future disputes between the two nations would be settled through nonviolent means rather than with bullets, a truce that Hitler began dissolving even as Chamberlain infamously returned to Downing Street announcing "peace in our time."

By the summer of 1940, this all would have seemed laughable were the results not so transcendentally tragic. Czechoslovakia's inevitable capitulation in September 1938 made it the second nation to fall under the swastika, joining Austria, which had been annexed seven months before. After the Munich Agreement, England was forced to stand idly by as Poland fell in September 1939, as Norway and Denmark fell in April 1940, as the Netherlands, Belgium, and Luxembourg fell in May 1940. By the time Churchill replaced the disgraced Chamberlain on May 10, France was crumbling, and within weeks Hitler would be photographed smiling at the base of his latest play toy, the Eiffel Tower. Hungary and Romania would follow in November, Bulgaria in March 1941, and now Hitler had set his sights on both Yugoslavia and Greece. In all, a German empire that in 1937 had consisted of 182,471 square miles and a population of 70 million was now four times as large and nearly twice as populous.

And now, the Nazis had their sights set on London, the biggest prize of all.

This was of daily concern within the borders of England, of course, but it provided many moments of anxious disquiet in the United States also, because the one line in the sand that President Roosevelt couldn't allow the Nazis to cross was the one on the beaches surrounding the island of England.

That would mean war: unconditional, unequivocal, irreversible.

So Americans were especially enrapt by Churchill's eloquent and defiant declarations that he would never brook a German invasion, no matter how inevitable that seemed in the darkest hours of late 1940 and early 1941, no matter how much fire came raining out of British skies. People on two continents were equally emboldened by Churchill's most important—and most famous—speech, delivered not long after he ascended to the prime minister's office.

"We will fight to defend our island whatever the cost may be," Churchill vowed. "We will fight on the beaches. We will fight on the landing grounds, in the fields, on the streets and in the hills. We will never surrender and even if, which I do not for a moment believe, this island or a large part of it were subjugated and starving, then our empire beyond the seas, armed and guarded by the British fleet, will carry on the struggle until in God's good time the New World, with all its power and might, sets forth for the liberation and rescue of the old."

England would never be able to fight these fights on her own, though, especially as fires raged in her streets, as wounded packed her hospitals, as survivors fled her major industrial cities for the countryside, wishing to avoid the terror tumbling out of the sky. Roosevelt recognized that even if he were reluctant to disperse American men to volunteer blood for the cause of freedom, there was one thing the burgeoning American economy could provide: ships, planes, guns, bullets, the tools of war, the commerce of conflict, and so he proposed a sweeping lend-lease arrangement to England through House Resolution 1776 (many instantly clucked at the ironic issuance of such a number for a bill whose primary intent would be to offer aid and comfort to what was at one time the nation's oldest enemy), which would provide as much as $1.8 billion to England. There would be spirited debate between interventionists and isolationists—the primary red and blue demarcation in 1941—but Roosevelt's iron will, fierce words, and helpful Democratic majorities in both chambers would push the bill along until its final passage on March 11, 1941.

"To all of you, it will mean sacrifices in behalf of your country and our liberties," Roosevelt said. "Yes, you will feel the impact of this gigantic effort in your daily lives. You will feel it in a way that will cause you many inconveniences. A halfhearted effort on our part will lead to failure. This is no part-time job.

"We believe that the rallying cry of the dictators, their boasting about a master race, will prove to be pure stuff and nonsense. There never has been, there isn't now and there never will be any race of people on the earth fit to serve as masters over their fellow men. The world has no use for any nation which, because of size or because of military might, asserts the right to goose-step to world power over the bodies of other nations and other races. Never in all our history have Americans faced a job so well worthwhile. May it be said of the days to come that our children and our children's children rise up and call us blessed."

In England, for once, there was hope flashing across the gray sky, even as American trepidation at this strengthening war alliance began to grow. Churchill himself summed up the feelings of most of his countrymen in the moments after Roosevelt fixed his signature to the bottom of the Lend-Lease Act.

"The most powerful democracy has, in effect, declared in a solemn statute that they will devote their overwhelming industrial and financial strength to insuring the defeat of Nazism in order that nations, great and small, may live in security, tolerance and freedom," he said. "By so doing the government and people of the United States have, in fact, written a new Magna Carta which not only has regard to the rights and laws upon which a healthy and advancing civilization can alone be erected but proclaims, by precept and example, the duty of free men and free nations, wherever they may be, to share the responsibility and burden of enforcing them."

But the good feeling wouldn't last long in England, because in 1941 good feelings never did. On the evening of May 10, at around the same time in the American town of Baltimore, Maryland, that a racehorse named Whirlaway would attempt to add the second jewel of the American Triple Crown to his résumé, the single most fearsome and furious attack of the war would all but bring London to its knees, a relentless assault aimed straight at the heart of England. So intense was the blitz that the roof was blown off Westminster Abbey. The Commons Chamber in the House of Parliament received a direct hit, and so did Big Ben. Thirty-three German raiders were shot down, but not before they and the rest of the Luftwaffe dropped 100,000 incendiaries, an unprecedented pace that surely hinted at a coming invasion, fears that were confirmed by Field Marshal Albert Kesselring, chief of German Air Fleet II: "I consider total air warfare as having fulfilled its objectives when the energy centers of a land have been destroyed and the will to resistance of a people paralyzed so that an occupation can take place more or less without fighting or when the threat of occupation breaks the last opposition of a people."

The assault lasted seven hours and introduced a terrifying new Nazi technique, in which high explosives were dropped on a neighborhood before the showers of incendiaries, the idea to frighten away civilian fire watchers and fighters who were supposed to take cover and be caught off guard when the spluttering firebombs arrived. It didn't work that way in London. Fireguards and air-raid precautions workers toiled openly throughout the night even as the enemy bombers came over. Harsh screams of big bombs mingled with the clatter of Molotov breadbaskets and the ceaseless roar of antiaircraft guns.

It was perfectly horrific, and the images would stun England's chief benefactor when they arrived the next morning, in newspapers that dutifully reported the carnage alongside the daily doings of one equine reminder that in a world at war, the most peaceful of pursuits can sometimes restore a man's faith in the possible. And the impossible. If only temporarily.

———————————●———————————

Warren Wright had celebrated his Kentucky Derby victory by hosting a party long into the Louisville night, inviting anyone with a fleeting interest in his prized racehorse. Most prominent among these was the actor Don

Ameche, a thirty-two-year-old dandy who'd gained fame playing the title role in the 1939 movie *The Story of Alexander Graham Bell* (so much so that by 1941, calling the telephone "the Don Ameche" became popular American slang) and was about to open in *Moon over Miami*. Ameche was a big sports fan, always a dapper ringside presence at championship prize-fights, a regular box seat customer at the World Series, and a particular favorite at the track. Ameche had been behind Whirlaway from the start, and for his loyalty Wright presented him with the victor's blanket of roses. Whirlaway himself was content to rejoice in quieter surroundings, enjoying extra helpings of hay and oats and a few celebratory carrots.

Ben Jones, not surprisingly, had little time for self-congratulation. Since 1946 the Triple Crown series of Thoroughbred racing has followed the exact same schedule year after year: the Derby takes place on the first Saturday of May; the Preakness runs two weeks after that; the Belmont Stakes finishes things up three weeks after that. But in 1941, only six days separated the Derby and the Preakness, meaning that not only was a Derby winner's stamina and recovery tested to the max, but so were the logistics of moving a horse six hundred miles from Kentucky to Maryland, from sprawling bluegrass country to one of America's grittiest urban cities. If everything went well, it would take a minimum of thirty-six hours to make that journey, and things didn't always go well when you tried to contain a restless animal in a cramped railway boxcar. And since nobody in Kentucky did any meaningful work on Sunday, Whirlaway wouldn't be loaded and shipped until the break of dawn on Monday.

Not that any of this shook Jones's confidence. Not after what he'd seen the horse do on Derby Day. Jones and Arcaro shook hands Sunday morning as Arcaro boarded a flight back to New York to resume his contract duties for Greentree Stables, but they'd be reunited later in the week at Baltimore's Pimlico Race Course since Greentree again had no competing horse in the race.

"If Whirlaway runs back to his Derby level, I see no reason why he shouldn't repeat at the Preakness," Jones said as he boarded the train alongside his prominent protégé. He did concede that the one horse he feared in the Preakness was Bold Irishman, trained by Sunny Jim Fitzsimmons, who'd sat out the Derby and would therefore be fully rested by post time Saturday. But, Jones, added, "Any horse is capable of beating Whirlaway if he doesn't run his race. Although I don't know if that's true if Whirlaway runs the way he did in Louisville."

The trip east was uneventful, Whirlaway peacefully and blissfully unaware of the commotion his mile-and-a-quarter romp had caused. Jones didn't sleep quite as much, but that wasn't at all unusual. Already he was mapping out potential pitfalls and pratfalls. Though he'd given Bold Irishman his full respect, in his heart Jones didn't believe that that horse or any other could mount a serious threat to Whirlaway. Only Whirlaway could do that. And the Preakness itself did have some potential traps. For one thing, it was a sixteenth of a mile shorter than the Derby, meaning Whirlaway would have less time to recover in the event of a slow start. For another, it was a shorter track, which meant there were sharper turns, which meant a horse that was so inclined could easily drift wide.

No, Jones said. That wouldn't happen. Not with Arcaro. Not with Whirlaway getting a taste of what his life could be like with a measure of discipline. This was a horse, after all, clearly nourished by the affections of the masses, who could hear them as they chanted "Go Mr. Longtail!" and who responded to their cries of "Here comes Whirlaway!" The great horses are like that. Jones had heard all the stories about Man O' War, and about Gallant Fox, and, of course, about Seabiscuit, all the most popular horses, all of whom fed off the love of the spectators and all but sneered at any other horse who would try to get in their way, try to intercept the devotions aimed entirely at them. And right now Whirlaway was clearly the object of the nation's abiding affection.

But as Jones would discover as he hopped off the train in Baltimore, he was also the target of its underlying cynicism, too. While they were on their journey, the *New York Daily Mirror* had published an item by its star columnist, Dan Parker, speculating that on Derby Day Whirlaway had been suffering from such a bad cold that he'd been given a triple dose of medicine. Sixty-five years before his professional descendants would begin asking baseball players if they'd ever beaten steroid tests, Parker asked Whirlaway, in his column, if he'd been given a proper saliva test.

It was a serious charge, and it was one that infuriated Jones, whose reputation as a gentleman had never before been questioned, and who categorically denied that anything untoward had ever come close to entering Whirlaway's system, and who immediately issued a defiant challenge to

Parker and anyone else who doubted the veracity of what they'd seen at Churchill Downs: "Bring Whirlaway out of the stable at midnight, high noon, or anytime, and without any notice whatsoever throw a saddle and rider on him and let him show you what he can do to any horse of his age at any distance and under any conditions."

Parker quickly retracted his column, and the Churchill Downs authorities issued an immediate statement that Whirlaway had indeed been tested and come up clean, and the controversy dissolved before it could gain momentum. But the world had been granted a peek behind Jones's stoic front and seen just how passionately this trainer cared for this horse. For Jones, training Whirly was truly more than a job now. It was part of who he was. All by himself, Whirlaway seemed to justify all those endless years of lonely toil.

"I've never spent as much time on any two horses as I have on this one," Jones admitted on May 7, the day Whirlaway reported for his first day of work at Pimlico, the day that another object of American fascination, Hank Greenberg, reported for *his* first day of work at Fort Custer, Michigan. "But he's worth it. Because I truly believe this horse can do what Sir Barton, Gallant Fox, Omaha, and War Admiral did."

With that one sentence, Ben Jones said for the record what the rest of the sporting nation had been thinking for three solid days. Jones never mentioned the magical words "Triple Crown," but that's precisely what he meant. Even the great Man O' War hadn't won the Triple Crown (if only because he hadn't been entered in the Kentucky Derby), and while it had been only four years since War Admiral executed that trick, there was little doubt that a Triple Crown chase was precisely what this sport coveted, mostly because the world of 1941 was almost entirely different from the world in 1937. Where there were only shadows of darkness then, largely ushered in by economic gloom, now there was an endless barrage of bad news that bordered on the apocalyptic. People needed good news. It sustained them. It fortified them. They needed these respites. It's why movie houses reported turnaway business, why Broadway was selling more tickets than ever before, why nearly 200,000 people had swarmed to ballparks on baseball's Opening Day. And why there was little doubt that the Preakness would be the toughest ticket in Baltimore, or anywhere else, on the afternoon of Saturday, May 10, 1941.

Rain loomed heavy in the forecast, as it had in Louisville the week before, and while Whirlaway had a reputation as a good mudder, nobody wanted to see him have to slog his way through the race after the way he'd electrified the homestretch in Louisville. Luckily, as it had in Kentucky, the sun not only scared away the clouds, it dried the track by the time the horses were gathered at the starting gate at 5:55 P.M., Eastern Time. This time there was no trepidation on anyone's part to install Whirlaway an overwhelming favorite, and that was reflected in the terribly short price the horse commanded: To win four dollars, you had to bet five. Yet nobody seemed to mind; Whirlaway money kept rolling in all the way to post.

Arcaro, who'd spent the week as the toast of New York's racing community, guided Whirlaway into the number-one post position and admitted he was never more confident in a horse's ability to win a race. "I cannot see how Whirlaway can lose first money in the Preakness," he'd said boldly just the day before, and there was little reason to doubt him. Bold Irishman had been forced to withdraw due to a cough and a fever. The usual suspects— Our Boots, Dispose, Porter's Cap—were sprinkled in the eight-horse field, but most of them were still shell-shocked by Whirlaway's mighty dash a week before. Only an unspeakable calamity could ruin the day.

Two seconds into the race, unspeakable calamity nearly crashed the party.

"Whirlaway walks out of the gate counting the house!" is the way the voice of Ed Thorgerson would describe it for the Fox Movietone Newsreel that would be sent to theaters later in the week. It was true. As the gates opened, seven horses galloped wildly, clearly understanding that the fifty-first annual Preakness was officially under way. The eighth horse, wearing devil red and blue and a prominent number one on its side, seemed utterly disinterested. Whirlaway had taken Jones's earlier Derby instructions about getting left at the gate literally. Off the pack raced, off into the distance, before Whirlaway finally built up a head of steam. It was a quarter of a mile before he was close enough to even sniff the dust his competitors had left him in, and if what the world had heard a week earlier was the sound of 100,000 people in the throes of athletic ecstasy, what you heard now was the sound of 35,000 people having a shared nervous breakdown.

"It wasn't just that we were in last place that was driving me nuts," Arcaro said. "We were in last place and we were *ten lengths* behind the next horse."

In reality, as Whirlaway neared the five-eighths pole, just under halfway through the race, he sat an astonishing twenty lengths behind King Cole, the leader. It had long been said of Arcaro that of all the things that made him The Master—courage, swagger, confidence, strength—the one that separated him from his peers was the internal clock that clicked in his brain. And what that ticker told him now was simple, and it's something he yelled into Whirlaway's ears over the nervous din of the crowd:

"You gotta *go! Now!*"

Arcaro grabbed the reins tight, and that seemed to finally get the horse's attention. "He started fighting me," he said, "which is what I needed to get him started." In almost any other horse alive, it wouldn't have mattered; there was simply too much ground to make up and too little time in which to make it up. But as Whirlaway began to make his move, as his ears perked up, so did the crowd's spirit. Slowly the roar began to build, and slowly the horses out ahead began to wonder what all the commotion was about, something they'd learn sooner than any of them could have imagined.

On the grainy, unsophisticated film that survives from that 1941 race, at the moment Whirlaway makes his move it seems that a kind of twenty-first-century trickery invades the footage. It's as if through f/x magic, the other seven horses continue to gallop but stop moving forward, and the number 1 horse speeds ahead, passing each foe one by one with an ease that seems comical, otherworldly. But then you realize, that's precisely how it happened. No tricks. No bluescreens. And even though there is no sound attached to the movie, save for the sound of Thorgerson's grim monotone, it isn't difficult to discern what they were shouting at Pimlico Race Course as all of this was happening.

HERE COMES WHIRLAWAY!

Thorgerson couldn't keep up with Whirlaway's pace; as he announces Whirly's move into fourth, he's actually already moved into third; as the announcer credits him for sneaking into second he's already eye-to-eye with King Cole.

At that very instant Arcaro, intoxicated by the moment, appreciating the privilege of seeing a once-in-a-lifetime athlete at the peak of his game, up close, couldn't help himself. He turned slightly, made eye contact with King Cole's rider, Johnny Gilbert.

"Good-bye, Johnny!" he shouted.

"Good-bye Eddie," Gilbert yelled back, but by the time he did, Arcaro was already out of range, already a length clear of him, already on a final tear toward the finish. He eased across the line in one minute, fifty-eight and four-fifths seconds, not a record but plenty fast on a track that was listed at good but was still heavy and soft thanks to all the rain. More telling, across the final three-quarters of a mile, Whirlaway had made up an impossible total of twenty-five lengths—from twenty behind to five ahead.

"I've never rode such a horse in all my life," Arcaro gushed. "There's no three-year-old around that can touch Whirly. I think he's just about the best colt of his age I ever rode. He got away slowly today, but that's what we expected him to do and I never had any doubt that he could overtake the field. I look for him to take the Belmont Stakes in a walk and become the fifth Triple Crown winner."

There it was: out in the open, out there for the world to ponder. Leave it to The Master to verbalize what everyone else was thinking. But it wasn't just the brash rider who'd say the magic words this time. No, when Warren Wright first cleared his throat that day, after presenting the winning crown of black-eyed Susans to Don Ameche, he said it, too: "We'll win the Belmont. We want that Triple Crown now." And even Ben Jones, who understood more than the others that thinking about the Triple Crown was the best way to jinx yourself from ever winning a Triple Crown, saw no need to couch his words any longer: "We want the Triple Crown," he said. "And I think we'll get it."

Whirlaway, ducking his head into a triumphant bowl of oats, was unavailable for comment: But it's believed he concurred with his teammates.

———•———

West Australian was the first horse to pull off the original Triple Crown, in 1853, winning England's Big Three races and causing an international sensation. In America, the Belmont Stakes (first run in 1867), Preakness (born in 1873), and Kentucky Derby (which debuted in 1875) spent more than fifty years as separate, independent, quality horse races that had little to do with one another. Sir Barton was the first horse to win all three races in the same year (1919), but there was no official connection between the three, so relatively little fanfare was attached. The following season was the great year of Man O' War, who crushed the field in the Preakness and the Belmont but whose owners didn't like racing in Kentucky and believed the race was held too early in the year for a horse to run a mile and a quarter.

So while Man O' War ultimately earned a reputation as the greatest of all Thoroughbreds, there was a definite hole in his historical résumé.

This bothered many who cared about the sport's standing in history, and a sportswriter for the *Daily Racing Form* named Charles Hatton sought to rectify that. When Gallant Fox duplicated Sir Barton's trifecta in 1930, Hatton borrowed from the British and the name "American Triple Crown" quickly stuck. Omaha had followed in 1935 and War Admiral in 1937, and both those horses had earned prominent legacies thanks to their triumphs, but neither of them had ever captured the American imagination the way Whirlaway had. So Wright, Jones, and Arcaro weren't the only ones who held such lofty ambitions for the colt after the Preakness. In the United States, the countdown to the Belmont Stakes not only dominated the sports page, it infiltrated page one as well. And even in England, the BBC offered regular updates on Whirlaway's attempt to cash in the Triple Crown's third jewel.

Part of the reason for England's sudden interest in leisurely American affairs was that in the three weeks separating the Preakness and the Belmont, for the first time in far too long, their sagging national spirit had been given a series of boosts that further buoyed their resilience. As they had so often across the past year, Londoners not only survived the long aerial assault of May 10, they started almost instantly trying to rebuild and repair where the bombs had fallen. The feared invasion hadn't materialized, and now there was word that if it happened at all, it wouldn't come for months.

Then on May 12 came the bizarre story of Rudolf Hess, the number-three-ranking member of the Nazi Party and a trusted Hitler confidant. On May 10, Hess, an expert pilot, had put on a Luftwaffe uniform, stepped into a Messerschmitt Me-110 fighter plane sitting on an Augsburg runway, fired the twin engines, and began a five-hour, nine-hundred-mile flight across the North Sea with the intention of landing at the residence of the Duke of Hamilton's estate, near Glasgow, Scotland. At six thousand feet, within thirty miles of the Duke's residence, Hess bailed out, parachuted safely to the ground, encountered a Scottish farmer, and told him in perfect English: "I have an important message for the Duke of Hamilton."

Churchill—unsure whether this was a ruse, a put-on, or a genuine Nazi olive branch—had him interrogated by army officers. To them, Hess proposed that if the British would allow Germany to dominate Europe, the

British Empire would not be further decimated by Nazi attacks. He declared that German victory was inevitable and hinted that England would be slowly starved to death by a coming Nazi blockade ringing the British Isles. Hitler, learning of his ex-aide's flight, quickly disavowed him as insane, and Churchill slowly came to realize that he probably was, too, after interviewing him personally. If nothing else, it was a massive humiliation for Hitler, and that alone was enough to cheer English souls.

Two weeks later there was another meaningful victory—the sinking of the German warship *Bismarck* on May 27. Three days earlier the *Bismarck* had scored a direct hit on the British battle cruiser HMS *Hood,* the world's largest battleship, during an engagement between Iceland and Greenland. The *Hood* exploded and sank, and all but three of 1,418 men were lost, another blow to England's psyche. But Churchill immediately declared that all of the Royal Navy's resources would be utilized to stalk, find, and ultimately sink the *Bismarck*.

At nine o'clock on the morning of the twenty-seventh, the *Bismarck,* already disabled and surrounded by three British ships, absorbed the first of a battery of attacks. The crew refused to surrender, and within ninety minutes the ship disappeared beneath the water, ending some 2,100 German lives. For the first time, those whose hopes were linked with England— both within the United Kingdom and in the United States—started to believe that the English were not lambs waiting to be led to slaughter. It was a pivotal perception change that not only emboldened English subjects, but also started to convince a larger majority of Americans that if the nation would have to enter the conflict, it would not be for a lost cause. Eighty-two percent of the respondents in a Gallup poll said as much.

In New York City, where so many sailors were based, where all of them had kept a watchful eye on the pursuit of the *Bismarck,* they happily allowed themselves to get swept up in Whirlaway fever. It had been a slow spring in New York thus far. The Yankees had spent much of May languishing in last place, thanks mostly to a stifling slump suffered by Joe DiMaggio. The Giants were already out of the race. The Dodgers were trying to stay with the Cardinals in the National League, but after so many years of fruitless folly, Dodgers fans knew better than to expect that to last very long. So the Belmont couldn't have come at a better time. Best of all, as June 7 approached, it seemed race day was going to arrive less a celebration than an all-out coronation.

For one thing, after weeks of speculation, Eddie Arcaro's primary employer, Greentree Stables, opted not to enter any of its horses in the race, freeing Arcaro to ride Whirlaway and try to gallop jointly into the ages. There also weren't many horsemen who wanted to serve as sacrificial steeds at the altar of Whirlaway, either: Only three other names were entered in the Belmont, and race officials were happy to have that many as it appeared for a time that Whirlaway might be allowed to run unopposed, so great had his aura already grown. There would be little money to be won, not with Whirlaway going off as a one-to-four lock. But that hardly mattered. The forty thousand people who would jam Belmont Park were there for something else, hoping to secure a slice of history in return for their entrance fee.

Only there were three conspirators hoping to blot this happy ending: Tom McCreery, Max Hirsch, and E. L. Snyder, the trainers for, respectively, Robert Morris, Itabo, and Yankee Chance, the other three horses in the field. In the days before the race, the three men sat together and acknowledged that, individually, none of their horses had a prayer against the people's horse. But collectively, if they could set a slow pace and lull Whirlaway to sleep, perhaps one of them would have enough, by the homestretch, to outsprint Whirly and give the race quite a shocking jolt. The strategy made perfect sense, especially since they all knew of Ben Jones's reluctance to allow Whirlaway to run early in a race. And since the Belmont was the longest of all three races at a mile and a half—a distance that would kill off too many Triple Crown bids to count in the years to come—there was no telling how Whirlaway would react to a slow pace.

What the trainers hadn't banked on, and should have, was the man who was steering Whirlaway, who was never more on top of his game than he was in the spring of 1941. Arcaro spotted precisely the kind of trap his rivals had set for him, and he knew he wanted no part of it. Besides, the Whirlaway running today bore little resemblance to the scatterbrained colt who'd run all over the track in Florida. *This* Whirlaway relished rising to the moment. He coveted a challenge.

In a move that would be unheard of just a few years later, Jones had actually entered Whirlaway in a race between the Preakness and the Belmont, the Henry of Navarre Purse, and even with Eads riding him—and Arcaro on another pursuing horse, Hash—Whirlaway had eased to a three-length win. He had gotten a taste for winning, and liked it. No longer nervous and restless, Whirlaway had actually fallen asleep in the paddock moments before the race, as he was being saddled up. Racing was like breathing to him now. There had also been a feisty workout two days before the Belmont. With trainers lined up at the finish line armed with stopwatches, Whirlaway had run a mile and a quarter in a crackling 2:02 2/5, just a second off his Derby record time, an unheard-of speed for a training run. Trainers up and down the rail were seen shaking their watches in disbelief.

So the horse liked putting on a show, too.

Ben Jones delighted in that, and delighted in the day, too. He wasn't impressed by much, and certainly wasn't given to self-reflection, yet here he was, the man most responsible for filling Whirlaway's legs with confidence and the Belmont Park grandstands with humanity. Jones's father had been a banker and a farmer in Parnell, Missouri, at a time before Parnell had even risen from the prairie to earn a dot on a map. The Joneses raised anything on four legs—hogs, horses, cattle, Missouri mules—and in the middle of the property the elder Jones constructed a crude horse track where, on Saturdays, folks from all over northwest Missouri and southwest Iowa would gather to race. Now, Ben watched over forty thousand New Yorkers stuff themselves into Belmont's rickety old bleachers, and he marveled at it all.

"I believe I have traveled a long, long way from Parnell, Missouri," he said to a friend as the two of them watched Whirlaway ease into the paddock, as he listened to the thrall of a full house whose eyes were all locked on the same horse, his horse, the one he'd waited his whole life to find. From somewhere deep in the crowd, a leather-lunged bettor yelled, "Hey, Ben! You think Whirly's gonna win?"

From atop the horse, a stableboy named Pinky Brown frowned and said, "You better believe he'll win" just before dismounting and ceding the saddle to Eddie Arcaro. Jones laughed. He didn't often engage crowds, but the crowds had come to see his horse, this was his day, and he played along. "I hope so," the trainer said. "If he doesn't they better spread a net to catch the fellows who bet him because they'll be jumping off the roof of the grandstand by the thousand."

Arcaro felt energized, too. In the sparsely populated starting gate, he sensed a calm about Whirlaway, even as his own heart was racing at track-record speed. When the gates opened, he followed his usual blueprint for a few moments, until his eyes told him what his gut had already hinted: He was on to his rivals' conspiracy. He knew what they were doing. And so one last time, thirty seconds into the race, he leaned over and shouted into Whirlaway's ear.

"You ready, boy?" he asked.

The shift in the horse's gait told Arcaro that he certainly was. Now he looked left, looked right, and delivered one final message to the other three riders, and their horses.

"I'm leaving, boys," he yelped. "Get the hell out of our way. We'll see you back at the house."

With that, Whirlaway was gone, and so were anyone else's hopes of winning the 1941 Belmont Stakes and knocking the Triple Crown laurels off Whirlaway's mane. For the first time, Whirly ran with the lead for a full mile, and he loved every step of it, loved drinking in the adulation of the crowd, loved the whooshing roar as he sped past the main grandstand, crossed the finish line, and etched for himself a lasting piece of glory. There was no need to urge him on this time, but out of habit the people did anyway: *Here comes Whirlaway!* The final margin was three lengths. There wasn't a soul inside Belmont Park who didn't believe it couldn't have been thirty if he'd wanted it to be.

"There must be jam on my face," Arcaro crowed, "because this is the sweetest thing I've ever tasted!"

Warren Wright was absent on this day, and missed his greatest triumph as a horseman, because he was in Denver attending his son's college graduation. But Ben Jones, speaking for his boss, said, "I think this is a day people will remember for as long as they race horses." Then, like a hard-ass football coach who doesn't want his players to get too giddy after a big win, Jones had this to add: "We don't intend to shut up shop just because we won the Derby, Preakness, and Belmont. Why, we're going to run until Heaven knows when—through the summer, the fall, and probably the winter. We've still got a lot of work and a lot of races ahead of us and while we aren't talking about Seabiscuit's record . . . we have it in mind."

Seabiscuit had earned $437,730 in his career. With the $39,770 he earned with his win at the Belmont, Whirlaway stood at $236,111, with a whole lot of racing left in his legs. In a country where the median annual salary was just north of $3,000, it may have seemed a little extravagant to be talking about such figures. Of course, elsewhere in the newspapers of Sunday morning, June 8, 1941, there were stories about Vichy France inching closer to full collaboration with the Nazis, to the growing rift between former allies Germany and Russia, to Britain's "extremely grave" naval positions. There was also this editorial in the Rome paper *Popolo di Roma*, picked up by the wire services, criticizing Italians for being too soft with the "Jew problem," wondering: "Where are all those Jew-haters who appeared suddenly as if by magic soon after the enunciation of racial principles? How many of these opportunists today notice the danger of Jewry, which is a corrosive element and a denial of every sacred moral and patriotic principle? The Jew today, more than yesterday, must be watched."

Given that world, given these times, rooting for rich guys to get richer didn't seem quite so obscene.

4

"THERE'S NO USE KIDDING MYSELF."

JOE DIMAGGIO SEARCHES FOR ANSWERS
AT THE EDGE OF THE ABYSS

Charles A. Lindbergh greets a crowd at New York's Madison Square Garden with a triumphant gesture after speaking at an America First rally. Lindbergh, once America's preeminent role model, saw his star fall drastically in 1941, as the nation reached out to other heroes, such as Joe DiMaggio.

Who started baseball's famous streak
That's got us all aglow?
He's just a man and not a freak,
Joltin' Joe DiMaggio.

Joe . . . Joe . . . DiMaggio . . .
We want you on our side . . .

From Coast to Coast, that's all you hear
Of Joe the One-Man Show.
He's glorified the horsehide sphere,
Joltin' Joe DiMaggio.

Joe . . . Joe . . . DiMaggio . . .
We want you on our side.

—Alan Courtney, Summer 1941

———————●———————

The advertisement appeared early in the spring, first in the pages of *The Sporting News*, the baseball bible, later in the newspapers of New York City, later still all over the country's sports pages. Joe DiMaggio was in his sixth season as the most famous player on the most famous baseball team in the media capital of planet Earth, so this wasn't the first time his smiling face had appeared hawking product. Still, as even his teammates would kid him, they'd never seen the twenty-six-year-old Joe look as happy as he did in these cigarette ads, a wide grin creasing his face, a freshly lit Camel sitting between the index finger and middle finger of his right hand, the smoke curling invitingly from the lit tip. In 1941, there was no greater status symbol than this among the cognoscenti. You could peddle breakfast cereal, chocolate milk, Rawlings sporting equipment, chewing gum. You could attach your name to the local brewery, or the local distillery, or the local car dealership, or the finest local restaurants. The money was just as good there, the exposure just as wide. But when you were asked to be a spokesman for Camel . . . well, you'd not only made it, you'd made it *large*.

Just Smoke It.

"You bet I smoke Camels," were the quotes crafted for DiMaggio that ran in the copy underneath his picture. "Along with all that swell flavor, Camels are EXTRA MILD. Camels have been my cigarette for years. There's less nicotine in the smoke and that extra mildness is important to a smoker like me. On top of that, Camels just always taste better. They're a cigarette that's really fun to smoke."

It was good that DiMaggio derived such pleasure from this profitable pastime, because by the middle of May he was smoking his Camels just about as fast as the company could cultivate the tobacco, roll it, box it, and send it off. DiMaggio had been a heavy smoker for years, but when he was nervous, or when he was uncomfortable, or when he was in a black mood, he barely ever drew a smoke-free breath.

And when he was in a batting slump?

"When Joe wasn't hitting," Tommy Henrich, his longtime friend and teammate, would say many years later, "then he was a human chimney."

Joe wasn't hitting. Outside, sheets of rain were falling on Fenway Park, and the Red Sox–Yankees game scheduled for two o'clock this afternoon of May 10 was soon canceled, the Yankees' first rainout of the season. Usually this would fill DiMaggio with more than a twinge of dread, because the ballpark was always a place where DiMaggio could find sanctuary, no matter what else was going on in his life. At the ballpark he would be guaranteed four solid shots a day to hit a baseball as hard as he could, he'd be allowed to roam the vast lawns of center field to his heart's content. The splendid geometries of a baseball field provided the one place on earth where he truly felt at home. It was usually a gift.

But the past few weeks, DiMaggio hadn't even hit his weight. Just nineteen days earlier, his batting average had been a gaudy .528. The baseball scribes had already assumed he would be winning his third consecutive batting championship, and now the only question was whether he'd become the first American League player in eighteen years to hit .400. Hell, why couldn't he take a run at Rogers Hornsby's modern single-season record of .424? He was the Jolter, the Yankee Clipper, maybe the greatest player since Babe Ruth, and he made playing the game look ridiculously easy.

What *couldn't* he do?

For the past nineteen days the simple answer had been, just about everything. Since April 22, DiMaggio had come to bat fifty-six times and collected only nine hits, a .161 clip that chopped 224 points off his average. Things had gotten so bad that before squeezing out a couple of scratch hits in the Yankees' most recent game, a 5-4 win over the Cleveland Indians on May 8, DiMaggio's average for the season stood at .295—the first time in his five-plus-year major league career that he'd sat south of .300 after May Day.

DiMaggio's teammates—especially pitcher Lefty Gomez, his best friend on the club, his roommate on the road—tried keeping his mind off his worries, tried joking with him, but it was no use. For the second straight year, the Yankees were in danger of falling out of the American League pennant race, they were barely playing .500 ball, and DiMaggio believed there was one man responsible for these unacceptable failures: He was wearing the number 5 on the back of his pinstripes, hitting fourth in the batting order, and staring glumly back at him in the clubhouse mirror. So DiMaggio smoked, and smoked some more, and guzzled cup after cup of coffee as black as his spikes, and smoked more Camels, and chased them with more coffee, and as the rain fell in Boston he finally shared with the world the wars raging within his soul.

"There's no use kidding myself," he said by his locker, shaking his head, crumpling a cardboard cup after draining its contents dry. "I'm in the worst slump I've ever experienced in all my years in the game. Believe me, I don't know the answer to the problem. I wish I did.

"They say the battle's half won when you know the cause of something.

Then you can go and try to discover the solution. I guess I know what's happened to me but why it happened or how to remedy it—well, that's something else."

Someone asked him, "Joe, are you feeling all right?"

"I feel fine," he sighed. "My timing is off. I've been getting a couple on the fat part of my bat and managing to get some base hits now and then, but for the most part I'm catching the pitches on the handle or some other part of my bat where it doesn't do much good. You go up there saying to yourself, 'Here's one that's going out of the park.' The pitch comes in and it looks like a fat one and then instead of smashing it the way you want to, you only get a piece of it. There's only one thing you can do. Just go up there, keep on swinging, and hope that sooner or later—much sooner I hope—you'll come out of it."

Then DiMaggio laughed, asking no one in particular: How do you figure this game out? His whole career, DiMaggio had been a notoriously slow spring starter. When he wasn't holding out for a bigger contract, he was fighting off injuries, spending more time in the trainer's room than out in the glorious sunshine of St. Petersburg, the Yankees' spring headquarters. This time there'd been a brief holdout, he'd gotten to camp a little late, but almost as soon as he unpacked his suitcases he'd started to see the ball fantastically, smashing it all over the South. DiMaggio had played in twenty spring exhibition games, and he'd gotten at least one hit in all twenty. After the first eight games of the regular season, he'd hit in all eight, accruing that .528 batting average. Every pitch he saw looked big as a beach ball, and even when he didn't crush a ball, he'd been incredibly lucky— every broken bat seemed to yield a bloop single, every grounder seemed to find a hole or hit a pebble that sent it sailing over a shortstop's head like a golf ball hitting a cart path. There were moments he felt he might never go a game without getting a hit. Twenty-eight and counting; how high could that number go?

The game was never designed to look that easy.

And the game has a funny way of taking its revenge.

Lester McCrabb was the first pitcher to figure DiMaggio out in the spring of 1941. McCrabb was a twenty-six-year-old right-hander for the Philadelphia Athletics who would pitch in precisely thirty-eight major league games in his career. As the papers gleefully pointed out, his $2,800 yearly salary was about half of what Joe DiMaggio pulled down in a month. But on April 22, he handed DiMaggio a stiff 0-for-3 collar in earning one of his nine lifetime victories, 6-5. Could McCrabb have been the trigger for this puzzling slump that had now lasted eighteen infuriating days? DiMaggio scoffed.

"He's not too fast and his curve is a dinky one. He's got something like a sinker but nothing to get excited about. McCrabb didn't come near equaling some of the pitching we've seen so far this season," he said.

He lit a fresh Camel.

"Off the figures, I look terrible. But I have belted a good many hard balls, only to have them caught. Mind you, I am offering no excuses. It's my timing. It's a way off. How do slumps like that hit a batter? Well, the boys have been trying to dope that since baseball began. I don't know what brings it on but I certainly know it's here. When it hits you, you do some lunging. You hit some on the handle. You start pressing and it gets worse than ever. Then you decide to concentrate on your timing, and the harder you try the tougher the going. There is no remedy. Time and confidence in yourself are about all you can look to."

Joe McCarthy, the Yankees' manager, was walking past and heard both the interrogations and his star slugger's self-analysis and decided to interject his own two bits: "DiMaggio is hitting the ball all right, but he's also hitting into some bad luck."

DiMaggio was eager to get back to the hotel on that May 10. No game meant he'd be able to find a radio somewhere around a quarter to six and listen to his pal Eddie Arcaro try to guide the great horse Whirlaway to the second leg of the Triple Crown that afternoon at the Preakness. "I hope he doesn't get rained on," DiMaggio said. "I could use the day off. But those fellows, they keep working through the storm."

Whirlaway survived fine. And so, it seemed, would DiMaggio. The next two days at Fenway Park, he had five hits in nine trips to the plate and beefed his average back up to .327 (already forty points behind Ted Williams, his likely rival for the batting title, who went 4-for-9 during the series), but the Yankees lost both, so his mood remained cloudy and so did his hotel room. The great Bob Feller did nothing to improve the situation on May 13, as he muffled DiMaggio all four trips to the plate, and when Joe followed that with an 0-for-3 the next day, not only was the average back down to .306, but the Yankees had lost four games in a row. They were sitting right at sea level at fourteen wins and fourteen losses, and they were already five and a half games in back of the streaking Indians, who were starting to look like the smart bet in the American League.

And things *still* hadn't hit rock bottom for the once-proud Yankees. Just two years before, the plaintive wail of "Break up the Yankees!" had drifted out of the front offices of each of the other fifteen major league clubs. The Yankees were ruining baseball. They not only won all the time, they crushed everyone. From 1936 through '39—which also happened to be Joe DiMaggio's first four seasons with the team—they won two out of every three games they played, averaging 102 wins against 51 losses and winning four World Series in a row, the last two in 4-0 sweeps over the Chicago Cubs and Cincinnati Reds.

How dominant were they? Consider that early in 1939 they suffered one of the most staggering blows a team ever absorbed, losing Lou Gehrig in early May with what was diagnosed as amyotrophic lateral sclerosis, a disease that would soon bear his name and lay him on his deathbed inside of two years. And how did they respond to missing one of the five greatest players of all time? They won 106 games. They scored 967 runs—over 400 more than their opponents scored, meaning that the average Yankee game that year was a 7-3 win for the men in pinstripes. DiMaggio hit .381, and seemed a shoo-in to hit .400 until an eye infection late in the year caused him to slump.

Break up the Yankees indeed. They were unstoppable.

But in 1940 they won only 88 games, finishing third behind the Tigers and Indians, and this simply wasn't acceptable to the men who ran the Yankees. They sought change. They needed to get younger, and so in 1941 they'd started playing Tommy Henrich and Phil Rizzuto and Jerry Priddy more regularly, but none of the kids was hitting, the pitching was spotty, and they were starting to hear about it from a press corps that until now had been almost ceaselessly fawning. In the *New York Post,* for example, columnist Stanley Frank summed up the yesterday's-news vibe the Yankees were giving off by asserting that they "may wind up fighting Detroit to keep out of the second division. The Yankees have a fine nucleus for re-building a pennant winner, and if this sounds like the kiss-off, I'm sorry, but that's the way things are. The great Yankees belong in the past or future tense, but not the present."

Even Yankees fans, spoiled by success, had started to actually boo the locals when they bothered to show up at all. On May 15, only 9,040 of them trickled into 65,000-seat Yankee Stadium for a matinee with the White Sox, and those who came were sorry they made the effort. The Sox drubbed the home team 13-1, sinking the Yankees south of .500 for the first time all year, pushing them six and a half games out of first. Worst of all, it turned out that one of the main culprits for the bludgeoning was the one man they figured would make the cost of admission worthwhile: In the top of the first, DiMaggio had picked up a single by Luke Appling on the dead run and whistled a throw to third base, hoping to gun out Chicago second baseman Bill Knickerbocker. But the ball skipped in the dirt, ricocheted off Knickerbocker's elbow and into the lower grandstand, and Knickerbocker came trotting home with the game's first run. Yes, DiMaggio did try to make amends in the bottom of the inning, lining a two-out single off Edgar Smith that scored Rizzuto and briefly cut the White Sox lead to 2-1, but what was so unforgettable about that? What was one hit in one game in the context of a 154-game season?

It wouldn't be until later, much later, that DiMaggio—and everyone else—would understand just how significant it really was.

The truth was, unless something *REALLY BIG* came along to capture the people's attention in that uncomfortable spring of 1941—Whirlaway roaring down the homestretch of a Triple Crown horse race, for instance, or Joe Louis defending his heavyweight championship one more time, against that month's designated patsy—it was going to be difficult to keep gazes focused on the back pages of the paper, since every day the front pages were chockablock with the grim, the gruesome, the grisly, and the guttural.

Almost all of it due to the machinations of one deranged man.

On April 20, Adolf Hitler celebrated his fifty-second birthday in the Balkans, in a railway car set up as a temporary field headquarters while his armies crushed a Yugoslavian uprising, folding that haphazard nation of Croats, Serbs, and Montenegrins into the Reich.

The day before, the Nazis captured Mount Olympus in Greece, and would soon enough seize the Acropolis, too. These were heady times for the Germans. Even as Hitler had begun his slow march to power in 1933, bringing with him loud slogans of nationalism and, later, anti-Semitism, few on the European continent believed him capable of whipping the defeated German people into even a minor international force. Yet here he stood, eight years later, on the threshold of European domination, the Nazi standard flapping atop most of the Continent's major landmarks. Once Greece capitulated, as it would on April 27, only England would remain an obstacle in Germany's path toward a complete European monopoly. Later, Hitler was said to be already contemplating reshuffling toward a name change, dubbing the coerced union the "United States of Europe."

"Germany's road to victory has already been illuminated by the light of faith," Joseph Goebbels, the Nazi propaganda minister, had declared during a national birthday celebration for Hitler. "It is the path to final victory. Never have we believed in that so firmly as today. The Fuehrer is bringing that to us. When Mr. Churchill recently spoke regarding the prospects of this war, he declared that Britain would win although he does not yet know how. We can only reply to him: The Fuehrer will be victorious and chiefly because he also knows he will be victorious. He has filled the nation with his spirit."

And the rest of the world with dread. Even Pope Pius XII seemed to accept the inevitable, calling on "whoever wins this terrible war to show humility to the innocent," but knowing that only one potential victor would be a scourge to those very innocents.

With each new conquest, Hitler's confidence would grow tenfold, and soon he understood that his words were no longer merely piercing the shattered hearts of his conquered neighbors, but also the frightened observers across the sea. Hitler would have preferred if the messages of his proxy spokesmen—chiefly the isolationists, particularly Charles A. Lindbergh—had resulted in a greater American resistance toward war than the poll numbers indicated. But he so dismissed the American will to fight, he had started issuing sterner warnings, especially after the passage of the Lend-Lease Act, especially when Roosevelt hinted that he might use American ships as convoys, essentially serving as nautical bodyguards for the vulnerable British supply fleet.

"Whoever believes he will be able to help the English must definitely know one thing: Every ship, whether with or without a convoy, that comes before our torpedo tubes will be torpedoed," Hitler declared in early spring, and there was little doubt who he was talking to. "[England has] hopes—they must have hopes, but what do they expect? What do they hope for? Outside help? America? I can only say one thing: We have taken every possibility into our calculations since the beginning. Everyone who does not wish to distort the truth and who claims the opposite knows the German people have nothing against the American people. Germany has never had interests on the American continent unless it be that she fought along with this continent for its freedom. When the states of this continent now attempt, perhaps, to interfere in the European conflict, then the war aims will only change more quickly. Then Europe will *really* defend herself."

In the conquered lands, people had already gotten an eyeful of what poor winners the Nazis could be. In Serbia, the German army stripped towns bare and randomly lined citizens up against walls for mass executions, sometimes dozens at a time, sometimes hundreds. In Poland, there were already sketchy tales of atrocities that would only grow grimmer and more stunning with time. In occupied France, it was not unusual for large groups of locals to be rounded up and, occasionally, shot on sight if the local Nazi authorities believed even a whiff of resistance swelled underground. And this occurred as official "collaboration" between the Nazis and French grew ever more likely, ever more real.

"It is inconceivable that the people of France will willingly accept any agreement for so-called collaboration which will in reality imply their alliance with a military power whose central and fundamental policy calls for the utter destruction of liberty, freedom and popular institutions everywhere," Roosevelt said. "The people of the United States can hardly believe that the present Government of France could be brought to lend itself to a plan of voluntary alliance implied or otherwise which would apparently deliver up France and its colonial empire."

But given the current shape of the planet, anything was possible. In Europe, that meant the people would try to seize upon any personal victory, great or small, to divorce the mind from an encroaching, ever-corrosive world. Even in Switzerland, it was all but impossible to remain completely neutral. On Hitler's birthday, some 40,000 people had flocked to a stadium in Bern to watch a soccer game between the German national team and a collection of Swiss all-stars. Six thousand of the spectators were German nationals, and before the game, accompanied by a military band, they sang "Horst Wessel Lied" at ear-splitting volume. When they were done, as the German players responded with a collective Hitler salute, just before the first ball was dropped on the pitch, the other 30,000 people in attendance shattered the solemnity and broke out in an impromptu version of "Rufst du Mein Vaterland (You Call My Homeland)," the Swiss national anthem, and they sang renditions in both German and French as a sign of quiet solidarity with the bloodied victims on both sides of the broadening conflict. The Swiss won the game 2-1, and the celebration lasted well into the night in Bern and throughout Switzerland as word of the victory spread. The next day, in Paris, in London, in The Hague, in Brussels, in all the places that used to be free until Nazi jackboots trampled that liberty into the dust, as the news spread even further, there was quiet but evident rejoicing. Small victories.

———•———

Part of the curse of being Joe DiMaggio was the hard truth that for all the expectations heaped upon his shoulders by others, those standards were always dwarfed by what he demanded from himself. His limitless ambitions had helped lift a high school dropout to a place of prominence in American society that only a few other citizens could match. DiMaggio wasn't merely a hero to young baseball fans, who are always the first to select and then lionize their idols, he was also an icon to adults—especially to immigrants who drilled into their children that if DiMaggio, son of an Italian-born fisherman, could attain such high hopes, then America really was the land where dreams could come true. In the Italian American community, especially, he was revered, and that wasn't limited to New York City. In Boston, where the Yankees' chief American League rival team played, DiMaggio would go his entire career and only hear sporadic boos, a testament not only to the large number of Italian American Red Sox fans who flooded Fenway Park, but also to the presence of Dominic DiMaggio, Joe's kid brother, who patrolled center field for the Red Sox during much of Joe's career.

"Sometimes," DiMaggio would confide in Lefty Gomez during that summer of 1941, "it's only when I sleep that I don't feel thousands of eyes staring right at me. And that's only if those eyes don't follow me into my dreams."

DiMaggio's perfectionism didn't come cheaply, however. Every spring, he and Yankees general manager Ed Barrow danced the same dance, haggling over a few hundred dollars here, a few thousand there. Even as a kid, it wasn't strictly about the bottom line with DiMaggio, because what he made off the field soon dwarfed his Yankees salary. No, DiMaggio may have been the most prideful—pride-filled—athlete of his generation. He simply demanded what agents more than half a century later would term "fair market value." If baseball fans are slow to swallow that sort of spin now, they were perfectly repulsed by it during the Depression. In 1938, prior to his third season, DiMaggio demanded $40,000. When Barrow and Jacob Ruppert, the Yankees' owner, countered with $17,000 and a horrified explanation that "Even Lou Gehrig doesn't make that much," DiMaggio countered with what might have been the pithiest quip of his public life: "Then Mr. Gehrig is badly underpaid."

DiMaggio's dispute lasted through the spring and bled into the first few days of the season, and he was helped neither by Gehrig's willingness to sign on for $39,000 nor by this public rebuke from Ruppert, who on Opening Day that year scornfully declared, "I have nothing new on DiMaggio. I've forgotten all about him. Presidents go into eclipse, kings have their thrones moved from under them, business leaders go into retirement, and great ballplayers pass on." The public, most of whom were still stuck in the throes of economic ruin, quickly sided with the millionaire owner, and when DiMaggio ultimately did settle (for $25,000), he was greeted with the first and only boos of his career. That hurt, sure. But it didn't sever DiMaggio's willingness to fight for what he considered a reasonable piece of the Yankees pie. So as winter melted into spring in 1941, as the Yankees headed south to their Florida home in St. Petersburg, one more time they opened for business with DiMaggio sitting three thousand miles away at home in San Francisco. The Yankees had offered $32,500, the exact amount he'd earned for winning the batting title in 1940. DiMaggio looked around the league, and this is what he saw: Hank Greenberg, $55,000. Bob Feller, $45,000. Bobo Newsom—Bobo Newsom!—$40,000.

There was no way DiMaggio could report in good conscience without asking for at least what Bobo Newsom—lifetime record to that point: 121-107—was getting. "They're entitled to as much as they can get," DiMaggio said. "And the more, the better."

"I know nothing of DiMaggio's returning his contract," Barrow insisted from Florida after the Yankees had officially hung out their shingle there and after he'd actually received a third unsigned contract back from his star. "We haven't heard a word from him since we mailed the contracts. If it is on the way back it hasn't arrived yet. That's all I can say except to emphasize that DiMaggio is not a holdout. I do not regard any player as a holdout unless and until he fails to present himself at the training camp."

DiMaggio certainly considered himself a holdout. On February 26 he appeared on the popular radio program *The Eddie Cantor Show,* and when the host asked if DiMaggio intended to work at all in 1941, Joe replied, "You'll have to ask the Yankees that question." Weeks dragged past. Reporters staked out the DiMaggio family restaurant on Fisherman's Wharf in downtown San Francisco, tried to get a read on the negotiations, and came away with nothing until finally, on March 6, they spotted DiMaggio's wife Dorothy, smiling a broad smile as she exited the joint.

"Yes, it's true Joe has signed his 1941 contract," she happily reported. "We are leaving tomorrow for Florida. He is very satisfied with the contract."

He'd get $35,000, which didn't make him happy; but he had bled an extra $2,500 from the tightfisted Barrow, and that made him *extremely* happy, so much so that before the DiMaggios had even made it clear of the California border in their new Cadillac, he was pulled over by a highway patrolman named Wayne Langston, who cited DiMaggio for going seventy miles per hour. The newspapers declared this proved just how anxious Joe was to get going, and DiMaggio didn't argue with them when he arrived. The boys in the press did scrape an old nerve with DiMaggio, though, when they asked if missing some spring workout time could hinder him from playing a full schedule.

That was always the great unspoken worry about the young DiMaggio: he had a hard time keeping himself on the field, especially early in the season. He was late beginning his rookie season because of X-ray burns on his left foot; in 1937 he was sent home from Knoxville, Tennessee, for a tonsillectomy during the Yankees' trek north; in '38 he was a holdout and didn't open the season, and then, in 1939, while he played the first eight games of the season, he then hurt his leg and missed a week. Just before the start of the 1940 season he was hurt sliding into second base in an exhibition at Ebbets Field. Maybe none of this would have been such a big deal if he weren't the natural heir to Lou Gehrig as the Yankees' designated marvel, but he was. And Gehrig had played in 2,130 consecutive games without once being sidelined by any of the ills that kept afflicting his successor.

"If I have any special ambition, it's playing a full schedule," he said, sweat glistening off his brow after his first full workout of the spring. "I've read reports that I get injured easily because I miss spring training, but that's bullshit. It won't take me long to get into shape. I think that within a week or ten days I'll be able to step into the lineup and play nine innings. I don't want to start too soon."

The usual questions followed: How much did he weigh? *A hundred and ninety-four, right on my playing number.* How'd he keep in shape over the winter? *Went to a gym for a few weeks, went hiking in the Minnesota snow.*

And then a few new ones.

Draft number? *It's 5,425.* Why so low? *Well, I'm married, head of household. And since you fellows will find out soon enough, Dorothy and I are expecting our first child.* When? *Hopefully, a few weeks after we win the World Series, hopefully it'll be a boy. . . .*

With that, he was off, looking as good in the batting cage as he'd ever looked this early, getting hits in all twenty of those exhibition games, in the first eight of the regular year, seeing his average climb as high as .615 after an 8-for-13 start. He thrilled everyone, including Franklin Roosevelt, who threw out the first pitch on Opening Day, April 14, and then settled into his seat to watch DiMaggio get two hits against Washington in four times up, with a triple, an RBI, and a stolen base. On April 26, the day that a poll of 17,000 American kids conducted by the Boys Athletic League revealed that DiMaggio had surpassed Babe Ruth as the nation's number-one sporting idol, the day when "The Star Spangled Banner" was first piped through the public address system at Yankee Stadium before a game (Barrow said that daily rite would continue indefinitely), DiMaggio, asked about his hitting strategy, shrugged his shoulders: "I'm swinging at every pitch that looks good to me," he said. "Just swinging. I'm not looking for anything in particular. I'm just trying to get as many base hits as I can."

Of course, within a few days, it would occur to him that those hits weren't coming quite so frequently. There was his slump. There was the Yankees' slump. There was that 13-1 loss on May 15, when he'd gotten that meaningless first-inning hit, when he'd confided afterward to sportswriter Dan Daniel: "I just have to keep believing things are going to get better tomorrow. Tomorrow is what sustains me."

When tomorrow arrived, with the White Sox in town, it *was* a little better: In the third inning he crushed a Thornton Lee fastball deep into the left-field bleachers at Yankee Stadium, 440 feet away, a place that only Hank Greenberg had reached in the eighteen years of the stadium's existence. That was good. What was better was later, in the ninth inning: the Yankees losing 5-4, DiMaggio leading off with a triple, promptly scoring the tying run on another triple by Joe Gordon, then watching Red Ruffing—a Hall of Fame pitcher who was good enough at the plate to be used as a pinch hitter—win the game with a single. The Yankees were back at .500. The Jolter had finally gotten some good wood on a couple of balls. Maybe this was a mirage, and maybe tomorrow it would all go away, because in baseball the good and the bad always melded into a mysterious fog.

DiMaggio wasn't prepared to declare himself back in a groove, not after a couple of good days in a row, but he *was* swinging the bat better, the Yankees *were* playing better, he did *feel* better about the way things were going. On May 18, "I Am an American Day" at Yankee Stadium, he went 3-for-3, and all three were gifts in one way or another. Once he reached on catcher's interference. Once he got a cheap double when St. Louis Browns outfielder Chet Laabs dropped a ball after a long run, the official scorer, Dan Daniel, figuring he ought not punish Laabs for his effort. And once he got a single off a squirt hit that third baseman Harlond Clift couldn't handle. None of those balls would have broken a pane of glass, but DiMaggio wasn't going to give them back. Sometimes you have to take what the Good Lord gives you. What had he said at the start of the year? *I'm just trying to get as many base hits as I can.* They didn't all have to be line drives. Every day for a week, he got a hit or two, every day, finding his swing, finding his stroke, every day, whaling away in the batting cage, fiddling in the batter's box, every day. That's what baseball was. A struggle. A grind. Every day.

On May 28, in the first night game ever played at Washington's Griffith Stadium, in front of twenty-five thousand curiosity seekers, DiMaggio waited until the eighth inning before he launched a one-out rocket off Senators pitcher Sid Hudson, just missing a home run by a few feet. The ball crashed into the fence, DiMaggio slid into third, and the Yankees would soon score five times to rally for a 6-5 victory, pulling to within four and a half games of the Indians. And the next afternoon, in the *New York World-Telegram,* Dan Daniel would point out, as an afterthought, as a throwaway note that easily could have been chopped for space, that three Yankees had extended hitting streaks in the game: Frank Crosetti (ten), Johnny Sturm (eleven), and Joe DiMaggio (thirteen), a veteran, a rookie, and a legend so vast that Daniel and others sometimes just referred to him as The Great Man on first reference.

Daniel forgot about it almost as soon as he wrote the words. If readers reacted at all, it was likely with relief: *DiMag is finally off the schneid. 'Bout time. He sure makes enough dough.* It was easy enough to ignore. In a week, Whirlaway would be racing for the Triple Crown. In a month, Joe Louis would defend his heavyweight belt for the eighteenth time against a chatty kid from Pittsburgh, Billy Conn, the beefed-up light-heavyweight. No need to get too rambunctious over baseball games in May. There'd be time enough to catch up with the Jolter and the Yankees. It's a long, long summer.

5

"HELL WITH THE LID TAKEN OFF"

BILLY CONN, JOE LOUIS, AND THE BRUISING
PURSUIT OF FAME

Promoter Mike Jacobs, left, and manager Johnny Ray, right, flank Billy Conn immediately after the fighter took on Joe Louis for the heavyweight championship on June 18.

"Watch the birdie" folks will say
As Conn and Louis sign today
And when the battle comes in view
Will Billy hear the birdie, too? . . .

The hopes of Conn are built upon
A good left jab, left hooks that stab
The will to train, a speedy brain
And—precious aid—he's unafraid!

—Tim Cohane, *New York World-Telegram,*
June 3 & 9, 1941

———————●———————

Here was a day that would test most cities' patience and shatter their attention spans, two momentous events simultaneously slicing up the metropolis, one uptown and one downtown, one shrouded in sadness and the other aflame in pomp and circumstance. In New York City, they simply called it Tuesday, June 3, 1941. Just another big, busy day in the biggest, busiest city of all.

Up in the Riverdale section of the Bronx, some five thousand men, women, and children solemnly filed past a bier at Christ Protestant Episcopal Church, trying to move at a respectable pace while lingering long enough to take one final look at the famous face at rest inside the casket. Hours earlier, a few thousand others had performed the same sad ritual in Manhattan, at the Church of the Divine Paternity on Central Park West and Seventy-sixth Street. Neither church was supposed to be open to the general public, both wakes were supposed to be simple, private affairs with only friends and family present, but the crush of bodies barricading both sites convinced the eminent man's widow that the doors should be flung open and his fans be ushered in to pay their final respects. In Manhattan, it took three hours for all the people to file past. In the Bronx, it seemed certain to take just as long.

Everyone in New York City, it seemed, wanted to say farewell to Lou Gehrig.

Gehrig had hoped he would best be remembered for his accomplishments on baseball fields and in the office of the New York City Parole Commission. From 1925 until 1939, he'd played in 2,130 consecutive games for the Yankees, a staggering string of stamina that most baseball observers believed would stand as a record for all time. And he hadn't just shown up for work every day, either. In those fifteen seasons he compiled one of the truly outstanding careers in baseball history: 493 home runs (second only to Babe Ruth on the day he retired), 1,995 runs batted in, a .340 lifetime batting average, and a .632 slugging percentage. In his second career as parole commissioner, he'd taken great delight in talking straight truths to the troubled teens of the city's hardest neighborhoods, his most successful reclamation project a tough-talking kid from Manhattan's Lower East Side named Thomas Rocco Barbella. Later in his life, by then known as Rocky Graziano, he would win the middleweight boxing championship of the world and say of Gehrig, "If not for him, I would have wound up in the electric chair."

Despite these splendid legacies, though, Gehrig was already destined to best be remembered as a tragic figure, felled in his prime by a largely unknown and deadly neurological disorder called amyotrophic lateral sclerosis, a syndrome that would henceforth be given the universally euphemistic name "Lou Gehrig's disease." He was only thirty-five years old when he was handed this death sentence in June 1939. And he was seventeen days shy of his thirty-eighth birthday when, after months of rapid degeneration, he'd died just after ten o'clock on the evening of June 2, 1941. Now, one day later, an eclectic assortment of mourners gathered to say good-bye, thousands of anonymous fans and dozens of famous ones. Bill "Bojangles" Robinson, the dancer, was there, and so was Babe Ruth, and so were nine representatives of Commerce High School, Gehrig's alma mater, and so was a firefighter named Patrick McDonough, who was supposed to start a family vacation that evening but said through his teardrops: "I had to pay my respects to one of the greatest men of all time."

Still, if the upper half of the city sat in a sullen, somber mood, its emotions fringed with black crepe, the lower half was busy reminding itself, and the rest of the city, and the rest of the world, that life in New York would continue to rumble forward at its usually rabid, rollicking pace. In that spirit, two men had gathered at noontime inside an office building on Worth Street in Lower Manhattan, they shook hands warmly and exchanged pleasant greetings, and they signed their names to the bottom of a stack of contracts. They had taken wildly different pathways to get here.

One was black, from Detroit by way of LaFayette, Alabama. His great-grandfather had been a slave owner, his great-grandmother a slave, his father a sharecropper, and the only reason why the world had come to know Joe Louis at all was because as a teenager he'd taken the money his mother had given him for violin lessons to rent locker space at a boxing gym.

The other was white, from the hardscrabble East Liberty section of Pittsburgh, Shakespeare Street to be exact, a place where you either learned how to use your fists or how to run very fast, where the vocational outlets of choice mostly consisted of P's: police, politics, priesthood, prison. That was just fine with Billy Conn, the son of Irish immigrants, who accepted from an early age that some men could make a living with brains, some with brawn, and God had simply placed him from birth in the second category.

They were an unlikely pair. Louis had been a boxing prodigy, and he'd already fought in two of the most famous matches ever contested, winning once and losing once to a charismatic if clumsy German thumper named Max Schmeling. As Louis took his seat inside the offices of the New York State Athletic Commission this afternoon, he'd successfully defended the world heavyweight championship seventeen times in the four years since he'd first won the title by knocking out James J. Braddock, the popular "Cinderella Man," at Chicago's Soldier Field on June 22, 1937. Through a brilliant blend of power, grace, and unfailing manners, to say nothing of his first-round thrashing of Schmeling—favorite of Hitler, friend of Goebbels, emblem of Nazi athletic preeminence—in 1938, Louis had done what only a handful of African Americans had ever been able to accomplish, his fame transcending color lines, crossing culture lines, bashing economic barriers. At his fights white men and black men cheered together, gambled together, thrilled together. At a time when major league baseball was still six full years away from dipping a cautious toe into the waters of integration—when the U.S. Army was still a *full decade* shy of doing that— Louis managed to inspire color-blindness in the most racist hearts and the most prejudiced souls, if only for fifteen rounds at a time every few months.

Conn's ascent had been a little more improbable, a little more roundabout, because when he'd first started in the fight racket at age sixteen he was barely a welterweight. He was skinny, he was brash, he was quick with a quip and faster with a jab, and he never once stepped into the ring without getting paid because he was taught that only suckers put in their time as amateurs, bruising their brain for the love of the game. Conn was a quick study, and in a city as boxing-obsessed as Pittsburgh, where five men between 1937 and 1940 won championship belts, he rapidly earned his credentials as a fine master craftsman. But even as he developed, even as he filled out, it didn't seem possible Conn could ever be anything more than a light-heavyweight—a terrific one, sure, good enough to win the title and defend it three times. Still, in the Darwinian world of boxing, ruling the light-heavies was like being captain of the freshman team. It was fine. You could make a living. But to make it big, to make a *score,* you had to swim in the deep water. You had to bust into the big room.

The one ruled at present by Joe Louis.

As odd a couple as they may have seemed, they needed each other, which is why they sat and they smiled and they shadowboxed and they fixed each other's neckties as flashbulbs crackled, as reporters fired questions, as newsreel cameras whirred. Louis's dominance was so complete that it was impossible to find anyone who could give him a competitive fight. The past year he'd given up finding a quality foe and settled instead for quantity: He stepped into a ring every three or four weeks, feeding off a diet of forgettable opponents, a rogue roster of mediocrity famously dubbed the "Bum of the Month Club." In his own way, Conn faced similar tedium among the light-heavies: He was simply in a different class than the rest of his contemporaries. He could hit harder than any of them, box smarter than any of them, and beat all of them practically without breaking a sweat, and where was the challenge in that?

More to the point: Where was the *cash* in that?

Mike Jacobs was the man who ruled boxing in 1941, the most influential promoter in the most important boxing city, the proprietor of the Twentieth Century Sporting Club. They said he could snap his fingers and fill Madison Square Garden, and in fact he would hold some 320 events in that boxing Mecca between 1937 and 1949, but Jacobs knew that as great as Joe Louis might be, as big an attraction as Billy Conn might be, keeping them apart was putting his sport to sleep. Interest was dwindling because there was little mystery left in the heavyweight division, even less in the light-heavies. Who wanted to spend money to watch sure things? Once Conn started making noise about moving up in class, abandoning his light-heavyweight title, and once he started knocking out heavyweights in his spare time between title defenses, this was a match Jacobs had to make.

"The Polo Grounds, gentlemen," he said. "Wednesday night, June the eighteenth, ten o'clock at night, Mr. Louis and Mr. Conn, fifteen rounds to decide this once and for all. I think if we're lucky, and if the weather cooperates, we could expect to see a gate of forty thousand, easy."

Jacobs believed he'd get more than that, of course. He knew a blockbuster when he had one on his hands, and this one had all the makings. Forty thousand? Please. He had two weeks to sell this fight, two weeks for the great New York hype machine to whistle and grind, and the people had waited a hell of a long time for a boxing match worth spending their money on—both at the box office and with the bookmakers. Jacobs didn't say much that day. He let the stars do the talking for him.

"You look good, Champ," Conn told Louis.

"You do too, Bill. You gainin' weight?"

"You bet I am, Joe."

"Looking forward to seeing you in a few weeks, Bill."

"You too, Champ. I'll be there."

Mike Jacobs smiled. They'd both be there. He'd be there. The whole world would want to be there, and they'd bring their wallets, and they'd keep the Polo Grounds turnstiles clicking, the bookies clucking, the sportswriters' typewriters clacking, and what in the world could possibly be better than that?

———————●———————

Even if he hadn't endured the brutal internships the bruising streets of East Liberty regularly offered, Billy Conn likely would have pursued a pugilistic path, because fighting was in his bloodstream, had coursed through his family's veins for centuries. Conn traced his immediate paternal ancestry back to County Down, in Northern Ireland, but his ancient forebears included the famed Irish warrior king Conn of a Hundred Battles, born around A.D. 110, who ruled the whole of the Emerald Isle and was so fierce a fighter that it was said even the legions of Caesar steered clear of his path. Conn of a Hundred Battles organized the Fianna, one of the hardest-fighting mobs of the day. Men who wished to join the Fianna had to prove their worth by first standing up against nine enemy soldiers, pledging to fight until victory or death. As tough as Joe Louis was, there would be only *one* of him waiting for Conn at the Polo Grounds on June 18.

Conn *did* come off those seething streets of East Liberty, however, and he was a natural by-product of a city that had been leading with its chin for nearly a century. As early as 1866, journalist James Parton had described Pittsburgh in the *Atlantic Monthly* as "hell with the lid taken off," a grim salute to the steel mills and blast furnaces that filled local skies and locals' lungs with a ceaseless chalky blackness. This was the ultimate shot-and-a-beer place, a city devoid of pretentiousness, comfortable in its blue-collar ways and rough-hewn traditions. It was a town rigidly divided along ethnic lines—the Irish mostly settling in Greenville, the Germans in Troy Hill, the Jews in Squirrel Hill, the Poles on the South Side—where East Liberty was seen as being oddly progressive because there the Irish and Italians actually shared the same blocks. Yet one thing united these diverse provinces: Fighting. Not necessarily boxing, although that was big, too, the Duquesne Gardens serving as both a gathering place and proving ground for a deep roster of local fistic hopefuls.

No, fighting meant just that: Sometimes, with little notice, you'd find yourself deep in a scuffle, with little reason for it other than that's what folks did for shits and giggles on a Friday night in western Pennsylvania.

Sometimes it was the Jews and the Micks mixing it up; sometimes the Wops and the Krauts; sometimes little rhyme or reason was needed for two men to exchange blows, regardless of cause or creed. It just happened. You took your licking, you got your whacks in, the loser brought the winner another round, and that was that.

Sometimes you didn't even have to leave your living room to take a beating. In the Conn household, where Billy was the middle brother between Frankie the eldest and Jackie the youngest, they would often pretend the family dining room was the ring at the Duquesne Gardens, sometimes starting before breakfast. When that happened it meant that the old man, Billy Sr., who worked nights as a steamfitter for Westinghouse, would often arrive home just as the preliminaries were getting under way, and he'd quickly take off his coat and his shirt and join in the bruising fun. Years later, after young Billy had earned a measure of fame by profitably employing some of the same tactics he learned in these intramural scraps, Pittsburgh sportswriter Harry Keck asked Conn's sainted mother, the former Margaret McFarland, "If Billy ever left home, you wouldn't know what to do with all the quiet, would you?"

"Glory be, yes," Mrs. Conn said. "They're all just big boys. That one—" she pointed at her husband "—the worst of all."

Conn's father was a colorful character who'd gotten into his own share of barroom dustups in his day, who'd spent some time as a rumrunner in his younger years and who delivered his middle son the most important lesson of his life when young Billy was twelve. Senior took Junior to one of the steel mills in town, snuck the boy inside, where the dreadful heat, foul smells, and frightening sparks attached to his senses.

"Take a good look around, son," Billy Sr. said. "This is where you're gonna spend the rest of your life if you don't find something better."

There *had* to be something better than this, Billy Jr. thought to himself. But what? Some of the neighborhood kids would talk about boxing as a career, that's how Harry Greb had gotten out, and Teddy Yarosz, and a batch of other Pittsburgh kids who otherwise would have gotten lost in the vortex sucking them all into the mills. Billy would join the talk, sometimes be the loudest of all of them, but who could take this skinny punk seriously? Every time words led to fists, he'd get his ass kicked by the bigger, stronger neighborhood kids, so often in fact that one day Billy Conn Sr. decided to pay a visit to the boxing gym in East Liberty, run by a broken-down old lightweight named Johnny Ray. "He's having some troubles with the tough kids on our block," Billy Sr. said. "I want him to be able to take care of himself."

Around this time, Ray had a unique business arrangement with a group of kids at Sacred Heart Parochial School, near his gym. To save the cost of a janitor and lighten his chores, he let the boys work out at his place every afternoon in exchange for sweeping the place out. Conn wouldn't be long for Sacred Heart, not after one of the nuns helpfully pointed out, "You're getting a little too big to stay in the same grade for so long," but he was smart enough to recognize a ticket out of the mills when he saw one. Conn asked Ray to teach him the sweet science.

Ray said, "Take this pail and start mopping. We'll worry about fighting later."

Conn worked the mop, he worked the broom, he cleaned the toilets and the showers, he snuck in some time on the speed bag and the heavy bag, and would hop in the ring and shadowbox whenever he had a few spare minutes. He was hooked from the start. Later in his life he would put it this way: "I felt like I started to breathe properly when I walked into Johnny Ray's gym. It was like my life had finally begun."

Ray noticed. He saw how hungry Conn was, literally and figuratively. But he saw something else, too. After a few weeks, he ran into Billy Conn Sr. at a neighborhood tavern and made the old man a deal.

"This kid is hell-bent on being a fighter," Ray said. "You don't need any education for that. In fact, as I've found out, the dumber you are, the better. Let me have him from now on. If I see he ain't going to make the grade, I'll get him a job in a steel mill and make him go work for a living."

"He's all yours," Billy Conn Sr. said, clinking a glass of whiskey with Johnny Ray's before downing it with a hard gulp, ordering a backup.

Ray didn't completely dismiss the idea of higher education, though, because to him his gym was a lecture hall, the ring was a laboratory, and this skinny kid was his star pupil, eager to begin a highly unorthodox work-study program. Ray's textbook was the tattered remains of his own failed career as a boxer. Twenty years before, Ray had been the most promising fighter in all of Pennsylvania, the popular local choice to swipe the middle-weight crown someday, the brightest of a crop that also included Harry Greb.

But Ray had already started drinking too much, smoking too much, chasing too much. Any one of those vices will kill a boxing career before it starts; you combine all three and it explains why Johnny Ray was running a shithole gym underneath bleak Pittsburgh skies while Harry Greb had become a world champion; while one of Ray's own brothers, Jake Pitler, had become a major league baseball player with the Pirates and was now GM of the Brooklyn Dodgers' affiliate in Olean, New York; and another brother, Dave, had played quarterback for a national championship team at the University of Pittsburgh before earning a law degree. "I know from two things," he would tell friends. "Fighting and fucking up."

To Conn he delivered a similar message. "I want you to profit by my mistakes," Ray told him the very first day they worked together. "Consider me a horrible example. Don't do what you see me do. In fact, do the opposite of everything you *see* me do. But do everything I *tell* you to do."

Conn obeyed, he behaved, and by the time he was sixteen, Johnny Ray figured it was time to throw him into the deep end of the Monongahela, to see if he could float. The first fight was in Fairmont, West Virginia, on July 28, 1934, a four-rounder with a lightweight named Dick Woodward, and the kid took a beating, losing a decision, but he stayed on his feet and collected a purse of $2.50, of which he saw exactly one dollar. He was raw, he was unpolished, and he bounced between Pittsburgh and West Virginia a lot in the months to come, losing six of his first fourteen fights, but the middling record didn't bother either of them, especially Ray, who would talk up his protégé to anyone, especially the disbelievers, and there was never a shortage of those. One long night, Ray was chatting up Havey Boyle, Pittsburgh's most respected sportswriter, who'd already gotten an eyeful of Conn and an earful of Ray and finally screamed, exasperated: "You oughta be ashamed of yourself. Send this child home to his mother or I'll have you both arrested."

As Boyle stalked away, he could hear Ray yell after him: "Talk to me again when the kid's a champ!"

A funny thing started to happen, though; the more Conn fought, the more he earned, the more he ate (one time at breakfast, he was said to put away thirteen fried eggs, a pound of bacon, a large stack of pancakes, and a huge pot of coffee, then after sparring three rounds he told Ray: "I sure could use a nice thick steak"), the more he grew up and matured. He started to get stronger, punch harder, work smarter. He could outslug smaller men and outbox larger ones. He developed a signature punch, a left hook he could often administer twice, rapid-fire, a double blow that rattled an opponent to his bones because even if he saw the first hook coming, he could never suspect the second one lay in reserve. In 1936, Conn fought eighteen times, a grueling pace even then, even for a kid on the make. He won all eighteen, capped three days after Christmas by the first truly important bout of his life, a ten-round decision against Fritzie Zivic, another Pittsburgher who would soon become welterweight champion of the world. There were 5,000 people crammed inside Duquesne Gardens that night, and another 8,000 milling around outside, hoping to gauge the action through the crowd noise. Zivic, the more established of the two, dominated the first half of the fight, but Conn came back, owned the last half, and earned a narrow decision.

But it would take another full year's apprenticeship before Billy was truly ready to make his first genuine splash, and even in a proud pug town like Pittsburgh, everyone knew what that meant: He'd have to fight, and win, in the smoky basilica on Fiftieth Street and Eighth Avenue in midtown Manhattan, Madison Square Garden, the holy place where so many boxers arrived for either coronation or cremation. Ray had fielded phone calls from minor New York promoters before, had mulled offers to bring his boy east to fill out an undercard here and there, but he always refused. In the same way he didn't want Billy to waste time and brain cells fighting amateurs, he figured when the kid's time was right, he might as well hit the big city as a main event. So they waited. And it was after a brutal twelve-round decision over Solly Krieger in November 1938 that the telephone call finally came.

"Jacobs here," came the famous, familiar voice. "Let's work something out."

What they decided on was a ten-round bout pairing Conn with Fred Apostoli, who didn't officially hold the middleweight title but was acclaimed by almost all of the New York writers to be the best fighter in that division. Apostoli was an overwhelming favorite when he stepped into the ring with Billy Conn on January 6, 1939. But Conn survived, winning a tough decision, then added another in fifteen rounds five weeks later in a rematch, and now everyone knew Billy, and everyone seemed to like him, and everyone was drawn to his good looks and his fast lip (the words coming out tangled in a Pittsburgh drawl that sounded perfectly exotic to the street poets of New York), and if there was one man smitten most of all, it was Mike Jacobs.

For all the money he earned pushing fights, Jacobs was never much of a fan of the sport, preferring to lock himself in his office counting receipts. But now, on the nights when Conn fought at the Garden, he was spotted ringside, occupying one of his own priciest seats, cheering madly, throwing his hat in the air whenever his boy fired off a particularly devastating combination of punches. Joe Louis was still Jacobs's meal ticket, but Billy Conn was rapidly becoming his surrogate son.

Jacobs introduced him to a brand-new world, one where you didn't have to con your next meal, one that didn't include grinding, hourly toil just to make the rent. The fighter started spending weekends at the promoter's country place on the Shrewsbury River in Rumson, New Jersey, or at his Miami Beach estate, or inside his duplex on Central Park West. He began wearing expensive suits cut by Jacobs's personal tailor, wearing silk shirts and five-dollar ties that Jacobs comped him. Conn was spotted driving a cream-colored roadster, another Jacobs gift. A guy could get used to living this way. Of course, there was only one way a boxer *could* live this way. And it wasn't on a middleweight's salary. It wasn't on a light-heavyweight's salary, either, so even after the 170½-pound Conn completed his swift rise on July 13, 1939, taking a fifteen-round decision from southpaw Melio Bettina in front of 15,295 at the Garden and winning the vacated light-heavyweight title, there was something missing.

It was after the last of his three title defenses, at Detroit's Olympia Stadium, when Conn finally and formally identified what he really wanted. Conn survived a fifteen-round decision against Gus Lesnivich, but only 6,075 people had bothered to show up, meaning the champion would pocket less than $2,500 for his effort, and he'd had enough of that. "Gus," Conn said in the shower room, "if you want this title, you can have it."

Really, he was just heeding his father's cautionary advice. He'd taken a good look around the sparsely populated boxing hall and realized: This is where I'm gonna spend the rest of my life if I don't find something better.

Only this time, he knew exactly where he had to go to find it.

The man who had what Billy Conn wanted could certainly appreciate the journey his opponent had taken to the moment, all the famished hours, all the sweaty hustle, because on the day *he* was born there was no way that anyone could have predicted that within twenty-five years, Joe Louis Barrow would become one of the five most recognizable faces in the country. If not the world.

He was born at the foot of Buckalew Mountain in east-central Alabama on May 13, 1914. LaFayette was the seat of Chambers County, ninety-eight miles from Atlanta and ninety-five miles from Birmingham. To get any deeper in the Deep South you'd have to dig yourself a pit. Joe was the seventh of eight children born to sharecropper Monroe Barrow and his wife, Lillie, but he barely knew his father, who was declared insane when the boy was two and vanished into the institutional mist. Lillie remarried, and her new husband, Pat Brooks, brought five children of his own into the blended family. Fifteen black mouths simply weren't going to be fed in a rural hamlet sparse with work and lousy with the Klan, and so in 1926 the Barrows joined the great migration of blacks to the industrial havens of the north, and the family settled into an eight-room house on Macomb Street, a few blocks north of the Detroit River. Joe was a naturally quiet kid, and his reticence grew deeper in such a large family, but even when he was young he had a physical presence about him. While he was at Bronson, a vocational training school, one of his instructors said, "This boy should be able to do something with his hands," and that was true enough, for in the mornings, before school, Joe worked in the Eastern Market, and after school he'd deliver frozen sixty-pound blocks for Pickman and Dean, a Detroit ice company, which explained why he was soon bursting out of his shirts.

Quiet as he was, young Joe Louis Barrow badly needed an outlet for his ever-growing physical prowess. For a time he became loosely affiliated with a band of street toughs known as the Catherine Street Gang, recruited mostly whenever there was a need for an extra set of fists. One of the neighborhood kids who first felt the wrath of what would soon become the world's most famous punch was Coleman Young, who would grow up to become Detroit's first black mayor. This wasn't the kind of training that was ever going to lead to a happy ending, though, and it was here that Louis received precious guidance from the first in a series of advisers who would shape his life and coauthor his unlikely rise. Henderson "Ben" Turpin was a police officer, one of the most respected voices in the black community, and an occasional "enforcer" when the situation called for it. Turpin figured there had to be a way to put Joe's natural gifts to better use, and he brought him one day to a small training facility, Bronson Gym. There, Joe put on gloves for the first time, he made his first solid contact with an opponent's jaw, he felt the rush as his foe hit the canvas, and he was captivated. He figured he could put the fifty cents a week his mother gave him to take fiddle lessons to better use at Brewster Recreation Centre, where all of Detroit's best amateur fighters gathered to hone their vicious craft, where he rented out locker space, bought third-hand equipment, and officially traded in violins for violence.

Unlike Billy Conn, who never once laced up a pair of boxing gloves without expecting a payday, no matter how modest, Joe Louis Barrow learned the sport in a city that had a rich and distinct amateur boxing culture, and he would fight fifty-four times as an amateur, winning fifty of them. Like Conn, his debut was less than auspicious, a match in 1932 with a future Olympian named Johnny Miler, who knocked him down seven times. That was enough to make an eighteen-year-old wonder if there weren't less hazardous ways to make a buck, so he stayed away from the Brewster for a while and took a job at Ford's River Rouge plant, spending countless mind-numbing hours manning a conveyor belt. He was back in the gym before long, and soon his skills were catching up to his body, his punches coming in faster and harder bursts; he won thirteen bouts in a row. During this stretch, while registering for a tournament, there wasn't enough space on the entry blank to fit his whole name. Thus was "Joe Louis" born, the "Barrow" a gift he would pass along to his children as a surname but one he would never use himself for the rest of his public life.

His first trainers at Brewster were Atler Ellis and Holman Williams, who hooked him up with George Slayton, manager of the Detroit Athletic Club, and his amateur career really started picking up. He made it to the Golden Gloves finals in Boston in 1933, losing to a football player named Max Marek, and by the time he won the national Amateur Athletic Union light-heavyweight championship in St. Louis a few months after that, he figured it was about time to start making some money for his labors. A wealthy black Detroit impresario named John Roxborough had taken notice of Louis, and the two quickly agreed to a management arrangement. Roxborough's listed vocations were "insurance" and "real estate," but in truth he ran the Detroit numbers racket. As a partner he enlisted a man named Julian Black, who occupied the same place of iniquitous prominence in Chicago.

Still, despite having spent much of their adult lives in the shadows, Roxborough and Black both understood that their new client would have to have an image that embraced the opposite extreme. Boxing wasn't ruled by the immovable color barrier that so infected major league baseball, for instance; the ring had long been a place where white fists met black jaws, where black fists collided with white noses, but by the mid-1930s it was clear that if a black man were ever going to be given another chance at the most coveted title in sports, the world heavyweight championship, he would have to be a most specific *type* of black man. Namely, he wouldn't remind anyone of Jack Johnson, the powerful black man from Galveston, Texas, who in 1908 had won the championship from Tommy Burns and proceeded to rub white America's collective nose in that triumph. He was loud, he was brash, he was, to use the word the papers always used, far too "flamboyant" for most sensibilities. Once Johnson surrendered the title in 1915, a padlock was fixed on the belt, and no black man since had gotten anywhere near the key.

Anyone who saw Joe Louis fight realized he had the goods to be champion one day in a fair world. But Roxborough, Black, and the man they recruited to train Louis, Jack "Chappy" Blackburn, also knew there was nothing fair about this challenge. So they drew up a very detailed, very specific blueprint for Louis, one with rules and absolute laws, and presented it to their fighter. These were their ten commandments:

1. Never be photographed with a white woman.
2. Never enter a nightclub alone.
3. Never participate in soft fights.
4. Never participate in fixed fights.
5. Never gloat over a fallen opponent.
6. Never talk poorly of him before the fight.
7. Always maintain a deadpan expression in front of cameras.
8. Live clean.
9. Fight clean.
10. No gold teeth.

"Can you do these things?" John Roxborough asked.

"I can," Joe Louis said, "and I will."

He started quickly and ferociously. His first pro fight was against Jack

Kracken on July 4, 1934, at Bacon's Arena in Chicago. Three times Louis knocked Kracken down before the end of the first round, and on the last he sent him completely out of the ring. He picked up fifty-nine dollars for his trouble, along with an instant reputation.

Blackburn was delighted with his fighter's work ethic and his insatiable appetite to talk boxing, both traits that warmed an old trainer's heart. Louis thought nothing of rising at six in the morning, running twice around Washington Park on Chicago's South Side, settling in for a long afternoon of training and a longer evening of boxing films and boxing chatter. All of that groundwork yielded remarkable results in the ring: twenty-seven straight wins to start his pro career, twenty-three of them by knockouts, more than half of them finished in four rounds or less. True to the ten commandments, few of them were against hazy bums, either, but rather against a roster of increasingly well-known names: Primo Carnera, Kingfish Levinsky, Max Baer, Paolino Uzcudum. He looked unstoppable as a locomotive.

On June 19, 1936, Louis entered the ring at Yankee Stadium as an overwhelming ten-to-one choice over German Max Schmeling, who'd briefly held the title three years earlier and had retained an international prominence thanks chiefly to his nationality. As Hitler rose to power, as the Nazi Party became more and more of an ominous synonym for Armageddon, Schmeling's status as a ticket seller had remained strong, but it was believed his best days were behind him. As a result, only 39,878 tickets were sold that evening, partly due to the anticipated one-sided nature of the fight, partly because of a boycott called by local Jews, outraged that this alleged tool of Hitler was being allowed such a public stage. In truth, Schmeling had never joined the Nazi Party, and his whole public life he would try to stay as detached from his homeland's politics as he could without incurring the wrath of the Reich. But that didn't matter much. Those who came that night wanted to see a Nazi's blood spilled on a baseball field in the Bronx.

What they got was one of the most shocking upsets in sports history. Schmeling had insisted time and again in the months before the fight that he'd spotted a weakness in Louis, a claim that was dismissed as blather and public posture, but it was true: Louis dropped his left shoulder whenever he was about to throw his devastating straight left. Armed with that intelligence, Schmeling now attacked Louis as no one ever had before, he hurt the man the papers called the Brown Bomber, he knocked him down in the fourth round and then, eight rounds later, moved in for the kill. And at two minutes, twenty-nine seconds of that twelfth round, the impossible happened: Joe Louis was knocked out, sprawled flat on the canvas. It was a staggering sight. And the experience could have destroyed a lesser fighter, a lesser man, especially one with so much of Black America's hopes, dreams, and aspirations pinned directly to his boxing gloves.

Louis went another way. He trained harder. He sharpened his focus. For two years he punished himself and his body for being so careless, he brutalized a string of foes, and after serving a bloody penance he was granted a modicum of consolation on June 22, 1937, when he pounded James J. Braddock in Chicago and became the first black man in twenty-two years to carry the title of undisputed heavyweight champion. But he was still unfulfilled. He defended the title four times, but it wasn't until his one-year anniversary as champion, June 22, 1938, that he finally had the chance to rid his résumé of its most appalling stain.

That night, he finally got his rematch with Max Schmeling, who by now had become completely demonized in the eyes of Americans, his nation now more than just an ornery nuisance but an imperialistic menace; and who, if he won, could take the heavyweight crown back home with him, where it might disappear forever behind steel Nazi gates. Schmeling himself had never willingly nor publicly embraced the Nazi philosophy, and while he had once been a friend of Joseph Goebbels, Hitler's propaganda minister, that was no longer the case. In fact, on *Kristallnacht,* the most infamous night of the Nazi reign, November 9–10 of 1938—when thousands of Jewish homes and business were vandalized in the "night of broken glass"—Schmeling was staying in a Berlin hotel and provided secure harbor for two teenage boys, Henry and Werner Lewin, sons of a Jewish friend, before helping to smuggle them to safety.

None of that would be known for decades, however, and so on the evening of the fight, the 70,043 people who jammed Yankee Stadium didn't see a proud old champion, but rather a jackbooted slug wrapped in a Nazi flag. Louis smelled blood early, pouncing on the soon-to-be-thirty-three-year-old German, breaking two of his ribs during a furious fusillade of punches, bloodying Schmeling's face, inflicting such a beating that Goebbels, at home in the Fatherland, ordered the national broadcast of the fight cut early, so the millions of Schmeling's countrymen glued to their radios wouldn't have to listen to the details of his ruination. The fight lasted all of two minutes and two seconds before referee Art Donovan finally, mercifully, ended the whipping. Schmeling's career, in essence, was over. And Louis solidified himself as the most frightening finisher of all time, issuing a warning to all future foes of what damage he could inflict when stirred to action.

The memory of that night could sustain a boxing fan for a long time, but it was close to three years now since Louis had been even remotely tested. Could Billy Conn be the one to do that? Really? The history of light-heavies rising from the dust to challenge for the varsity belt wasn't a favorable one, and a lot of veteran observers believed Conn bore more than a passing resemblance to Georges Carpentier, the French boxer who'd been the last to attempt that mighty leap, twenty years before, an audacious ambition that had ended just a minute and sixteen seconds into the fourth round at the powerful fists of Jack Dempsey.

Boxing fans hoped so. Because even as they gathered steam looking forward to what they hoped would be the Next Great Bout, the present state of the world made it certain that Max Schmeling's shadow, and the specter of his people, would never be terribly far away.

———•———

Losing to Louis hadn't been easy on Schmeling, and not only because there isn't a fighter alive not owned by the mob who likes the idea of getting his brains beaten out in public. Schmeling knew he was about to lose more than a chance to regain the heavyweight championship. Once he returned to Germany, there would be an army uniform waiting for him, and an airplane for him to jump out of, and live bullets to try to avoid. As inconvenient as the American draft might have been to the athletes it claimed, as difficult as it might be for Hank Greenberg to abandon the Tigers, for Porky Oliver to leave the golf tour, for Maj. Robert Reese Neyland to vacate the head football coach's office at the University of Tennessee, they weren't exactly facing hazardous duty working for an army without a declared enemy.

It was an entirely different story for Schmeling, whose entire nation had been mobilized and scattered throughout Europe. He was thirty-two on the night he lost to Louis, which may have been old for an American soldier but fit comfortably within range of uniformed personnel in the German paratroopers, whose numbers he finally joined in April 1940 and who boasted a membership ranging in age from boys in their late teens through men in their late forties. But he still struggled with the notion that his days as a fighter were over, that he was now merely a full-time *Fallschirmjaeger*. In January he was denied a furlough to defend his European heavyweight title and had to simply relinquish it. Later that month, he admitted to an American journalist, "Joe Louis is still the best fighter in the world, he is the best you have over there and I would love the chance to fight him a third time. Luftwaffe parachute training is lots tougher than camp training for a fight, but I like it." A few weeks later, Schmeling's wife, Annie Ondra, put to rest all such folly that might still be dancing in Max's head: "Max will fight soon," she said, "but not in the boxing ring."

She was correct. In late February 1941, Schmeling appeared in a German propaganda film and was seen smiling as he tumbled out of an airplane door. Around that time he also gave one final interview to *Der Angriff* (literal translation: *Attack*), the newspaper run by his former friend Joseph Goebbels: "I am no longer so young and don't know if it will be possible to take up such a project as fighting Joe Louis again. At a quiet moment I thought about it, but it is not a quiet moment now to bother with such things."

———————●———————

On May 26, 1941, 27,042 pilgrims flocked to Forbes Field in Pittsburgh to watch their favorite son, Billy Conn, take on Buddy Knox in a bout that was suddenly of huge importance to both Conn and Joe Louis. Three days earlier, in Washington, D.C., Louis had knocked out Buddy Baer (kid brother of Max, the former heavyweight champ) late in the sixth round, but not before Baer managed to hit Louis flush with a first-round left hook that sent him through the ropes and sprawling onto the ring's apron, right in front of a row of startled sportswriters. Louis was back on his feet at the count of four and never let Baer get that close again, but he did absorb enough punishment early that he had to lie down on the training table for twenty minutes at match's end to gather himself. Now Mike Jacobs was pondering a Louis-Baer rematch and pushing Louis-Conn back to late summer or early fall, depending on how impressive Conn looked against

Knox. But Conn handled Knox easily, finally giving the crowd what it wanted by knocking him out, and Jacobs was duly satisfied. Conn would soon officially be given the chance to provide Joe Louis with his toughest assignment in three years.

That same night, on the opposite side of the planet, the last man to make Joe Louis sweat—and bleed—was one of the first German paratroopers to jump out of a plane and glide toward the Greek island of Crete, where the Germans were engaged in a furious battle with Greek and British forces for control of that strategic stronghold, days after the Royal Air Force had been forced to abandon it. The jarring juxtaposition of those two stories may have seemed especially jolting the day they appeared.

Two days later it was even worse.

May 28, 1941: The sad news that was plastered above the fold in just about every important newspaper in the United States:

SCHMELING, FLEEING CAPTORS, IS REPORTED DEAD

The story, emanating out of Britain's journalistic headquarters in Alexandria, Egypt, told a stark, simple tale of how war can kill indiscriminately, how not even worldwide fame can serve as a bulletproof shield, a reality that certainly hit home with just as many would-be American draftees with names like DiMaggio and Arcaro and Louis and Conn and Williams as with anyone else on earth. Max Schmeling, the story somberly reported, had been killed in Crete while trying to escape from British soldiers escorting him to a prison camp. The piece was attributed to "reliable British sources."

British field ambulance men reported that Schmeling had been wounded slightly in the first days of the Battle of Crete. He was taken to a dressing station as a prisoner, and he showed papers identifying himself as the former champion. The story then quoted an ambulance driver from New Zealand:

"Early in the battle of Crete, a husky German soldier was captured, slightly wounded. Speaking English with a strong American accent, he said he was Max Schmeling and his papers bore that name. He was truculent and surly. After talking with him at length, our officers were convinced he was Schmeling. Later in the day he was being taken to a field hospital by our ambulance corps when more German parachutists descended on top of us and a dogfight opened.

"Schmeling grabbed a rifle from one of our soldiers who had been wounded and went into action like a wild bull. Before he did any damage, however, someone let him have it. And that was the end of Max."

The end of Max brought a sober response from Americans, who suddenly had a face to put to all the carnage, even if he happened to be fighting for the wrong side.

"I hate war and killing," said Max Baer, who'd famously beaten Schmeling years before while wearing a prominent Star of David on his boxing trunks, even though his Jewish heritage was more than a little in doubt. "I think Schmeling did, too. He probably didn't want to fight, but Hitler made him do it. His death is a pitiful example of what happens when men bring war to this world. In my racket we can fight and still be friends. But not in war."

Added Jack Dempsey: "He was a great fighter and a great fellow. And he really wasn't in favor of the Nazis at all. He told me that once in a private conversation."

Billy McCarney, Schmeling's onetime manager, echoed this: "Schmeling was never a Nazi at heart and never approved of Hitler, but he was caught in a vicious system. I hope the report of his death isn't true but if it is, perhaps Max is better off."

Actually, Schmeling would argue that he really *was* better off, because he was actually very much alive, a fact the Nazi propaganda machine churned out as quickly as they were able to confirm it. The ambulance driver had gotten it wrong. Back from the beyond, Schmeling was just as chatty now as Americans remembered him being in the run-ups to both Louis fights.

"Our group was assigned to occupation of the northern coastal road in Crete," he explained. "We were subjected to machine gun and rifle fire from snipers in trees and houses as soon as we cleared our planes and dropped down by parachute. We fought our way clear with some casualties and finally cleaned up enemy nests. Two hours later we contacted and gave battle to regular British troops.

"The Tommies fought our group hard and finally surrendered. During the battle I became separated from the rest of my group and for some time wandered about in fields and wooded hills, cautiously alert for ambush. Some time afterward, I met up with others of my group and by nightfall we were back with the main German bodies. Fighting was continued the next day.

"Once again the Tommies fought stubbornly until they were compelled to surrender. There is no excuse for the mistreatment of many of our parachutists. General headquarters will be justified in dealing drastically with such violations of the international rights of fighting men. All of us wear regulation parachute uniforms. I'm sure glad I had a chance to get into this fight."

That last paragraph came more from Goebbels's mouth than from Schmeling's, because it was Schmeling's belief that the English had actually treated their German prisoners quite well. In fact, a week later, talking to another reporter, he made a comment that would make him essentially persona non grata with the Reich for the rest of the war: "Some of my comrades who were captured by the English said they'd been treated well," he said. "I've got a lot of friends in the United States. I hope the war ends soon and we can get together again."

Schmeling was being Schmeling again, trying to work the room, trying to get back in the picture with Joe Louis again, but it was Mike Jacobs who silenced those ambitions forever when, a few days before his big show on June 18, he let Max down easily, and permanently.

"Right now," said Jacobs, one of the most prominent and visible of all American Jews, "he wouldn't be any more welcome here than I would be over there."

Indirectly, that ambulance driver turned out to be right. At least as far as his boxing career was concerned, this was the end of Max.

———————•———————

It wasn't the end of boxing, however, not by a long shot. Not with the freshly signed contracts sitting in Mike Jacobs's filing cabinets. Louis would head off the next morning to Greenwood Lake, New York, up in the state's rustic Catskill region. Conn opted for Pompton Lakes, New Jersey, a training site familiar to fight fans because that's where Louis had prepared for the second Schmeling fight and where he'd done most of his training for his first few title defenses. It was June 4, and in the morning Lou Gehrig was memorialized at Christ Church in Riverdale without a eulogy. "We need none," Rev. Gerald V. Barry said, "because you all knew him." In the afternoon came word that Kaiser Wilhelm II, the German face of another generation's global crisis, had died at age eighty-two in Doorn, Netherlands, of an intestinal ailment; Adolf Hitler, who believed it was his sacred duty to right the wrongs that Wilhelm's surrender had wrought, sent official condolences.

In the evening came this hopeful if dubious declaration from Kichisaburo Nomura, the Japanese ambassador to the United States, who decreed, "Between America and Japan, the way of peace is the only way . . . now, even if our present problems overshadow those of the past, there is no reason to lose faith in our ability to work out a peaceful solution."

And just for kicks, somewhere in the middle of all that, a feisty upstart boxer named Billy Conn sidled up to the aptly named Hype Igoe of the *New York Journal-American,* the most influential boxing journalist in town, and dropped a few tantalizing hints foreshadowing the kind of hyperbole the people could expect the next two weeks: "I won't be so anxious about pleasing the customers at the Polo Grounds. I'm not stupid enough to think I can trade wallops with Louis . . . the crowd is going to see a Conn they little dreamed existed. I've never had to show everything in New York."

And then, the firecracker:

"I think," Conn said, "that I'll make him look like an amateur."

Yep. Just another big, busy day in the biggest, busiest city of all.

6

"You're in for a fight tonight, Joe."

A challenger takes his best shot while a champion seeks his finest hour

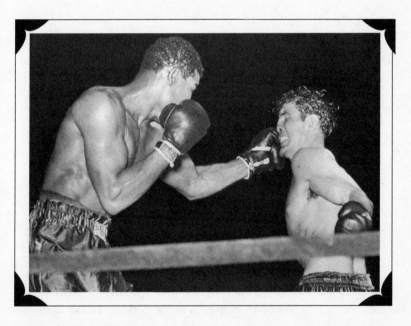

Billy Conn swings for Joe Louis's head with both hands, as the champion connects with a left to the nose during the title bout in the Polo Grounds on June 18.

I know that Conn has brains and heart
And knows his share of boxing art
I know Joe's not quite what he was
When he tagged Schmeling on the juzz
I know he's got to lose some time
When he's not moving off a dime
But I won't bet it, not tonight
I still like Joseph's left and right.

—Tim Cohane, *New York World-Telegram*,
June 18, 1941

———————●———————

There is nothing comparable in our world now, not the Super Bowl, not the Final Four, not Wimbledon or the World Series, the Olympics or the World Cup. Certainly not anything that takes place on a twenty-foot-by-twenty-foot slab of canvas, bordered on all sides by three nylon ropes. In the twenty-first century, boxing has devolved into a fringe sport, visible mostly on cable television or via pricey pay-per-view extravaganzas, shrouded in mystery and corruption, diluted by a glut of alphabetized ruling bodies and the sad fact that the world's best athletes long ago discovered easier, less brutal outlets for their skills. Every now and again a boxer will emerge from these shadows and carry the sport back to the public eye—a Mike Tyson, a Sugar Ray Leonard, an Oscar De La Hoya—but for the most part boxing sits uncomfortably in the second tier of spectator sports, battling for the same entertainment dollars as professional wrestling and ultimate fighting.

In our world, it is a sport that means practically nothing.

In the world of 1941, it meant everything. It meant *more* than everything. It was a means of escape for millions of poor, hopeful athletes. It was regularly accessible to the common man, the biggest fights aired for free on national radio. At a time when the most famous baseball players in the country, playing the nation's titular pastime, often struggled to squeeze $30,000 a year out of tightfisted owners, top fighters regularly pulled that down for one night's work. On July 2, 1921, more than eighty thousand fans had swarmed a swatch of New Jersey farmland called Boyle's Thirty Acres to watch heavyweight Jack Dempsey fight Georges Carpentier, a light-heavyweight, and they paid the staggering sum of $1,789,238 to witness Dempsey slaughter Carpentier in four rounds. In 1926, in Philadelphia, Dempsey lost his title to Gene Tunney in front of an announced (and, some thought, conservatively estimated) crowd of 120,557; when the two men fought a rematch in Chicago the next year, they drew another 104,943 who paid the astonishing total of $2,258,660, a record that had yet to be approached. And considering that a champion's standard cut was 40 percent of the gate, and the challenger's 20, there was little surprise that Dempsey and Tunney were able to spend much of the latter part of the Roaring Twenties living like a Rockefeller.

Joe Louis's lone million-dollar gate had been the $1,015,012 that came in for his rematch with Schmeling in 1938. The Depression had worked boxing over pretty good, and so had Louis's relentless dominance in the sport's most glamorous division. That's why, as early as 1940, a regular feature of the buildup to every one of his title defenses included variations of the same question: Is Louis slowing down? Is he the same fighter he was, the same terror who'd pulverized Jimmy Braddock in earning the title, who'd damn near killed Max Schmeling in defending it? Does he have the same fire? Does he still work as hard? Has he grown soft? Fat? Lazy? Satisfied? If it seemed odd that there was so much concern about the eroding skills of a man who wouldn't even turn twenty-seven until May 13, 1941, it really shouldn't. Much of that speculation came spinning out of the offices of Louis's own promoter, and out of the typewriters of his favored scribes, and it was designed to inject a modicum of mystery into the sport at a time when there was hardly any. Seventeen times Louis had defended his title. Seventeen times he'd barely broken a sweat.

Would number eighteen be different?

The world certainly hoped so. The Mutual Broadcasting Company was expecting its largest audience ever on the evening of June 18, when it would present the Joe Louis–Billy Conn bout after wresting the rights away from NBC. Mutual's broadcast would feature a young announcer named Don Dunphy, known to New Yorkers as the man who brought them condensed and reconstructed baseball games each evening at 7:15 on radio stations WINS. His partner would be Bill Corum, the widely read sports columnist for the *New York Journal-American,* and their audience would be vaster than even they could possibly know. Out in the South China Sea, the U.S. Navy battleship *Ticonderoga* would steam to a halt moments before the opening bell, the commanding officer ordering the ship's radio tuned to the fight. At Forbes Field, a baseball game between the Pittsburgh Pirates and New York Giants would draw an advance sale of some twenty-five thousand people, which seemed surprisingly good for a midweek game between second-division opponents until you considered the Pirates announced they would halt the game around ten o'clock and pipe the broadcast in over the public-address system. Thus, Pittsburghers unable to make their way to New York could still gather with their neighbors in one mass setting, hoping if they roared loud enough, perhaps a favorable jet stream could carry their pleas 370 miles east.

People wanted this fight. They needed this fight. June 1941 was shaping up as one of those months when you wondered how thirty days could possibly contain everything that was happening around sports, around the country, around the world. Lou Gehrig was dead. So was the Kaiser. Whirlaway was practically lighting Belmont Park on fire with his training runs as he pursued racing's Triple Crown. On June 5, Joe DiMaggio smacked a sixth-inning triple off Hal Newhouser at Detroit's Tiger Stadium to quietly extend his hitting streak to twenty-one straight games, a feat greatly overshadowed by the fact that a couple hours away in Cleveland, Boston's Ted Williams had extended *his* hitting streak to twenty games and fattened his batting average to a gaudy .434.

All of this was plenty interesting. But it was all background music. That same day, Billy Conn had settled into his training camp in Pompton Lakes,

New Jersey, a rustic getaway less than a forty-five-minute drive from Manhattan whose primary claim to fame was that it had formerly been the place where Joe Louis prepared for his New York–area fights. On his first day there, as Conn wandered around the Colonial House, the Revolution-era center of the camp, he quipped, "Joe didn't leave any left hooks lying around here, did he?" Louis meanwhile had set up headquarters in Greenwood Lake, New York, sixty miles north of the city in that part of the Catskill Mountains that New Yorkers referred to as the "Jewish Alps." He was still nursing a cut above the eye sustained when Buddy Baer had flipped him out of the ring, so he spent the day tooling around a golf course, promising, "I'll put in my work for Mr. Billy Conn, don't you worry about me."

For the next two weeks, every grunt and every groan would be duly noted in dozens of notebooks, every grimace and grin would be frozen by dozens of flashbulbs, every offhand comment, boastful pledge, or witty observation would be sent out to a famished public as one of the largest media corps ever seen assembled at the two camps day after day. Seven hundred reporters would be credentialed to cover the fight; each day a rotating mob of forty to fifty of them arrived early, stayed late, typed furiously, chewed an endless string of cigars, plowed through a mountain of free food, adding to the hype and (Mike Jacobs hoped) to the fight's bottom line. The close proximity of the camps meant that the writers could bounce back and forth breezily and easily, swapping gossip with the fighters, with the managers, with each other.

Joe Louis was used to this game, and to this relentless spotlight, and if he wasn't bored by it, he'd been trained to feed it as little as possible. Billy Conn was another matter. Not only was he enjoying every second of the spotlight, drinking the attention like the milkshakes he was gulping down daily in a fruitless attempt to pack on pounds, but he was surrounded by talkers, too. Johnny Ray, his manager, had waited even longer than Conn to become an overnight sensation.

"Hell, I've had Billy with me since before he knew how to talk," Ray said one day.

"Yeah," Billy said, feeding off Ray's straight lines. "You pulled me out of grade school and taught me how to row drunks."

Mostly, though, it was Conn doing the talking, and the boasting, and the predicting, and the instigating. Conn had been leading with his lip for as long as he could remember, and while it sometimes caused that lip to fatten and bleed in his younger days when he'd talked too much around the feistier folks on Shakespeare Street, he was an endearing fellow, naturally funny and likable. Each day his trainer, Freddie Fierro, would punish him, and each afternoon Conn would settle down for a splendid lunch prepared by Billy Handler, a cook Ray had recruited from the kitchen at Lindy's Restaurant, and he would sit down for extended sessions of blarney and bullshit. And the writers ate up every syllable.

Conn would need the bluster to bolster both his own self-esteem and the confidence of the wagering public, who knew well the inglorious history of light-heavyweights taking the leap across the great chasm, challenging the big boys. Only two had ever done it successfully, and both came with explanations: Ruby Bob Fitzsimmons, a lean, oddly built Englishman, knocked out Gentleman Jim Corbett in Carson City, Nevada, in 1897, but he never defended the title, losing his next time out to Jim Jeffries. In 1906, little-regarded Tommy Burns outpointed Marvin Hart, but Hart wasn't really considered a true champion since he'd won an elimination series after Jeffries retired. Then, two years later, Burns nearly drowned in a pool of his own blood while taking a vicious beating from Jack Johnson in Sydney, Australia. Conn knew that people thought there was a great possibility that he wouldn't just lose, but be crippled. Or killed.

"I'm nobody's dope," he said, dripping with sweat after a workout on June 9. "I didn't come to town on the last load of hay. I've been fighting for as long as this Louis and while I admit I can't punch the way Joe could before he softened up and started to slip, I know as much, if not more, about the game than he does. Joe cuts easily. He's going in there with that bad eye Buddy gave him. Wouldn't there be hell to pay in the champ's corner if I opened that eye? It could be. Of course, Joe won't have a sign on that injured optic saying, 'Please keep off this eye.' And I'm a pretty fair sharpshooter when I get my mind on it. No rough stuff, you understand. But Louis had better keep a glove in front of that glimmer—just in case of a tie."

Later, to the venerable columnist Grantland Rice, Conn elaborated, "Louis never has fought anybody like me. He got to the top beating fellows like Carnera, Max Baer, and Jim Braddock, who either couldn't box or were too slow to move around. Even Schmeling was slow. Max was a fair boxer and could punch, but he fought in a straight line and lost his early speed.

All Louis had to do to lick him was move in on him constantly. He still doesn't know what it's like to be in there with a fellow who can step around and make him hustle through every round."

These nuggets were dutifully relayed to Greenwood Lake, where Louis mostly met them with a shrug and a sleepy smile. "Billy's a good fighter," he said. "He *should* believe he can beat me."

It wasn't until a few days later that Conn would finally find a way to break through Louis's stoic façade and truly scrape a nerve. Jack Miley, formerly a columnist for the *New York Post,* had signed up to run public relations for the Conn camp. One afternoon, stretched out on the vast lawn in the middle of the camp's grounds with Conn, Miley and the writers engaged in a familiar game for the era, heavy with ethnic stereotypes that, lacking the filter of six and a half decades, sound a lot like slurs. Conn had endured this for years, alternately hearing that he was doomed to be a drunk, that his quick temper would inevitably be his ruination, that his stubborn Irish streak would eventually get him knocked flat somewhere. It was the way things were. Miley mentioned that Conn's entourage included an Irishman (Conn), a Jew (Ray), an Italian (Fierro), and a German (Handler).

"It's like one of those old League of Nations meetings," Miley crowed. "Suddenly you got a bunch of 'dese and dose' guys getting all Tunney on me"—Gene Tunney, the ex-champ, was famous for being the most intellectual of all boxers, a voracious reader who often brought books to the gym with him—"and basically saying that Louis is licked mentally before going in the ring. When guys like Conn's guys start shrinking *my* head, I'm gonna quit."

The writers all laughed. So did Conn. Then the fighter piped up.

"Louis is just a big, slow-thinking Negro," he said. "Nobody knows this better than Joe himself. He's a dangerous fighter because he can punch and because he's been taught well. But he's a mechanical fighter doing only what he's been told. He can't think under pressure in the ring, and he knows it. He showed this every time he met a man who wasn't a rule-book fighter. Schmeling started hitting with right hands in the second round of their first fight and kept on hitting him with those sucker punches until Louis was out. In twelve rounds Louis lacked the savvy to put his left hand up and block those punches."

Then it was Johnny Ray's turn.

"Louis is as slow on his feet as he is in his brains," the manager said. "When he breaks out of his shuffle, he's gone. If he gets all tangled up in his feet like he [sometimes does], Billy'll move around him so fast, Louis won't be able to hit him with a shotgun. Louis knows this and when he thinks about Conn, it's like a kid thinking about matching wits with one of those magic guys."

Many years later, Conn would cringe when those words were read back to him; he would hold his hands up and say, "You have to remember that times were just different then. It really wasn't personal. I think Joe knew that."

Eventually, he would. But as soon as he saw those quotes, as soon as they were verified as being truthful, Louis's whole demeanor changed. He started arguing with Roxborough, who thought he was training too hard, sparring too often, but Louis was heard to scream, "Ain't no such thing as training too hard to fight *this* fight!"

Normally the blandest quote anywhere, Louis was suddenly quite chatty himself.

"Why does Conn want to say all those bad things about me? He's got no right to shoot his mouth off. What's he done, anyway? I fought some boys as fast as Conn, guys who were much better boxers than Conn, and I licked 'em all. He ain't done nothing yet."

Someone asked, "Joe, could Billy hurt you?"

He smiled at that. "He'll hurt you if he hits you often enough," Louis said. "You get enough raindrops on your head and you'll begin to feel them."

Now everyone else was laughing, too. This was a side of Louis they rarely got to see.

"It doesn't always happen that the puncher beats the clever man," Louis said. "Little, clever, light-hitting men have beaten big punchers before, and they'll do it as long as there is boxing, I guess. Only, in this coming case, the puncher will beat the little man who can't hit. Sure, that Conn's got a pretty good left. But I got a pretty good left, too."

He shook his head, took his gloves off, wrapped a towel dipped in ice water around his neck. "Some days you get tired and bored with this training. But then another day you don't and you figure it's your business and you keep going. Especially for this fight. That Conn, he makes some nasty cracks. I never make nasty cracks."

The writers went scurrying, looking for telephones, eager to call their offices and tell their sports editors how much smoke their newest dispatches would contain. The editors couldn't get enough, because their readers couldn't get enough. In New York City, every one of the eight daily newspapers reported serious spikes in circulation for the first two weeks of June 1941 and gleefully presented that information in page-length house advertisements. It was like that all over the country. For one night, June 18, the entire nation's attention would be fixed on one thing, in one place, and for once the only blood that would be spilled would come voluntarily from the combatants, who would be handsomely compensated for their wounds.

This would be a welcome change of pace.

———————●———————

Blood covered the front pages of the newspapers by the time summer arrived in 1941. It flowed inaudibly over the radio, as the newscasters in their dour voices introduced another horrific tale from Montenegro, or Athens, or Warsaw, or Amsterdam. It pooled in the frightened imaginations of boys just now growing into manhood in the United States, who would soon be old enough to have a draft number, and who knew what that could mean in the years to come?

For so many months the stories had been bloodless and cold, no matter how ominous they'd sounded. The bluster of dictators can be terrifying if you hear the words up close, if you're near enough to feel their venom, but from a distance, with an ocean of insulation, they can lose their impact. They're just words. Until the blood spills. Until the blood belongs to real victims, and the victims have names. There's nothing abstract about that.

One name that reached the papers on June 17, 1941, the day before Joe Louis and Billy Conn would meet for the heavyweight championship of the world, belonged to Janusz Kusocinski. In a world before the rise of the Nazis—a world that, in Europe, seemed barely real by the middle of 1941—he had been Joe Louis, Joe DiMaggio, and Babe Ruth rolled into one spectacular, heroic icon for the people of Poland. Born in Warsaw to a family of railroad workers, he'd rocketed to stardom at the 1932 Olympics in Los Angeles by capturing the ten-thousand-meter run, outlasting a pair of Finns, Volmari Iso-Hollo and Lasse Virtanen, setting a world record in the process. He retired to what should have been the easy life of a hero in his native land and had aspirations to be a race-car driver on the European Grand Prix circuit, but the German invasion obliterated that comfortable pathway. He volunteered for army service, was wounded twice, then captured by the Gestapo on March 26, 1940. His death was formally announced on June 17, 1941, but he'd actually been executed almost a full year earlier, on June 21, 1940, in Palmiri, a suburb of Warsaw and a regular Nazi killing field where so many Poles were slaughtered it sometimes took an agonizing, endless time for the names of the dead to eventually surface. Even the most famous names.

"Anyone who saw Janusz walk in ahead of Iso-Hollo that August day in 1932 would know he wouldn't be the kind of a guy who would bow to an oppressor," is the way sports columnist Paul Zimmerman eulogized Kusocinski in the *Los Angeles Times*.

A mounting stack of similar atrocities had finally forced Franklin Roosevelt to take an active hand in the United States' relationship with Germany. On June 16, Roosevelt ordered all Nazi consulates operating in the United States closed by July 10, a step just shy of completely breaking diplomatic relations—which would be about a half-step shy of war. He informed the Reich that its agencies in North America indulged in activities of "an improper and unwarranted character inimical to the welfare of the United States"—which was simply a more genteel way of accusing the Nazis of openly spying. Winston Churchill's reaction was predictably effusive—"United we stand. Divided we fall. Divided the dark ages return. United we can guide and save the world."—while the German response was predictably grim: "The Third Reich does not allow itself to be provoked," was the official communiqué. It also announced that some $450 million of U.S. assets in German banks were being immediately frozen.

Roosevelt didn't reach this line in the sand easily, but he did sense the inevitability of what was happening across the Atlantic. For one thing, he was privy to firsthand evidence that illustrated precisely how vast were the Nazis' atrocities in the conquered lands, especially in regard to what the Nazis euphemistically referred to as "the Jewish question."

Actually, you didn't need access to classified documents to understand just how grave things had gotten for Jews under Hitler's thumb. You might not have been able to foresee the wretched horrors that would be visible only four years later when the concentration camps would be liberated—

What right-thinking human being possibly could?—but if you scanned the newspapers every day in 1941, you knew *something* was going on, something ominous, something menacing, and had been ever since *Kristallnacht* in 1938. It might take some careful searching to find them; few of the subsequent stories found a home on the front pages of any of the nation's newspapers. But they were there if you knew where to look.

On January 3, for example, the *New York Times* ran a photo on page 3 showing a concrete wall, eight feet high, which had been built to surround more than one hundred city blocks in Warsaw, an area designated as a ghetto for five hundred thousand Jews in the former Polish capital. Twenty-one days later, a buried item deep inside the same newspaper reported that "scores" of Jews in Berlin were being led into basements there for "summary executions."

Hitler never had been shy about this, actually. In the Reichstag meeting of September 1, 1939, in which the invasion of Poland had been formally announced, he'd declared that "if the world were pushed into a general war by Jewry, all Jewry will have exhausted its role in Europe." Now, less than two years later, he believed his message, however subtle, however brutal, had gotten across well. "Already, our racial views are gripping people after people," Hitler said on January 30, "and I hope that also those people who are today our enemies will one day recognize their internal enemy and that they will enter into the front with us—the front against the international Jewish exploitation and corruption of peoples."

Three days later the official Nazi newspaper, *Voelkischer Beobachter*, predicted the complete elimination of Jews from the European economy by the close of 1941, saying such a "victory" would lead to a similar process in the cultural and political fields as well. "National liberation," it declared, "can be achieved only by eliminating all Jews." With all European economies linked with those of Germany and Italy, the paper argued, "the result is obvious."

"What German merchant or businessman can be expected to do business with Jews? Beyond this a revolutionary revision of economic thought is in the process of development on all continental nations. Everywhere the German ideas are gaining ground. These ideas lead automatically to the elimination of Jewry."

Germany itself, of course, was only a part of Hitler's great sinister plan, and throughout the spring and summer of 1941, news of anti-Semitism leapt from the pages of newspapers, tumbled out of radio speakers, with the datelines varying depending on the day.

In the Netherlands, in March, Dr. Arthur Seyss-Inquart, Reich commissioner for the Netherlands, ordered the registration within four weeks of all Jews and "part-Jews" in the country. In Italy, a measure issued by the Ministry of the Interior further restricted the activities of Italian citizens who were Jews, forbidding them from taking jobs as salesmen, middlemen, appraisers, and canvassers for "firms or authorized agencies"—such as travel agencies, auction sales, and publicity bureaus or the like. Under laws issued the previous three years, Jews in Italy could not hold jobs in government administration, the stock exchange, and universities. Moreover, they were forbidden from joining the Fascist Party and the armed forces. They could not practice the liberal professions or own shops of any kind.

In Vichy, the transfer of Jewish-owned businesses to non-Jews was carried out in the occupied zone under German regulations. The local war counselor told the press in Paris that German authorities were eliminating Jewish influences entirely from the economic life of the occupied territories. To achieve this end, all Jewish-owned businesses or industrial enterprises must be registered. Eleven thousand had already been listed in the Paris district.

The Jewish owners were permitted to sell to non-Jews if the German authorities were satisfied that the sale was not being made to a dummy proprietor representing the previous owner. If the Jewish owner failed to declare his business, his property was confiscated, and if he declined to sell, a commissioner was appointed to carry out the transfer of the business to a non-Jew. This affected some 4,000 small businesses and 500 larger ones, and the routine was always the same: The stores were first placarded with yellow signs labeling them as Jewish; when those were replaced with red signs, it meant that an "Aryan" purchaser had been found.

Every day the roster grew thicker, angrier, more desperate; every day brought more of the same: Reichsmarshall Hermann Goering's *Essener National Zeitung,* in a dispatch from The Hague on February 28, asked whether the "Jewish question" on the Netherlands was about to receive a "total solution" that would make it impossible in the future for even a single Jew to be in a position "to sow hate and dissension in the Netherlands, to beat up Netherlanders with their cowardly machinations." In Romania, the next month, all Jewish property was expropriated as an "act of national reconstruction" by premier Ion Antonescu. In the former Yugoslavia, Jews were given a rapid taste of what their new life would look like; they were quickly aggregated and forced to wear yellow armbands under penalty of execution. Jewish men were organized into labor groups to clear the immense bomb wreckage and excavate bodies buried in the ruins since the first week of April. No Jew was permitted to buy in the public market before 10:30 A.M., after which point most stocks were exhausted. Any Jew found trying to escape the country was shot without questions.

"And this," one German soldier reported excitedly, "is only the beginning."

On June 18, a day that would seize the United States because that night two men would meet each other inside a twenty-by-twenty ring to determine the world's greatest fighter, as people discussed tales of the tape and the latest gambling odds and all manner of numbers, a more portentous set of statistics was released that stated, unequivocally, that fully one-third of the 15 million Jews presently on planet earth were living under Nazi rule. It's possible that no one reading that fact understood just how disquieting a truth that really was. If not, there was this accompanying bit of news from Berlin: "A rule that Jewish laborers must not be paid for time spent in air-raid shelters was among the regulations recently passed into German law. Also, Jews are not entitled to compensation for damage incurred during the raids. . . ."

Now, more than ever, if you were lucky enough to be living in America, it meant you had the option of leaving these horrors behind, if only for a few minutes, and flipping a few pages forward, to sports sections that were no longer providing relief from the rest of the world, but exile from it. Young Phil Rizzuto was right. People not only read these pages, they *devoured* them.

Because you really were afraid of what you'd see in the other parts of the paper.

———————●———————

Billy Conn hid it well, kept it camouflaged behind all the bluster, but he was trapped in turmoil as the days and the hours clicked away to the defining moment of his life. The two women in his life were each battling for his spirit and for his attention, and in different ways, for different reasons, both were about to take turns breaking that oversized Gaelic heart.

Before he'd left Pittsburgh for the train that would take him to the city and to Joe Louis, Conn had paid his mother a visit. She wasn't well, hadn't been for a year, the cancer eating away at forty-one-year-old Margaret McFarland Conn's bones, locking her in a bed upstairs in the house that her prizefighting son, Billy, had bought for her. Conn's image as a flashy spendthrift helped sell newspapers, but the truth was that virtually every nickel he'd earned in a boxing ring over the past two years had been funneled into his mother's care. She would have the best doctors, the best hospitals, and now, as her days grew shorter, the most comfortable escort possible away from her temporal existence.

"Mom," Billy had said that day, "the next time you see me, I'll be the heavyweight champion of the world."

"Sonny," Margaret replied, "the next time *you* see *me* will be in Paradise."

One of their last conversations had been about a sweet young lass named Mary Louise Smith, eighteen years old, the daughter of a rakish Pittsburgh character named Greenfield Jimmy Smith. Greenfield Jimmy had played a bit of ball with the Pirates, the Phillies, the Reds, and the Dodgers as a light-hitting infielder, and after his playing days he'd invested wisely during Prohibition and bought himself a first-rate nightspot, the Bachelor's Club, once the new laws allowed him to go legit, and now he was a prominent figure in Pittsburgh sporting circles. As such, he'd befriended a kid boxer on the make named Billy Conn, the two had hit it off, and he'd invited Conn to spend some time at the Smith family summer home down the Jersey Shore. There, Conn had been smitten by Mary Louise Smith, Greenfield Jimmy's young daughter, then only fifteen.

"Someday," he announced one day in the surf, with all the innocence of the 1930s coursing through his Irish blood, "I am going to marry you."

Someday, with luck, would arrive the day after Billy Conn won the heavyweight championship of the world. Billy and Mary Louise, now eighteen, had already taken the blood tests, already gotten the license. Mary Louise had never seen her intended fight, he wouldn't let her, but he'd gotten her a room at the Waldorf-Astoria and the room had a radio in it, and she planned on listening, and then meeting him later on, and then hurrying home to Pittsburgh to become Mrs. Billy Conn.

What Billy and Mary Louise *didn't* have was Greenfield Jimmy's permission to walk down the aisle. And on the morning of the fight, Greenfield Jimmy informed the world that before Billy and Mary Louise became man and wife, they would first have to hop across his dead body. But not before he broke all four of their legs.

"Champion or no champion, I'll punch hell out of that fellow, and he'd probably be the first one to say I could do it," Smith snarled. "I hope he wins, but I want him to stay the hell away from my family. Billy always has been a good friend of mine and I've seen a lot of him, probably because I'm interested in all kinds of sports. But I'm against him—as I would be against you, or you, if you tried to interfere with my little family. My little girl has just turned eighteen and that's just a baby to me."

A Conn never took fighting words sitting down, of course. Informed of Greenfield Jimmy's low opinion of his son, Billy Conn Sr. responded with all the subtlety of a brick to the back of the skull: "Jimmy might lick Billy, but I'll be goddamned if he can lick me. Who does this guy think he is? There is one thing certain: He ain't ever punched a Conn. And it'll be a sorry day for him when he tries. Listen, this guy never punched anybody without having a couple of guys hold the other fellow's arms. He was even a light hitter with a baseball bat."

In the middle of all this fun, the groom/challenger reported for work on Wednesday morning, June 18, and was flabbergasted by the furor. "I got to look out," he said of Greenfield Jimmy as he returned to the State building on the corner of Worth and Centre, where he and Louis would finally be weighed. "He's a wild-eyed Irishman."

Soon, though, the man who best fit that description was Conn himself. He'd shown up on time at 11:45, eager to be done with the formalities so he could head back to the hotel and take a nap. By noon, Louis still hadn't shown up. By 12:15, nothing. As the clock barreled toward 12:30, Conn said he was through. "I'm not waiting on him anymore," Conn barked. "Weigh me and let's be done with it."

He stripped, stepped on the scale, and Jacobs was horrified at what he saw: The challenger for the "heavyweight" title was barely 167 pounds—eight pounds under the maximum allowed for *light-heavies.*

"One-seventy-four!" Jacobs announced, before anyone could prove otherwise.

"Who the hell does Louis think he is? How long do I have to wait?" Conn asked.

"You ain't waiting on anyone," Johnny Ray told him. "Let's get the hell out of here." The photographers begged him to keep his boy around, so they could take the perfunctory pictures, but Ray said no. "The kid's a fighter," he said. "He ain't no movie star." On his way out the door, Conn left the reporters from the afternoon papers one last bit of sizzle for them to include in their final advance stories.

"Louis has lost 50 percent of his punch and has slowed way down," he said. "He's just another guy now. They can say what they want about how I'm not heavy enough, and how I lose my temper. Well, all I'll say is I'll be heavyweight champion by about eleven o'clock tonight. I'm a cinch to win a decision." And then he was gone.

Louis finally arrived about forty-five minutes late, apologizing, saying the traffic from Greenwood Lake had been hell, and he was quickly hustled to the scale, and again Mike Jacobs began to sweat. The champ was at 202. That was a fine number for a heavyweight. But it was thirty-five pounds more than what Conn had weighed.

"One-ninety-nine and a half!" Jacobs proclaimed.

Louis, told of Conn's prediction of a "cinch" decision, decided to play along and slightly violated a few of his ten commandments.

"That Billy Conn talks too much about what he's gonna do," he said. "There'll be a knockout in this fight and you know who I think will do it. Conn ain't no faster than a lot of fellows I met. Don't forget, I can do a little boxing myself. I guess it'll be over inside eight rounds."

By now the bookmakers were more than satisfied with the business the fight had attracted, and Mike Jacobs's fiddling and fudging wasn't going to change that. An influx from Pittsburgh of thousands of fans on the "Ham and Egg Special" and the "Shamrock Special" had already filled city hotel rooms and balanced the bookies' ledgers, because a lot of them were actually throwing serious money behind their boy. That included a couple of well-known Pittsburghers named Johnny Ray and Billy Conn. Ray had always schooled Conn, "Never bet on yourself. If you lose, you don't ever wanna lose twice." But now, Conn made an exception. He got himself at three-to-one. He liked those odds very much.

By the time Mike Jacobs returned to his office on the sixth floor of the Brill Building at Forty-ninth Street and Broadway, he realized he had one last hassle on his hands. Before storming off in a huff, Conn had insisted he would wear purple trunks. Nobody had said anything about that. But then Louis had been asked what color trunks *he* planned to wear, and quietly he'd said, "Purple." Usually, this was the champion's call. And usually, that would mean Mike Jacobs or someone else would have to make a most unpleasant call to Johnny Ray and tell him his boxer would have to wear different colors.

Jacobs called John Phelan, the boxing commissioner, and told him of their dilemma. After a few awkward seconds of silence, Phelan laughed.

"Mike," he said, "the idea of the contrasting colors in the fighting trunks is to enable the spectators to tell the contestants apart. Look at who our contestants are. I don't think that'll be a problem tonight."

———————————•———————————

There had been a terrible threat of thunderstorms all day, but except for a brief sprinkling early in the evening the sky remained clear, and by the time the gates opened at seven o'clock there were already about twenty-five thousand people milling in front of the Polo Grounds, an old horseshoe of a stadium at 155th Street and Eighth Avenue in the heart of Harlem. The Polo Grounds had long languished as the third-most-popular boxing venue in the city, behind Madison Square Garden a hundred blocks downtown (and used only during the foul-weather months, due to its limited capacity of twenty thousand seats) and Yankee Stadium, which sat just across the Harlem River in the Bronx. But Jacobs was a firm believer in the *Farmer's Almanac,* which always insisted the best time to schedule an outdoor event well in advance in New York City without fear of a rainout was between June 16 and June 22, which is why all of Joe Louis's seminal summer fights fell in that range. And in 1941, the Yankees were in the midst of a two-week home stand that covered all of those dates. So the Polo Grounds it would have to be.

The Yankees themselves were delighted about this, because, for one of the few times, they'd actually be in town when one of these boxing burlesques took place. Joe McCarthy, the Yankees manager and an old friend of Johnny Ray's, picked Conn because "he's climbed the ladder and he's earned his shot." McCarthy would be ringside. So would pitcher Lefty Gomez, a huge fight buff, who warned, "Skill beats brute force." So would Joe DiMaggio, who in the afternoon had stretched his hitting streak to thirty-one straight games in a 3-2 loss to the White Sox at Yankee Stadium with a hard fifth-inning smash that Sox shortstop Luke Appling couldn't quite handle. When DiMaggio entered the Polo Grounds and made his way to his seat, he received one of the three loudest ovations of the night, up there with the two boxers themselves, a staggering concession to a Yankee deep in the heart of Giants country.

Famous faces were dotted throughout the growing crowd. Bob Feller arrived just before the lights went down, having hopped an express train from Philadelphia, where the Indians had pounded the Athletics, 14-2. Al Jolson was there. Bob Hope was there. J. Edgar Hoover was there. A young singer and fight fan from Hoboken, New Jersey, badly wanted to be there, but that night Frank Sinatra, along with Buddy Rich, Ziggy Elman, Connie Haines, the Pied Piper, and the rest of the Tommy Dorsey Orchestra were opening at the Astor Roof at the Hotel Astor in Times Square. Pittsburgh mayor Cornelius Scully occupied one of the twenty-five-dollar ringside seats, as did Pennsylvania governor Arthur James. Jersey City mayor Frank Hague didn't have a ringside seat, but instead sat as a credentialed member of the press corps, representing his hometown *Greenville Gazette,* and seated nearby was Jimmy Cannon, former boxing writer, future legendary columnist, presently a guest of the U.S. Army at Fort Dix.

By 10:15 the Polo Grounds could barely restrain the electricity bouncing within its ancient walls. Mike Jacobs could barely suppress his delight as he looked around and saw that they had, indeed, surpassed expectations (the final official crowd count would be 54,487, although, security being what it was, there were surely five or six thousand more than that inside) and the gate would come close to a half million bucks, a splendid figure indeed. By 10:16 both fighters were in the ring, Louis wearing a blue bathrobe and Conn a white one, and they were being introduced by famed ring announcer Harry Balogh, and heavyweight contender Lou Nova was shaking hands with both of them, and nobody could hear a single word. This was about to happen, for real, for good, for keeps.

The Polo Grounds was ready. The world was ready. Fifteen million radio sets were tuned to the fight, assuring Mutual of its largest audience ever. The *Ticonderoga* was ready. A few blocks south of the Polo Grounds, Harlem was ready, several thousand African Americans making their traditional pilgrimage to the corner of Seventh Avenue and 125th Street, site of the Hotel Theresa, where Joe Louis would return after the fight and where his wife, Marva, was inside listening to everything on the radio. Pittsburgh was certainly ready. At Forbes Field, where 24,738 watched the first three and a half innings of Pirates-Giants with one eye on the field and the other on the loudspeakers, waiting for the main event, the Pirates had taken a 2-1 lead when the umpires called the teams off the field and the first strains of radio station WCAE echoed out of the amps.

In the Conn homestead on Fifth Avenue in Pittsburgh, Margaret McFarland Conn remained in her bedroom (doctor's orders) and refused to have a radio wheeled in (her own maternal anxieties), but she could clearly hear the excitement building downstairs where her daughters, her sisters, and her friends had all gathered around a large RCA console. "Billy's promised to win for Mom," Conn's twenty-year-old sister, Mary Jane, reported. "That's all we needed to hear. We know he'll win now." Seventeen people in all were stuffed into the living room, including John Schaub, the Conn family doctor, keeping one eye on his patient and one ear on the radio.

"I don't want Billy to fight," Mrs. Conn had whispered to a Pittsburgh reporter earlier in the day. "I can't help worrying before a fight. I'm always afraid he'll get hurt, although I know Billy can take care of himself. He always has. I want my boy to be happy. And I know he'll never be happy until he wins the heavyweight championship. He's talked and dreamed of nothing else for years.

"I don't know much about boxing. But everybody's heard of Joe Louis. He must be a great fighter and a fine man. I know he's much bigger than my Billy. But I'm not worried about that. Billy was always fighting with the big kids of the neighborhood, even when he was six years old."

Now, as the world prepared to watch her Billy take on the biggest kid of all, Margaret McFarland Conn closed her eyes and opened her ears. The ruckus downstairs would tell her all she needed to know.

———————●———————

At first, it did not go well for the challenger.

Barely a minute into the fight, Billy Conn found himself in the last place he wanted to be: on the seat of his pants, looking straight up into Joe Louis's eyes. Louis hadn't put him there; Conn had slipped and fallen without taking a punch, stepping out of the way of a long left from Louis. But it did betray the brash confidence Conn had carried with him for two solid weeks. Just a few hours earlier, as he'd left the Edison Hotel on his way to the Polo Grounds, he'd told a Pittsburgh buddy who was with him, Sammy Baraf, "Louis knows that I'll win the title or die in the ring in front of him.

He won't suspect he's fighting a desperado until I start to knock his head loose on its hinges. We'll see who will score the best punches. I know he can't hit me and I know that I'll hit him plenty."

Baraf looked at his friend as if he'd taken one too many uppercuts to the brain stem. Conn laughed. "Listen," he said, "I'm going to be a millionaire in a few hours. I can afford to be different." Actually, his take would be 20 percent of the gate (about $70,000; Louis, the champion, would take home roughly $140,000), but that was still more money than he'd ever seen sitting in one pile before.

Now, suddenly, Conn was learning what seventeen men before him had already discovered: Reports of Joe Louis's demise were not only greatly exaggerated, they were comically wrong. Louis wasn't only able to catch up with Conn, he was able to land a couple of blows, too. Conn had absorbed a few thousand punches in his lifetime; none of them ever felt like this. The second round was an almost note-for-note repeat of the first: Conn landed a few jabs that felt like mosquito bites; Louis countered with combinations that felt like they were going right through Conn's chest and his jaw. The crowd, frantic at the outset, quieted. It looked certain to be a quick night. As the two men retreated to their corners after the bell ended round two, all three judges—referee Eddie Joseph and the ringside monitors, Marty Monroe and Bill Healy—wrote the same verdict on their scorecards: Louis had easily won both rounds.

"You got dinner plans or something?" Johnny Ray asked Conn.

"This big son of a bitch can really hit," Conn said between oxygen gulps.

"Even so, you might want to join the damned fight at some point."

Soon enough, he did. Over the next two rounds, Conn slowly coaxed all 54,487-plus fans back to the edges of their seats. A left hook midway through the third round knocked Louis a stride off-balance, and the first roar of the night filled the hazy summer sky. Then, early in the fourth, he landed a crushing straight left to the champ's face, followed with a straight right, followed by still another straight right that actually buckled Louis's knees. Conn wasn't hurting Louis, but he also wasn't giving Louis much of a target, either. All three judges noticed. All three gave Conn rounds three and four. The idea of a quick knockout was gone. Suddenly it seemed that everyone might actually be there for a while.

In Pittsburgh, at Forbes Field, New York Giants pitcher Cliff Melton had started to warm up in the bullpen, knowing that he was going to enter the game as soon as play resumed, replacing starter Johnnie Wittig. He threw a couple of soft tosses, wanting to break a sweat. But suddenly he found himself unable to concentrate. He found Don Dunphy's voice mesmerizing. And before he knew it, he was caught up with what he was listening to, fascinated that all around him twenty-five thousand people were on their feet and screaming themselves hoarse without seeing a thing. He sat back down. "I never realized how powerful the imagination could be until that night," Melton would say years later, shortly before his death in 1986. "But I swear I could *see* what was happening that night. Everyone at Forbes Field could."

In some ways, they had a better view than most of the people inside the Polo Grounds, but even that didn't matter. Even from the cheap seats (which sold for two dollars and hardly guaranteed an unimpeded view of the action), fans could sense that something different, something *special* was at work here. Conn may not have packed cement in his boxing gloves, but he knew how to land punches; and Louis, for all the hand-wringing about his alleged deterioration, was still among the best fighters who ever lived and was showing everyone why, regaining control of the fight, cruising to claim the next two rounds, one more time reestablishing in everyone's mind who was the champion and who was the challenger. He opened a cut over Conn's left eye in the sixth and seemed settled in, ready to pummel Conn to a bloody decision if the stubborn Irishman wanted to play it that way.

"The guy's great," Conn reported to his corner after the sixth.

"So are you," Ray snapped. "Now prove it."

Stunningly, across the next six rounds, that is exactly what Billy Conn would do.

Across those eighteen minutes of boxing, as 54,000 people inside the Polo Grounds at last abandoned their seats for good, as 25,000 people inside a baseball stadium in Pittsburgh tried to shake to its core the very foundation upon which Forbes Field sat, as 15 million living rooms and saloons and recreation halls and patios rumbled with anticipation, it's quite possible that Conn turned in the most unforgettable boxing exhibition anyone had ever seen—or, in most cases, heard. It wasn't that he knocked the champion to the ground—he didn't, and really didn't come close to doing that. It wasn't that he turned Louis's face into a bloody pulp—for the most part, it remained scratch-free. It wasn't even that his relentless rounds of body punches hurt Louis all that badly, because for all of Conn's ranting, Louis had been right: He really had faced dozens of tomato-can heavyweights who packed a more vicious punch than this feisty light-heavy.

It was more than that. With each ring of the bell, Conn not only survived, he got stronger. His mere presence at the start of each round seemed to take a toll on Louis, and his tireless commitment to advancing and retreating, retreating and advancing, started slowing Louis's legs, too. Louis could still get off a wicked combination, and that would slow Conn down for a few moments. But then the challenger would come back twice as hard, twice as fast. He started picking up rounds. He evened the fight, and then, in the ninth, many believed he might have gotten ahead on points.

It was early in that round when Conn, coming out of a clinch, feeling awfully good about himself, whispered in his opponent's ear: "You're in for a fight tonight, Joe."

"That's right," Louis said.

All of Conn's toil, all of his patience, all of it nearly came crashing down in the tenth round, midway through, when he followed a left to the body with a left to Louis's face and then, for the second time, slipped on a slick patch of canvas and fell. This time Louis was right above him and could have easily—and legally—taken a free whack at a prone Conn, maybe sent him flying clear into Thursday morning.

"That wasn't his way," Billy Conn would recall, decades later. "Joe Louis was a gentleman. He didn't want to fight that way."

Louis stood frozen, arms at his side, waiting for Conn to recover. The slip had cost Conn the round, and a bit of momentum, but it hadn't shaken his confidence, not even a little. And so in the eleventh round the assault continued. In the champion's corner, Chappy Blackburn pleaded with his fighter to stay away from Conn, but he couldn't, Conn was too quick, had too much stamina, kept coming after Louis and then ducking back, seizing on Louis's tiring arms and weakening legs. Could he keep this up? It sure looked that way. Everyone could see that Conn didn't have enough punch to flatten Louis, but he sure seemed to have enough energy to keep running with him. He won the eleventh in a breeze, and now he was ahead on Joseph's card, 6-5, and on Monroe's card by the same number, and even though Healy had that number reversed in favor of the champion, that looked to be only a temporary inconsistency.

Because in the next round, it looked for all the world like Joe Louis was finished.

In the twelfth round, Conn's "fistic fusillade" as so many of the morning papers would describe it, turned Joe Louis, heavyweight champion, into a walking carcass for a few precious moments. Conn *still* couldn't finish him off, despite a left-right-left combination that almost seemed to extinguish the life from behind Louis's eyes, but each punch that landed seemed to strip away one more layer of invincibility. Louis was still fighting back, still landing his share of blows, but none of them hurt Conn at all. Just as the bell clanged, Conn got off one last beautiful punch, a left to the face, and it sprayed the ringside seats with Louis's perspiration.

The crowd—all of the crowds, everywhere—was beyond rabid now. Louis turned and staggered back to his corner. Conn did the same, only now he shot his right fist high in the air, acknowledging not only the crowd's mounting adoration but also the fact that he knew what everyone else knew: He was ahead on points, and he was about to take Joe Louis's title away. Him. Billy Conn. Punk light-heavy from East Liberty. Nine minutes from the championship.

The sixty seconds separating the end of the twelfth from the start of the thirteenth seemed to take sixty days. In Louis's case, he could've used the extra time. As it turned out, Conn would spend the rest of his life wishing that he had.

"Chappie, you're losing," Blackburn screamed over the din, directly into Louis's ear.

"I know I am," Louis said, huffing, gulping air, realizing he was about to suffer an upset that would probably be talked about for all time, a loss that would define his legacy every bit as much as all the wins that preceded it.

"You got to knock him out, Chappie," Blackburn screeched. "You got no other choice. You got to find a way to get him on his back."

"I know," Louis said.

Not surprisingly, Conn was far chattier in the opposite corner. Johnny Ray and Freddie Fierro and Manny Seamon, Fierro's second, knew they were in trouble the moment they saw Conn's fist shoot up into the air, the moment they saw his eyes as he fell onto his stool. The eyes were wild, they were on fire, they bore the unmistakable mark of a man whose grasp was about to seriously exceed his reach.

"Junior," Johnny Ray said, "you got the fight won, boy. You stay away from him for three more rounds, you're gonna be heavyweight champion. You hear me?"

"I got him," Conn said.

"You got him, all right," Fierro said. "Now stay the hell away from him."

"Nah, no way. I got him. I'm gonna knock him out."

Ray's heart fell to his ankles. *This crazy, crazy Mick . . .*

"Have you lost your fuckin' mind, Junior?"

"I got him," Conn said, not hearing, not caring, not worried about a goddamned thing right now. "I know what I'm doing."

For the rest of their lives, Billy Conn and Johnny Ray would tell and retell the story of what happened during those sixty seconds, Johnny pleading, Johnny begging, Billy not wanting to hear any of it, Billy talking shit about going out and knocking out Joe Freaking Louis. Always, they would reach the same punch line. Always.

"What's the point in being Irish," they would say, "if you can't be stupid?"

And so Billy Conn went after Joe Louis early in the thirteenth round, and he went after him often, intoxicated by the moment, overcome by the adrenaline flooding his system. Louis seemed helpless to stop the assault, didn't fight back, *couldn't* fight back, couldn't block Conn's machine-gun punches, one combination after another, five punches in a row, nine, thirteen in a row, *eighteen. . . .*

. . . and then . . .

Thwack! A right hand from Louis, delivered flush to Conn's exposed jaw.

Pow! A left, airmailed right to Conn's undefended ribs.

Blam! Another right hand, another blow to the jaw.

Conn's legs bent, then buckled, then gave out on him. His arms were dead, and they couldn't brace his fall. His head hit the canvas, which felt like a soft pile of cumulus clouds. Through the fog, he could barely make out the referee, Eddie Joseph, standing over him, slowly drawing out the count. All around him, fans were hoping that the bell ending the thirteenth round would beat Joseph's count to ten, and there was added hope when Conn sat up as Joseph reached seven, and started to regain his feet when he got to eight. But he wasn't quick enough. Over the next few days, as films of the fight began to fill movie houses across the country, people would study whether Conn had actually gotten to his feet before Joseph waved his hands, but it was a moot point. He was out.

And Joe Louis was still the champion.

The champion's final assault had been twenty-four unanswered punches, nineteen rights and five lefts, and it had been furious, the act of a desperate man, with those three punches—right to the jaw, left to the ribs, right to the jaw—making up for twelve and a half rounds of frustration.

For half a heartbeat, the Polo Grounds wasn't sure what it had just seen, but once it recovered, there was a relentless roar, louder and louder, partially for having witnessed a champion's finest hour, partially for having gotten twelve rounds (and two minutes and fifty-eight seconds' worth of a thirteenth) of unfettered brilliance, the kind of bout boxing fans always hope to get when they plunk down their money, and rarely do. Twenty blocks away, the crowd around the Hotel Theresa swelled in numbers and in noise as the final verdict was read, as the vigil for Louis's return began in earnest, blocking southbound traffic on Seventh Avenue. Eight hours to the west, Forbes Field was shrouded in silence, in disbelief, the words of Don Dunphy—"Conn is *out!* Joe Louis is *still* the champion of the *world!*"—hanging heavy in the musky air, the baseball players quietly retaking their positions after a fifty-six-minute delay. The Giants would soon scratch across the tying run, and when neither team could break that deadlock by the time the local curfew hit at one in the morning, after eleven innings, it was declared a tie. Hardly anyone cared. Pittsburgh had already lost.

Nowhere in the city was that loss felt more completely than in the house at 5435 Fifth Avenue, where the seventeen people downstairs began weeping, hugging each other, shaking their heads, and wondering who among them was going to have to deliver the devastating news to the house's top floor. Just a few minutes earlier, Margaret McFarland Conn's sister, Mary Herr, had scurried up with the wonderful news that Billy was leading, that he was safe, that all looked good, and Margaret's response had been a simple one: "Keep praying."

This time, another sister, Rose Shook, volunteered for the grim task. But it wasn't necessary. Margaret already knew. She had heard the giddy commotion turn funereal in an instant, and she knew what that had to mean. "It's all right, Rose," she said. "I know. I'm proud of Billy." Then she smiled weakly, turned to the wall, and vowed to stay awake a little while longer, until her son could call and she could tell him that herself.

Louis, as ever, was gracious later on, as the newsmen elbowed their way into his dressing room. "I knew I was losing, but I was sure Conn would lose his head," he said. "He was faster than I thought he'd be, faster than I could ever be. Maybe if we fight again Billy will win my title.

"Billy's a good fighter and he was hard to get to. I think he's the smartest fighter I ever boxed. Sure, he's faster than me, but I don't know how tough he is because I didn't hit him with much until I caught up with him. It was a tough thirteen-inning game."

Someone asked about how he could possibly have recovered so quickly, so completely, after looking to be perched right on the verge of disaster. Joe Louis shrugged his shoulders.

"I nailed him," the eighteen-time defending champion said. "And he lost his head."

Billy Conn couldn't argue with that simple assessment, because he knew how true it was. Even as he climbed out of the ring, spotting a friendly face, Hype Igoe, among the deadline-fueled sportswriters, he rasped, "I'm sorry, Mr. Igoe. You told me to box him, but that just wasn't good enough for me, I guess. How could I have made such a blunder?" By the time the rest of the newspapermen arrived, he'd already had a good, long sob, realizing exactly what he'd just done, what he'd risked, what he'd lost.

"I got too much Irish in me," he said. "I lost my head and a million bucks."

His parish priest, Father Patrick Hanrahan, sitting next to him, said, "It was magnificent, Billy. You made a grand showing. Everyone's proud of you, especially your mother."

But Conn wasn't buying.

"They begged me not to get too cocky back in my corner after I came back in the twelfth," he said over his sniffles. "I had him hurt, and thought I could get him in the next round. I gambled. Well, I went down fighting, I guess. That's just how I fight."

Around them, people instantly started identifying this as one of the greatest fights they'd ever seen. Julian Black, flushed with relief (and a few freshly won dollars, no doubt), said, "I thought Joe was through in the thirteenth. I really did."

Johnny Ray couldn't stay mad at his boy for acting as he did in the thirteenth because, who's kidding who, Johnny Ray would have done exactly the same thing. On one hand, he was a little annoyed that Eddie Joseph hadn't given Billy the benefit of the doubt on beating his count of ten, but on the other he realized that even if he'd been given a reprieve, his boy didn't have anything left. Louis would have still had two rounds to finish him off. He would have found a way. And maybe would have hurt him, too.

"The count was all right," Ray said. "Everything was all right. Louis won. He's champion. But Conn is the better fighter."

Someone asked Ray if Louis's reluctance to take advantage of Billy's tenth-round slip showed what a true sportsman the champion was. Ray chuckled at that one. "Maybe Junior would've done the same thing and maybe he would've kicked Louis in the teeth. I don't know. If that Louis is so damn polite, why didn't he step back in the thirteenth and give Junior a chance to come out of the fog? That's what I would have called being a gentleman."

Louis was dressed quickly and out the door, and soon he was mobbed by the waiting crowd back at the Hotel Theresa when his car pulled up in front around twelve-thirty. Seven mounted cops and fifteen foot patrolmen worked to clear a path, but they could do only so much with ten thousand fevered fans craning for a look at their hero. Boys in trees shouted deliriously at Louis, and twice the champ lost his hat running the gauntlet from car to stoop to lobby. The crowd milled around for an hour. They didn't want to go home, and the cops didn't force them, and so they stayed until all their energies dissolved, and they finally dispersed.

What a few of them soon encountered would stun them.

Conn had stayed and yammered on for close to ninety minutes, unable to stop talking, filling notebooks until the writers' hands were cramped. When the catharsis was finally complete, he lingered in the shower, dressed slowly, and by the time he and Ray were ready to leave, they were the last men left at the Polo Grounds. When they walked outside, the cabstands were empty and there wasn't a soul in sight.

Billy had to get back to the Waldorf to see Mary Louise, who'd been too nervous to listen to the fight, who'd stayed in her bathroom and kept the water running so she couldn't hear the muffled radio broadcast bleeding in from the neighboring rooms. He needed to tell her he'd be okay, and that they'd be okay, even if he knew there was no way in hell her old man was going to let them get married later that day. How to get there? They had to start walking, through the heart of Harlem, and even for a couple of fearless men like Billy Conn and Johnny Ray, this was something of a worrisome task. After all, he'd just spent an hour peppering the greatest of all African American heroes with his fists. He'd come *thisclose* to taking his title, and throwing all of black America into a deep funk. How would they respond to him if he walked in their midst now?

He found out. Soon he ran into a crowd that had just left Louis's hotel. Conn wasn't too hard to spot, a well-dressed white fellow whose face looked like it had just been worked over by a meat tenderizer. And then, the most amazing thing happened: Hundreds of people, thousands of them, almost all of them black, started applauding. They started cheering. They shook Conn's hand. They slapped him on the back. Some even hugged him. "You were great, Billy!" they crowed. "You were really something!" And then they got him a cab, and he was on his way to Mary Louise, and the rest of his life Billy Conn would never feel so good about losing anything as he did in that moment in Harlem during the longest night of his life.

———————⚫———————

Years later, after they'd become good friends on the rubber-chicken boxing circuit, a much older Billy Conn would turn to a much older Joe Louis and ask with a smile, "Jesus, Joe, couldn't you have let me borrow your title for just a little while? Just for six lousy months?"

"Billy," Louis said, "I let you have it for twelve rounds, and you didn't know what to do with it."

7

"THE ONLY TIME TO WORRY IS WHEN YOU'RE NOT HITTING."

A STREAK BECOMES A STREAK AS A NATION TURNS ITS LONELY EYES TO DIMAGGIO

Ted Williams and Joe DiMaggio celebrate the American League's victory in the 1941 All-Star Game.

Our Joe DiMaggio has hit
In thirty-two straight games
A batting streak that calls for cheers
From Yankee guys and dames

If there's a mental strain in this
Our Joseph doesn't show it
He merely takes his batting stance
And dares the bums to throw it.

—Tim Cohane, *New York World-Telegram,*
June 19, 1941

———————————●———————————

The day Joe DiMaggio first started thinking he might actually be able
to set the record was the first day a lot of other people started thinking about it, too, which made it the first day that the streak officially became *The Streak*. For DiMaggio, it took going 4-for-5 against the Detroit
Tigers on June 20 to finally pique his interest, capture his attention, because until that time, despite his daily visits to the basepaths, despite the
fact that he was hitting better and the Yankees were playing better, he really
hadn't felt like he was in a groove, still seemed as if he was fighting his way
through each at-bat. But on the afternoon of June 20 at Yankee Stadium,

against Bobo Newsom and, later, Archie McKain in relief, DiMaggio rapped out three singles and a double, and paired with the 3-for-3 he'd turned in the day before against the White Sox, that made him seven for his last eight. The average was up to .354—still almost seventy points behind Ted Williams for the league lead, but high enough that DiMaggio could finally believe his slump was a distant memory, and he could honestly say for the first time in a while that he felt he was in the middle of a hot streak (lowercase *s*).

He was also now in the thirty-third game of that *other* Streak, the one with the capital *S*, and now, finally, it was truly worthy of his concentration as he was now just eight games shy of George Sisler's modern mark of forty-one in a row. Later, and for the rest of his life, this was the moment DiMaggio would cite when The Streak became the first thing to occupy his mind when he woke up in the morning, the last thing in his consciousness when he went to bed in the evening, and was constantly in his thoughts during the six or seven hours he'd spend at the ballpark, a new obsession for him to smoke out with his Camels and drown with his coffee. DiMaggio wasn't unfamiliar with the art of building and maintaining a hitting streak. As a professional rookie with the San Francisco Seals in 1933, he'd hit in sixty-one straight games, a feat that had first landed his name in the nation's newspapers (although in both of his hometown outlets, the *San Francisco Chronicle* and the *San Francisco Examiner,* headlines that summer consistently butchered the name and spelled it *De* Maggio) and served as the official warning flare that a new folk hero was approaching the baseball horizon.

"I didn't make a big deal about it in '41," DiMaggio said in 1986, "until I felt like I was swinging the bat well enough to really do something about it. That was around the thirty-third game, when I got four hits and the baseball started looking as big as a beach ball to me then, and for the next couple of weeks. That's when people really started asking me about it, too. Until then, they seemed to have other things on their mind."

Until then, DiMaggio had been able to build his streak in relative secrecy. At the beginning, Whirlaway had stolen most of the attention away from the baseball teams, occupying most of the public's curiosity, so much so that one night at Toots Shor's saloon on Fifty-first Street, Eddie Arcaro had sidled up to DiMaggio, his pal, the regular occupant of Toots's esteemed Table Number One, and joked, "Joe, that damned horse is going to let me take that table away from you before long." As soon as Calumet Farms' great colt strutted away from the Belmont Stakes freshly fitted with the Triple Crown, Joe Louis and Billy Conn swaggered onto the sports pages and the nightly radio broadcasts, filling news cycle after news cycle and selling thousands of extra tickets. And even now, two days after the fight, you could hear the echoes of the hoarse, raspy voices that had filled the Polo Grounds because the fight was still the talk of the town, and the nation.

That very day, in fact, a great mystery that began on fight night was finally resolved. While most of the 54,487 fans and almost all of the sportswriters had walked away from the Polo Grounds believing that Conn was ahead on points when he'd foolishly tried to go for the knockout in the thirteenth round, no one could know for certain because the judge's ballots had, quite remarkably, vanished. Louis's knockout had rendered them meaningless, but the more people talked about the fight, replaying it in either their memories or their mind's eye, the more they wanted to know for sure if Conn really was as close to the title as they believed. There was no way to tell. Could someone really have been careless enough to throw the ballots away along with the used hot dog wrappers and empty beer cups and cigarette butts?

But just as DiMaggio was lining a first-inning single off Newsom at Yankee Stadium, the puzzle was solved. It turned out that Harry Balogh, the ring announcer, had gathered the slips amid the abrupt ruckus of the bout's aftermath and handed them to timekeeper George Bannon. This was standard. Bannon, as he'd done countless times before, was then supposed to hand the slips over either to Boxing Commissioner John J. Phelan or one of his deputies. This, too, was standard. There was only one problem: Bannon couldn't find anyone from the commission in the crowded craziness of the post-knockout ring. He took the slips home with him that night.

Bannon had no telephone back at his apartment, so he dropped the slips in the mailbox—but, incredibly, he failed to put sufficient postage on the envelope and it was returned to him. So this time he hand-delivered them to Phelan's office. Riddle over. Made public, the ballots confirmed what everyone had suspected: Eddie Joseph and Marty Monroe had the fight scored 7-5, Conn; Bill Healy had it even at 6-6. Conn hadn't cinched the fight, but if he'd simply won one of the final three rounds—and he was heading toward winning the thirteenth before losing his head—he definitely would have.

"I knew I'd goofed," Billy Conn said from Pittsburgh, where Greenfield Jimmy Smith had officially thrown a roadblock in the way of his plans to marry Mary Louise by using his considerable connections to warn every Catholic priest in the Commonwealth of Pennsylvania that the happy couple most certainly did not have a full parental blessing. "I didn't need anyone to tell me I goofed."

Watching from one of the twenty-five-dollar seats that night, Joe DiMaggio had received a very real reminder that once the fight was over, once the hype dissolved, he'd be resuming his role as the country's number-one sporting fascination. Summer was heating up, which meant baseball would assume its rightful place as a daily hot-weather companion. The Yankees were within three games of the Indians in the American League, and with the Dodgers also within three games of the Cardinals in the National League, there was a very real possibility of another interborough World Series visiting New York City in the autumn. The Yankees had played the Giants five times in the Fall Classic, but never the Dodgers, and that was enough to get baseball fans' juices flowing all over the boroughs.

So was a DiMaggio sighting anywhere outside Yankee Stadium. He showed up for the Louis-Conn bout impeccably dressed as always, the dreadful humidity not bothering him a bit, wrapped in his standard double-breasted blue suit, hand-painted necktie, French-cuff shirt, and spit-shined Italian shoes.

"He nearly started a riot," George Solotaire, a Broadway ticket broker and a close friend of DiMaggio's who accompanied him to the fight, would remember some twenty years later. "There were so many people asking for his autograph that he had almost as many cops around him as the fighters did."

The fame that DiMaggio brought with him to the front row that night was enormous, but not unparalleled. To that point in his career, DiMaggio had assembled a splendid set of lifetime statistics, he'd been a part of four World Series winners, he'd established himself as the best all-around player in the game, but those were ephemeral accomplishments. Eventually someone else would replace him as the game's best player, the same way DiMaggio had replaced Lou Gehrig. Theoretically, someone could put together better five-year numbers, could find just as much postseason success. Great as DiMaggio was, popular as he was, he'd yet to make a permanent imprint on the game the way Babe Ruth had with his 60 home runs in 1927, the way Cy Young had with his 511 lifetime pitching victories, the way Ty Cobb had with his 4,191 career base hits. Those were forever players.

DiMaggio, for all of his brilliance, wasn't. Not yet. He needed something to call his own. He needed The Streak.

"Joe tried to downplay The Streak almost from the moment people started talking about it," Tommy Henrich, DiMaggio's longtime teammate, would say some sixty years later. "But I think he knew that this was his chance to do something so amazing that other guys would be chasing him forever. Hell, he'd already had that huge streak in the minor leagues. He knew what it felt like to show up for work every day for two months and get a base hit. That's something no one else ever did."

Hitting streaks are organic, they are mystifying, they have their own personalities, their own rhythms . . . and their own fair share of fortunate hops and lucky bounces. There is never any pressure attached to maintaining one until someone slaps a number on it. Then, *like that,* it's out there. A hitter can have a blazing-hot month, can hit over .400 for thirty solid days, and he still might have five, six, eight games in there where he goes hitless. He's hot. But he isn't on a *streak*. The more it grows, the longer it goes, the more the attention flows, the greater the pressure mounts. New York sportswriter Dan Daniel may have first tabbed the hitting streak when it reached thirteen, but hardly anyone else paid attention to it then, which was interesting, because DiMaggio immediately encountered a difficult gauntlet that damn near killed the streak before it could ever grow into The Streak.

Game Fourteen, for instance: Both DiMaggio and Johnny Sturm, two of the streaking Yankees identified by Daniel in that very day's *World-Telegram,* had base hits in a five-run sixth inning that broke open a 2-2 game with Washington. There was only one problem: The skies opened before the Senators could bat in the bottom of the inning, washing the game out, reverting the score to the tie. Both DiMaggio and Sturm lost out on their sixth-inning hits, and that bit of misfortune cost Sturm his streak. But DiMaggio had already eked out a single off Steve Sundra in the fourth, hammering the ball off the plate and just beating the throw to first. By an eyeblink, the fledgling Streak survived and made its way as a small note into the pages of the next day's *New York Daily News* for the first time.

Games Fifteen and Sixteen, for instance: DiMaggio waited until the ninth inning of the front end of a doubleheader with the Red Sox before drilling a clean single off lefty Earl Johnson, then got a little help from the fates in the second game when he poked a lazy windblown fly right into a brutal sun in right field. Boston's Pete Fox circled around the ball but it never touched his glove; a newly installed feature of the Fenway Park scoreboard was a slot that relayed to the spectators whether a questionable play was a hit or an error, and when the HIT sign appeared, the crowd groaned.

The streak endured, and because it wasn't yet The Streak, there wasn't near the anxiety accompanying that first hit as there would be even two weeks later, and there was no controversy shrouding the official scorer for gifting DiMaggio that ultracheap double later on. In fact, nobody was much in the mood to talk about DiMaggio's offense at all, because the greatest center fielder of his generation suffered through the worst defensive day of his life, committing four errors in the twin bill—although the afternoon *Sun* was the latest to join the Streak watch, in between chiding DiMaggio for his follies with the mitt.

Games Seventeen and Eighteen, for instance: In a doubleheader with the Indians, DiMaggio got his first-game hit early, but in the second he waited until his final at-bat in the eighth—and reached base then only because Ken Keltner, manning third base for Cleveland, was playing him a little more shallow than normal and wasn't able to corral the hot shot that rocketed off DiMaggio's bat. The ball flicked off Keltner's glove, rolled harmlessly away, and Keltner made a mental note that from then on he was going to play DiMaggio as deep as the law allowed every time, a strategy that would prove useful in time. As DiMaggio and Keltner crossed paths at inning's end, DiMaggio laughed and told Keltner: "One more inch, Ken, and I start all over tomorrow." He knew he had a streak going, if not a Streak. So did the *New York Times* and the *Herald-Tribune*, which dutifully joined the cluster of chroniclers the next morning.

Game Twenty-five, for instance: This was the first time DiMaggio's palms might have gotten sweaty, because for the first time there was a target to reach—the Yankees record of twenty-nine games in a row, shared by Roger Peckinpaugh and Earle Combs—so for the first time, there was truly something at stake as he stepped to the plate in the seventh inning to face Johnny Rigney of the White Sox. And for the first time, evidence of how faithful an ally luck must be during a hitting streak came into play, for DiMaggio clobbered a Rigney fastball, but he hit it right at third baseman

Dario Lodigiani, who'd grown up with DiMaggio, who'd been a sandlot teammate years before in the North Beach section of San Francisco. Twice already DiMaggio had sent screaming shots Lodigiani's way, and twice they'd died in the soft, small pocket of Lodigiani's glove. This time, even the quick-handed Lodigiani couldn't scoop it up, but he'd blocked the ball nicely, like a lacrosse goalie, and he'd pounced on the ball and whipped it to first . . . where it either just beat or just missed getting DiMaggio. First-base umpire Stephen Basil extended his hands: *safe!* And the scorer made it official a few seconds later. No way could he charge an error on a smash like that. The streak lived another day, came a little bit closer to being a Streak.

Games Thirty and Thirty-one, for instance: On back-to-back days DiMaggio scratched out hits thanks mainly to the fact that the White Sox's Luke Appling, once the slickest-fielding shortstop in the American League, was now thirty-four years old, with reflexes that were still sharp but no longer spectacular. The first one, which officially set the Yankees team record, looked at first to be a routine seventh-inning ground ball, but just before it reached Appling, it hit a pebble, took a wicked hop, and bounced up off Appling's shoulder for a single. The next day, in the fifth inning, DiMaggio found Appling again, drilled a hard ground ball to Luke's left that, he later admitted, "I would have had in my back pocket when I was twenty-five," but this time he could only smother it. A few hours later DiMaggio was ringside at the Polo Grounds, signing autographs and shaking hands, a one-man undercard for the championship fight ahead, the owner of what was likely the single-most-photographed face in the United States.

A few days later, when he reached thirty-three against the Tigers, he would have something else, something better.

He had himself a Streak. Nothing would ever be the same again that summer.

Or for the rest of his life.

"We obviously knew what he was doing every day," Henrich would recall. "But it was almost as if all this other stuff had to go away first before anybody else started to take notice. But, boy, once they did, it was like nobody could talk about anything else."

Good thing, too. If people weren't able to lose themselves in the daily dramas revolving around DiMaggio's four or five daily trips to the plate, they may have been forced to ponder some other realities more closely. That wasn't an appealing alternative at any time during 1941, but during June the front pages started to bark ever louder, blaring news that was ever more unsettling.

June 9 was one of those days when the country could certainly have used the distraction, and it happened that June 9 was one of the slowest sporting days of summer: Joe DiMaggio had the day off, so did Ted Williams (whose own hitting streak had been snapped at twenty-two the day before, cooling his batting average to .416), and it was an unusually quiet training day at the boxing camps in Pompton Lakes and Greenwood Lake. So when the war in the Atlantic touched the United States, quite literally, for the first time, people had little choice but to follow every bulletin, absorb every report of Nazi aggression, and ponder what it would all mean.

Early in the day, Jefferson Caffery, the U.S. ambassador to Brazil, announced that an American freighter, the *Robin Moor,* had been sunk just north of the equator on May 21. A Brazilian merchant vessel had spotted a lonely lifeboat bobbing in the waters of the Atlantic Ocean, with eleven passengers aboard who had a shocking tale to tell. They'd been adrift for eighteen days, ever since their ship, containing twenty-eight crewmen and seven civilians, had been confronted by a German U-boat. The Nazi commander had stopped the *Moor* even though an American flag was clearly flying from her mast and told the thirty-five people on board—including one two-year-old boy and one couple in their late sixties—that they had exactly thirty minutes to lower themselves into the ship's four lifeboats before the *Moor* would be destroyed.

Melvin Mundy, the ship's chief officer, tried to reason with the German. "Your country has no issue with my country," he argued. "We are not at war with each other." But the commander was unbowed.

"You have supplies for my country's enemy," he said, "and I must sink you."

Half an hour later, right on schedule, the U-boat fired a torpedo at point-blank range right into the *Moor,* then left the four lifeboats to fend for themselves in the angry waters of the Atlantic, ignoring a promise to tow the rafts to safety. The eleven men rescued by the Brazilian boat feared that the others had been lost, since they hadn't had contact with the other three lifeboats in nearly a week. When this news reached the United States, it was met with outrage, even as President Roosevelt tried to head off a national panic by urging, "Let us not start screaming 'Remember the *Maine*' just yet," during one of his fireside chats.

Still, the prospect of all those Americans—including two-year-old Robin McCullough—drowning in the vast sea was almost too much for the nation to bear. This wasn't helped on June 13 when an authorized German spokesman issued the Nazi Party line, which was predictably unapologetic: "Germany won't be buffaloed by American or English discussions concerning the *Robin Moor*. Whenever any ship with contraband sails for England we'll shoot at it. There were railroad rails aboard the *Robin Moor*. The British have declared railroad rails to be unconditional contraband and in these matters we invariably adopt the British practice. What's contraband to them is contraband to us."

This shouldn't have come as a surprise, of course. Back on January 30, Adolf Hitler himself had boasted, "Whoever imagines he can aid England must, in all circumstances, know one thing: Every ship, whether with or without escort, that comes before our torpedo tubes *will* be torpedoed." He wasn't kidding.

And now, neither was Roosevelt. On June 16—despite receiving the splendid news that all of the *Robin Moor*'s victims were safe, accounted for, and heading for the safety of Cape Town, in South Africa—he had ordered those twenty-four German consulates on U.S. soil to be closed within thirty days' time, allowing only the main German embassy, the official Nazi news agency, and properly credentialed German newspapers to remain open. Not surprisingly, three days after that the Germans did likewise, shutting down thirty-one American consulates and ordering the deportations of eighty-six American citizens living in Berlin, and reaffirming, in case anyone had forgotten, just how quickly the dominoes of war can tumble, even between undeclared enemies.

"We are not yielding to this band of international outlaws and we do not propose to yield," Roosevelt told Congress on June 20. "The German Reich has disregarded the most elementary principles of international law and humanity, and is set on world conquest based upon lawlessness and terror on land and piracy on the seas."

The official German response was terse: "This is more or less what we are accustomed to with Roosevelt."

The unofficial response came filtered through two sources. First, there was Benito Mussolini, the Italian dictator whose practical usefulness to Hitler had diminished greatly but who still bore the gift of voluble oratory. "American intervention will not give victory to Great Britain but will prolong the war. American intervention will not limit the war in space, but will extend it to other oceans. American intervention will transmute the United States regime into an authoritarian and totalitarian regime which will very much surpass and perfect its European precursors—Fascist and Nazi. When one wants to remember a dictator in a pure classic expression of the term, one cites Sulla [who ruled Rome in the first century B.C.]. Well, Sulla seems to us a modest amateur compared to Delano Roosevelt."

Then there was Charles Lindbergh, speaking that evening at the Hollywood Bowl: "I tell you that the only way our American life can be preserved is by staying out of this war. I tell you the only way European civilization can be saved is by ending this war quickly."

And that day in Yankee Stadium, Joe DiMaggio—unburdened at last from the haunting slump that had strangled his spring, able now to focus on other matters at hand—first started thinking about his Streak after collecting those four base hits against the Tigers, and many of his fellow countrymen figured:

That's not a bad thing to be thinking about.

———————●———————

It sure as hell beat the alternative, which came crashing out of the nation's radio speakers on June 22, breaking news that would, as much as anything—at least anything prior to December 7—seal the inevitability of the European conflict turning into a global catastrophe. Tommy Henrich remembers hearing the buzz burning on the streets outside Yankee Stadium as he reported to work that morning. As Henrich stepped into the home-team clubhouse, located then on the third-base side of the stadium, players were huddled in small groups, trying to fit pieces of information into a terrible jigsaw puzzle of uncertainty.

It was a Sunday, so there would be no afternoon papers to clarify what was coming out of the radio, but the skeleton of the story was this: At 3:22 in the morning, sunrise in the Baltic region, German troops had stormed across the Russian border. Hitler and Joseph Stalin—who, only two years before, had been sinister coconspirators, partitioning Poland in a terrifying prelude to their plotting a joint carving of the Continent as a whole—were now at war. German artillery, backed by massive aerial support, had begun the assault in the middle of the night, and by dawn there was a staggering total of 146 Panzer, infantry, and motorized divisions rushing into the Soviet Union.

Much of the early information was sketchy and unreliable, second- and third-hand accounts relayed through heavily censored dispatches. By the time the Yankees had to report onto the field, this much was known: There were three large battle zones, in the north, middle, and southern regions of Russia. News out of the north was vague, although there were reports of massive Russian casualties. In the middle, the news was even worse, with the Germans driving on what seemed to be a direct course toward Moscow. And although the Russians were reported to be holding their own in the southern region, initial dispatches said the ground was already carpeted with corpses from both nations.

Hitler, in an explicatory message delivered through his propaganda minister, Joseph Goebbels, charged that Russia, along with Britain and the United States, had tried to "throttle" Germany, leaving the Nazis little choice. And in formally declaring war, German foreign minister Joachim von Ribbentrop insisted, "Contrary to all engagements which they had undertaken and in absolute contradiction to their solemn declarations, the Soviet Union had turned against Germany. They have first not only continued, but even since the outbreak of war intensified their subversive activities against Germany in Europe. They have second, in continually increasing measure, developed their foreign policy in a tendency hostile to Germany, and they have, third, amassed their entire forces on the German frontier ready for action."

The first voice to be heard from the middle of the war zone came from Russian foreign commissar Vyacheslav Molotov, who relayed Stalin's vow to "repulse this predatory assault" and called the German justification for the war a "sheer lie and provocation that has been belatedly concocted."

"This unheard-of attack upon our country is perfidy unparalleled in the history of civilized nations. The attack on our country was perpetrated despite the fact that a treaty of non-aggression has been signed between the U.S.S.R. and Germany and that the Soviet Government most faithfully abided by all provisions of this treaty. The entire responsibility for this predatory attack upon the Soviet Union falls fully and completely upon the German Fascist rulers."

Washington's immediate response was muffled; for the record, the president wanted to take a wait-and-see approach before committing to an official position. Privately, however, Roosevelt understood that he was about to make one of the most distasteful choices conceivable. On the one side of this conflict were the atheistic Communists, a menace against whom Roosevelt had railed his entire presidency. Though it was not yet known just how many millions of his own citizens Stalin had exterminated during his blinding rush to complete power over the past fifteen years, he was no fan of freedom, and in fact believed that he would live to see the Soviet sickle dominate each of the earth's quadrants.

And these were the *good guys*.

For no matter how great the standard against which you judged these shades and shadows of evil to be, Germany under Hitler knew no equal. In just under three years, Hitler's expanded empire now included sixteen formerly sovereign nations, more than 150 million conquered citizens, and more than 720,000 square miles of territory. If he was successful in adding Russia to those totals . . . well, the ramifications of *that* were too terrifying to ponder.

In England, Winston Churchill wasted little time declaring his empire's intentions: "Any man or State who fights against Nazism will have our aid. Any man who fights with Hitler is our foe." He called Hitler "a bloodthirsty guttersnipe." Then he added a none-too-subtle prod into the ribs of "our good friends in the United States":

"We have but one aim and one single, irrevocable purpose. We are resolved to destroy Hitler and every vestige of his Nazi regime. From this nothing will turn us. Nothing. We shall fight him by land; we shall fight him by sea; we shall fight him in the air until, with God's help, we have rid the earth of his shadow and liberated its people from his yoke."

Yet the American ambivalence was best described by John T. Flynn, who happened to be the head of the New York chapter of the America First Committee but on this issue seemed to speak for people of all political stripes, saying, "If Germany wins, Russia will go Fascist. If Russia wins, Germany will go Communist. There is no choice for us at all. The question now is: Are we going to fight to make Europe safe for Communism?"

With all of this swirling in the air like dust on the plains, with every hour bringing the most dire kind of news from the other side of the planet, Americans really had only two choices on the first full day of summer. They could sit in their stultifying living rooms and listen to the radio reports as they came faster and louder and more ominously. Or they could do something else. Like catch a ballgame. In Cincinnati, for instance, the largest crowd to ever see a baseball game in that city, 35,792, stuffed Crosley Field to watch the defending champion Reds get swept in a doubleheader by the Brooklyn Dodgers. And in New York City, some 27,072 came to Yankee Stadium to watch the team the Reds had beaten in the World Series the previous October, the Detroit Tigers, take on the home-town Yankees under a broiling 94-degree sun, the hottest June 22 in history to that point.

And they came to see Joe DiMaggio.

DiMaggio's Streak was not yet the national obsession it would soon be, but every at-bat was nevertheless a case study in just how popular he had become, certainly in Yankee Stadium. Even in the middle of rallies, the crowd would quiet to a hush, almost hoping with their silence to focus his concentration. On days when he took care of business early, the release was sudden and satisfying and the customers could go back to enjoying the ballgame. On days when it took a little longer, though, the pressure would build and mount and multiply with each successive grounder or pop fly or base on balls. On this day, it took a little longer. When DiMaggio strode to the plate in the bottom of the sixth, he was still hitless, and the overheated crowd was anxious and bustling nervously. But then Hal Newhouser tried to beat DiMaggio with a fastball away, a regrettable choice, and DiMaggio—who'd learned early on to spray the ball to all fields, knowing that all but his most titanic clouts would be contained by Yankee Stadium's murderous dimensions in the left-field power alley—drove the ball 370 feet over the right-field fence. The crowd didn't know whether to roar or sigh, and so it did both. Freed from his own tensions, DiMaggio later added a ninth-inning double that helped the Yankees turn a 4-3 deficit into a 5-4 win.

Thirty-five straight. Now DiMaggio could officially zero in on history. Six more and he would tie George Sisler's modern-day record of forty-one in a row, set in 1922. Nine more and he'd catch Wee Willie Keeler, the nineteenth-century star who'd played under more favorable offensive rules (foul balls weren't considered strikes until 1901, for instance) and coined a hitter's mantra that would define him forever: "I just try to hit 'em where they ain't." In 1897, playing for the old Baltimore Orioles of the National League, he'd piled up a forty-four-game hitting streak, something few remembered until DiMaggio inspired some amateur baseball historians to blow the dust off their annual reviews.

Joe Louis had sent Billy Conn back home to Pittsburgh, into the waiting arms of his beautiful young fiancée and the scornful glare of her father. Whirlaway had galloped off into history, a million hearts stuffed into his saddle. At a time when Americans needed more distractions, not less, when they actually heard themselves applauding en masse when Joseph Stalin asked for—and received—close to $2 billion in aid from U.S. coffers, they did precisely what a future generation would long to do, in the musical opinion of Paul Simon (born October 13, 1941).

They turned their lonely eyes to Joe DiMaggio.

And every day, without fail, they liked what they saw.

His teammates did, too. That was the other transformation in Joe DiMaggio in June 1941. He'd always been a well-liked member of the Yankees, from the moment he showed up in spring training of 1936, instantly popular with New York's melting-pot fans because of the various vowels scattered throughout his surname, quickly accepted by his teammates because of his breathtaking skill. Few men had ever broken into the big leagues quite the way DiMaggio had, his first five seasons standing in a rarefied place among all the thousands of men who had played major league baseball:

Year	Avg	R	2B	3B	HR	RBI
1936	.352	132	44	15	29	125
1937	.346	151	35	15	46	167
1938	.324	129	32	13	32	140
1939	.381	108	32	6	30	126
1940	.352	93	28	9	31	133

"From the moment DiMaggio joined our team," Joe McCarthy once said, "it seemed like he'd been a Yankee forever."

Still, as great as he'd been, as superb a career as he'd built for himself, the Yankees still weren't DiMaggio's team as 1941 dawned. That, sadly, could never happen as long as the captain emeritus, Lou Gehrig, was still alive. The Yankees had managed to shake off Gehrig's stunning retirement in 1939, going on to win 106 games and the World Series, but in 1940 his absence (and the rapid aging of other key team members) hobbled them badly. DiMaggio wasn't able to carry the Yankees by himself, leading some to wonder if he could indeed follow the pathway established by Gehrig, and before him Babe Ruth. Gehrig did his part to try to change that perception. In February 1941, just before spring training, he'd invited John Kieran, the sports columnist for the *New York Times,* to his home on Delafield Avenue in the Bronx for a chat. During their conversation, Gehrig implored Yankees fans to recognize that DiMaggio "may be the best you'll ever see here. He's that good. He's that strong." It wasn't in DiMaggio's nature to vocally change the culture around the Yankees, though. He would wait his turn.

On June 2, in Detroit, it arrived in an agonizing rush.

The Yankees filed into the Book-Cadillac Hotel in a cheerful mood, having taken two out of three from the front-running Indians in Cleveland. Phil Rizzuto and Joe Gordon had led the team in boisterous sing-along on the train ride from Ohio to Michigan, with Rizzuto, the popular rookie, absorbing a relentless ribbing over a flashy suit he'd purchased in nearby Canton. Just past eleven o'clock, as taxis started dumping the Yankees off in groups of two and three in front of the Book-Cadillac, the hotel manager, William Chittenden, approached McCarthy with a long, somber face.

"I've got bad news for you, Mr. McCarthy," Chittenden said.

"Bad news?" the manager asked.

"Yes. We've just heard it over the radio. Lou Gehrig is dead."

George Selkirk was standing nearby, as were Johnny Murphy and Lefty Gomez. They were too stunned to cry, too bewildered to even move. McCarthy, the cigar in his hands quavering between his fingers, found a chair in the corner of the lobby. He shook his head.

"Is there any way the news isn't true?" he asked.

"I'm afraid not, sir. It's all over the news."

Selkirk started tearing the slip showing his room number to pieces. Gomez looked off into space. A few minutes later, catcher Bill Dickey, Gehrig's former roommate and one of his closest friends, came bounding into the library after visiting a neighboring drugstore for his nightly malted milkshake, a ritual he used to share all the time with Gehrig. He saw the somber looks on his teammates' faces and didn't even have to ask what was wrong. An eerie sense of déjà vu filled him at once; it was in this very hotel exactly twenty-five months earlier that Gehrig had made the decision to take himself out of the lineup after playing 2,130 consecutive games. This was before Gehrig was told there was something gravely wrong with him; all he knew was that his skills as a baseball player had all but vanished. That night, in their room, Dickey had assured him, "All you need is a little rest. You've got the time coming to you, after all. You deserve a little time off."

Was that really only two years ago?

"My God, I only spoke to Lou over the telephone a few days before we left for New York," Dickey said. "He told me he felt fine. Henrich told me he had spoken to Lou, too, and had been told the same thing." His voice started to crack. "I've lost my best friend. It's like losing one of your own family. It's like losing a brother."

McCarthy, near tears, pointed to a spot in the lobby.

"It was here that Lou came to me and said, 'Joe, I always said I'd quit when I felt I was no longer any help to the team. I'm no longer any help. When do you want me to quit?' And I said, 'Today.' I was afraid he'd get hurt. His reflexes were gone. He couldn't get out of the way of the ball. I was fond of Lou. He was not only a great ballplayer, he was a fine man."

McCarthy and Dickey would hustle back to New York for Gehrig's wake and funeral. The rest of the Yankees, led by DiMaggio, would carry on at Briggs Stadium, where they lost two straight, but there was a tangible sense, right away, that something had changed with the team, and with the centerfielder. DiMaggio had been as devastated as everyone else by the news—"He was a wonderful ballplayer and a great individual and he was a good influence on us young ballplayers, to whom he was always an inspiration" was his simple eulogy—and now he quietly moved to fill the emotional void left by the departed captain. It wasn't a job he sought out, or necessarily wanted. But it was his nonetheless.

"From that moment on," Lefty Gomez said years later, "there was no question who the leader of that team was. No question at all. He might not have been the captain, but that was all right. A fellow like that, he deserved a higher rank than captain anyway."

There would be no speeches, no team meetings, no overt displays of leadership. That wasn't the Yankee way. That wasn't DiMaggio's way. This was: Starting on June 7, the Yankees rattled off eight wins in a row. DiMaggio had thirteen hits in those eight games. They were hot. He was hot. That, DiMaggio figured, was the only leadership anyone cared about.

———————————●———————————

Man, he hated Elden Auker.

It was nothing personal, you understand. But Joe DiMaggio had that wide stance, patently wide, forty inches separating left instep and right instep (he measured it), and while he would insist his entire career that this is what allowed him the proper balance to offer a mighty cut every time he cocked the bat, it didn't provide a terribly useful escape hatch if a baseball heading toward home plate wanted to take a circuitous path toward his rib cage or the back of his head. Auker was far from a headhunter, and was one of the best-liked people in baseball in the 1930s and '40s, but he had a slingshot delivery that, to a right-handed batter, seemed as if his release point came from the grandstand behind third base. DiMaggio could handle Bob Feller's flame-broiled fastball. He feasted on curveballs and change-ups, sinkers and sliders, forkballs and knuckleballs. Even the odd spitball that would flutter and dance his way never much bothered him. But, Jesus, did he hate those sidewinders. Especially good ones, like Elden Auker.

Years later, in the summer of 1961, having flown all night from Sweden to make it to Yankee Stadium in time for the annual Old-Timers Day ceremonies, DiMaggio made his one traditional appearance at the plate, pinch-hitting in the third inning as cheers rained down all sectors of the ballpark. Mickey Cochrane, managing a team of Tigers all-stars, waited for DiMaggio to step into the batter's box and then walked to the mound to make a pitching change. He summoned Auker. When DiMaggio saw this, he immediately set down his bat and started walking back to the dugout. When Auker saw *that, he* immediately walked back to the bullpen. They did that for a while, laughing, their old teammates cracking up at this dance even if nobody in the stands could understand quite what was happening. Finally, DiMaggio picked up the bat and a handful of dirt, and yelled out to the pitcher's mound.

"How are you going to pitch me?" he asked.

"I'm going to pitch low and behind you," Auker said. "Be loose."

DiMaggio laughed. And then ducked. Auker threw it behind him, as promised.

"If I knew I was going to have to hit off you," DiMaggio yelled before getting back in the box, "I would have stayed in Stockholm."

Had he thought of it, DiMaggio might have employed a similar strategy on the afternoon of June 26, 1941. Auker, near the end of a ten-year career in which he would win 130 games, was on the mound that day for the woeful St. Louis Browns. The Yankees, in the midst of a streak where they would win eighteen out of nineteen, were in a flat-footed tie with the Indians for first place, sixteen and a half games ahead of the Browns, who would put up little resistance this day, losing 4-1, scratching out only one hit against Yankees starter Marius Russo. Russo, a twenty-six-year-old left-hander in the middle of the best year he would ever have as a big-leaguer, was masterful, and took a no-hitter into the seventh inning. And here's the funny thing:

Nobody noticed.

Nobody cared.

There was officially a Code Red alert on The Streak. It was different now that The Streak had capital letters, now that the waters had parted and all eyes were fastened on DiMaggio's back. All of those calls in May and early June barely caused a ripple of discomfort because nobody could know what he was building toward. Now they knew. Now, George Sisler was in view, and Wee Willie Keeler was looming just beyond, and gradually a daily interrogation was integrating itself into the national conversation:

"Hey, did DiMaggio get a hit today?"

"Sure did."

"How many?"

By now, the unique quality of this particular chase had become clear. A few years earlier, Hank Greenberg had gone right to the end of the 1938 season pursuing Babe Ruth's fabled single-season mark of sixty home runs, and there was an enormous amount of pressure involved in that hunt. But the fact is, Greenberg could go a day or two—or even a week—without hitting a blast, and he would still have a chance, same with anyone who would ever pursue the Babe's record of 714 lifetime homers. You fail today, you still have tomorrow. But DiMaggio's streak was different. Five seconds after a ball would fall safely somewhere in fair territory, five seconds after he'd touch first base to make it official, and add another number to The Streak, it would start again. *What about tomorrow?*

DiMaggio tried to brush aside the importance of The Streak, and its effect on his nerves. "Why should I worry?" he'd asked a reporter who approached him two days earlier. "The only time to worry is when you're not hitting. I'm not worried now—I'm happy. It's no strain to keep on hitting. It's a strain *not* to be hitting. That's when your nerves get jumpy."

The reporter had approached DiMaggio cautiously, admitting that he hadn't wanted to jinx him by having him talk about The Streak, but DiMaggio waved off such talk. "Hell, talking's not going to stop it. No, I'm not superstitious. Hoodoos aren't going to stop me—a pitcher will, and hoodoos aren't going to help me. A little luck, of course, but mainly it's up to me to keep swinging."

Now, in the eighth inning against the lowly Browns, with a modest midweek crowd creeping to the edges of its seats, DiMaggio stepped up to home plate to face the one man in the entire American League against whom he liked hitting the least. All the Yankees players stood on the front step of the dugout. It was eerily quiet, too quiet for a ballpark. Everyone knew what was at stake here, and the only one who seemed unfazed was the unflappable Elden Auker, who years later would admit, "I didn't give a damn about that streak, to tell you the truth. I cared about doing my job and doing it well. I sure as hell wasn't going to lay one in there for him. But I wasn't going to pitch around him, either."

The tension was unbearable, and it had been building all afternoon. In his first at-bat, staring at a 3-and-0 count, DiMaggio got the green light to swing from his manager, Joe McCarthy, but flied out lazily to left. His next time up, in the fourth, he bounced a ball right at shortstop Johnny Berardino, who bobbled it and couldn't make a play. It was an obvious error, and the official scorer that day, Dan Daniel of the *New York World-Telegram*, knew it. In 1941 it wasn't yet standard on stadium scoreboards to inform fans whether a play had been ruled a hit or an error; most were content to get that information in the next day's box scores, if they bothered to check at all. And it was strict protocol that the members of a team never, ever checked with the official scorer in those matters, as it was considered a strong negative taboo to be too concerned with hits and errors and other minutiae when there was a game to be played.

And yet the moment the ball bounced away from Berardino, all eyes in the Yankee dugout instantly locked on Daniel, sitting behind his typewriter up in the open-air press box. Daniel didn't hesitate; he called it an error, which was exactly the right call. But that didn't stop the Yankees from shaking their fists at Daniel and offering some rather ungentlemanly suggestions. It wasn't the last time Daniel would sit on a griddle as the thermostat was ratcheted high, and it helps illustrate why, by the end of the century, newspapers would forbid their employees from serving as official scorers and potentially planting themselves in the middle of such dramas.

In the sixth inning, DiMaggio tapped out to third base, and now The Streak officially reached its first Crisis Point, because there was no guarantee DiMaggio was even going to get a fourth at-bat. "That was the trouble at the Stadium," DiMaggio would tell Pulitzer Prize–winning sports columnist Dave Anderson many years later. "On the road I always knew I always had nine innings, so I was almost sure to get up at least four times. But at home, if we were winning, I only had eight innings."

The Yankees were cruising, ahead 3-1, and they went out in order in the home half of the seventh, so in the eighth DiMaggio would be the fourth scheduled hitter. He needed someone to get on just so he could have one last crack at his side-arming nemesis. Johnny Sturm, the first baseman, opened the inning with a weak pop-out. The crowd, 8,692 of them, none of whom could be remotely stirred to action when it seemed Russo had a chance at the no-hitter, began murmuring nervously, but then let out a full-throated roar when Red Rolfe worked Auker for a walk. So now there was a chance, at least.

Tommy Henrich walked to the plate.

Two days earlier, DiMaggio had been robbed of a hit when Browns outfielder Roy Cullenbine snared a blast right in front of the white 457-foot sign in left-center field, the part of Yankee Stadium known as "Death Valley," where so many DiMaggio drives died over the course of thirteen seasons. Henrich got himself doubled off first base on the play, and years later he *still* got chills thinking of his gaffe: "You couldn't waste an out because you wanted to make sure Joe would get as many at-bats as possible," he explained. Henrich was spared a lifetime of collateral guilt when DiMaggio collected his hit a few innings later. Now, the man his teammates would in later years dub "Ol' Reliable" had a chance to do his part for the cause.

"I've never been scared on a baseball field," Henrich said in 2002. "I've played in World Series games, huge pennant-race games, never once felt butterflies or anything. But that day, when I dug in the batter's box, I was scared out of my mind, because all I'm thinking is this: If I hit into a double play, if I end the inning and Joe's streak dies, then I'm never going to make it out of this stadium alive."

Henrich had an idea, though, and he approached Joe McCarthy. "Is it okay if I bunt?" he asked. Old-school baseball etiquette said you *never* bunted with a two-run lead that late in a game, not unless you wanted one of your players to wind up with a baseball planted in his ear. But these were extraordinary times, and McCarthy figured the Browns wouldn't mind. He told Henrich he could sacrifice. "And I never laid down a more perfect bunt in my life," Henrich said, "and then I got the hell out of the way."

It's a testament to how other teams in baseball felt about DiMaggio that it never occurred to Auker, or to Browns manager Luke Sewell, to walk DiMaggio in that spot, even though there was a base open, even though the Browns were still very much in the game, and even though technically the Yankees had committed a glaring breach of protocol.

"No way," Auker said. "I was going after him."

One thing was sure: DiMaggio wasn't going to wait for a walk. A consummate team player, it bothered DiMaggio to a degree that his streak was getting so much attention, and he was sensitive to leaving himself open for critics who might wonder if The Streak was taking away from the greater goals of the team. Of course, there was little room to wonder that, as the Yankees were already a sparkling 25-10 during The Streak and were playing their best ball of the year just now. So DiMaggio was going up hacking.

Auker's first pitch was right around the plate, and in that half-second in which such decisions are made, DiMaggio figured it might be as good a pitch as he was going to see. He swung. He connected. And before he could even pick the ball up with his eyes, the crowd's reaction sent him a message through his ears: He was in. The ball had rocketed past third baseman Harlond Clift and was now rolling into the left-field corner. Rolfe came galloping home with the fourth run for the Yankees, maybe the most inconsequential scoring play of the season because no one was looking at him as he crossed the plate. The Yankees were exploding from their dugout, all of them yelling and laughing and pointing at DiMaggio, and a lot of veteran Yankee watchers swore they saw more joy emanate from the usually staid men in pinstripes that day than fourteen years earlier, when Babe Ruth had hit his sixtieth home run, or for any of the seven times the Yankees had won the World Series.

"I thought the old Streak," DiMaggio said later, "was gone for sure."

But it was intact, and alive, and for another day his adoring public could wrap itself up in news of The Streak, and it couldn't have come at a better time. A few hours after DiMaggio's double off Auker extended it to thirty-eight, Interior Secretary Harold Ickes stepped in front of a podium in Hartford, Connecticut, in front of a bank of microphones that carried his words live over the National Broadcasting Company. Then, for a feisty rally for the Committee to Defend America, he branded Charles A. Lindbergh, the erstwhile Lone Eagle, formerly known as Lucky Lindy, "a Hitler stooge."

In making a shockingly frank case for joining the war—the first such overt message delivered by anyone that close to Roosevelt—Ickes said, "Such a golden opportunity cannot be expected to come again. The American people must make their supreme choice not tomorrow but now. We have been living too long on borrowed time."

Sports couldn't always guarantee protection, couldn't always provide a cocoon. People understood that. The athletes themselves were far from bulletproof, far from invincible, far from infallible. Janusz Kusocinski had proven that point. So, for a few days, had Max Schmeling. Hank Greenberg's fame hadn't kept him from trading in steak dinners for the mess hall at Fort Custer, and Jimmy Stewart's Academy Award did him no use when the reveille bugle blared at 5:15 A.M. Soon enough, the long arm of the real world would tap everyone on the shoulder, and it didn't matter who you were, what you did, or how much money you earned. People all over the country were resigned to that now.

Still, if that reality bothered Joe DiMaggio, he didn't let on. George Sisler was in his sights now. Wee Willie Keeler was on deck. There would be time to ponder the world at large. Later.

8

"I'D LIKE TO HOIST THAT MARK WHERE NOBODY COULD REACH IT."

An unassuming hero, an unbreakable record, and an unforgettable night in Cleveland

Joe DiMaggio's Yankees teammates celebrate the home run that extended his hitting streak to 45 games on July 2, moving him past Wee Willie Keeler's record of 44 games.

He tied the mark at forty-four
July the first you know
Since then he's hit a good twelve more,
Joltin' Joe DiMaggio.

Joe . . . Joe . . . DiMaggio . . .
We want you on our side . . .

He'll live in baseball's Hall of Fame
He'll get there blow-by-blow.
Our kids will tell their kids his name,
Joltin' Joe DiMaggio.

Joe . . . Joe . . . DiMaggio . . .
We want you on our side.

—Alan Courtney, Summer 1941

T here wasn't a thing about him that didn't fascinate the nation now, and there was little that DiMaggio, an intensely private man, could do to stop it. One day he arrived home from the ballpark to discover a news reporter and a photographer from the *New York Post* awaiting him in the living room of the $300-per-month Midtown penthouse he shared with his wife, Dorothy, now midway through her pregnancy. Decades later, athletes of DiMaggio's stature would while away their free time behind gated communities and armies of bodyguards, but in 1941 access to DiMaggio was unlimited if you knew how and where to find him, and so he begrudgingly went along with the circus, posing for pictures in his bathrobe, on his patio, with his wife (who dutifully lit his cigarette for him). Mrs. DiMaggio, who delighted in the spotlight's glaring, prying eye every bit as much as her husband detested it, was asked how The Streak was affecting their home life.

"Joe is calm as can be," she reported. "But it has me all on edge and tense. I can't say that I've been a baseball fan all my life, but I certainly am one now."

The Streak wasn't only good business for DiMaggio, who was now receiving so many business proposals and so much fan mail he had to ask the Yankee public relations people to sift through the plentiful post each day. It was also a beautifully beneficial boon to the Yankees, who were rapidly gaining ground on the faltering first-place Indians, would catch them on June 28, pass them the next day, and never be bothered again as they sprinted off toward an unprecedented twelfth American League pennant.

It was equally fortuitous for the other seven clubs in the league, which normally would resign themselves to having thousands upon thousands of empty seats as their teams tumbled out of the race one by one, but now they used the prospect of DiMaggio's daily march on history as a marvelous marketing tool. A.L. president Will Harridge, in fact, salivating at what DiMaggio's commercial appeal could mean to his league's bottom line, even decided to remind the ticket-buying public what would happen if a team opted to walk DiMaggio every time he batted during the course of a game.

"My personal opinion would be that if he was not charged with an official at-bat in a game and was credited with a hit in his next game, his consecutive-game hitting streak should be continued," said Harridge, whose judgment was backed up by the *Official Rule Book*, specifically Rule 10.24 (d), which stated plainly that "a consecutive hitting streak shall not be terminated if a plate appearance results in a base on balls, hit batsman, defensive interference or sacrifice bunt."

Fortunately for baseball, the rule rarely needed actual application, although a Philadelphia Athletics pitcher named Johnny Babich vowed that he wouldn't be afraid to use the base on balls as a weapon if he had the opportunity to attain lasting fame (or infamy) as the man who muffled The Streak. Babich was a feisty San Franciscan with a long memory, and he had a couple of scores to settle. Eight years earlier, with DiMaggio twenty-eight games deep into his sixty-one-game Pacific Coast League hitting streak, the two men had run into each other one hot afternoon at Seals Stadium. Babich, pitching for the Mission Reds, the Seals' crosstown rival, completely shut down the hard-hitting Seals and held them scoreless as the 0-0 game entered the bottom of the eighth inning. But with a man on second, Babich tried to sneak a fastball past DiMaggio, who crushed it for a triple. The Seals won 1-0, DiMaggio (or De Maggio, as per the local dailies) had his streak pushed to twenty-nine, and Babich had a devastating loss he would never truly forget.

That distant memory was only part of the equation, though. In 1939, Babich won seventeen games for the Kansas City Blues, the Yankees' top farm team, and expected to get called up to the big club in time for 1940. But the Yankees left him unprotected in that winter's Rule Five draft, the Philadelphia A's picked him up, and Babich proceeded to win five games against the Yankees in 1940 (for a team that won only fifty-four games all year), single-handedly seeing to the business of knocking the Yankees out of the pennant race.

With his reputation as the greatest "Yankee killer" of his generation sewed up, Babich now went to work flummoxing the Yankee Clipper. Babich told his teammates of his plan: The first time up, he'd challenge DiMaggio, come right after him, dare him to hit his fastball, give him every opportunity to beat him. If he did, he'd tip his cap. If he didn't, then those would be the last hittable pitches DiMaggio would see from Johnny Babich. He'd throw nothing but junk the rest of the way, nothing but soft stuff off the plate. On June 28 he put his plan into practice, much to the waiting chagrin of the 13,604 who'd actually made the pilgrimage to Shibe Park (maybe the greatest testament to DiMaggio's drawing power, since that was the gravest graveyard in all of baseball; between them, the A's and the National League's last-place Phillies averaged barely two thousand fans a game that year). With two on and one out in the first inning, DiMaggio worked the count to 3-and-1, and Babich fed him a fastball with plenty of the plate, and Joe took a mighty whack and popped the ball straight in the air. When it landed in the glove of shortstop Al Brancato, Babich had executed the hardest part of his plan.

The problem was, Babich hadn't been shy in sharing his strategy with the Philly writers. They'd flooded the morning papers with warning, telling fans they might want to get to Shibe early unless they wanted to see DiMaggio trot down to first all day. DiMaggio knew he would have to take The Streak into his own hands, more than he had at any time before. He knew Joe McCarthy would give him a green light on any 3-and-0 count he might face—a rare license for the times—but he didn't want to wait that long, and he surely didn't want to linger until the seventh or eighth inning before making his move. So leading off the third, DiMaggio vowed he would swing at anything his bat could touch. The first pitch he saw was so high and so wide he would have needed an oar to catch up. But the second was a little better—still high and away, but reachable—and DiMaggio sent a pellet right back through the box, right through Johnny Babich's legs, the ball missing his most precious assets by a couple of millimeters, tops, and turning him as white as his uniform jersey. DiMaggio—who didn't appreciate Babich's tactics and would go the rest of his life without mentioning his name to interviewers, even as he delighted in retelling this story—added to the fun by roaring around first base and stretching his Streak-extender to a double.

He sat on forty now, one game shy of the modern record, and there wasn't a soul alive who wasn't aching for DiMaggio to break the record, and to see how far he could push it forward. That included George Sisler, the former St. Louis Brown who'd spent eighteen years with the mark, who'd reached forty-one during his greatest season, 1922, when he'd hit .420 and led the perennially lowly Browns to within a game of the A.L. flag, the closest they'd ever come.

"Sure, I'm proud of it," Sisler said when he was contacted in St. Louis, where he owned a popular sporting goods store. "I went through an awful lot to make it. You'd be surprised at the strain a batter is under. The newspapers keep mentioning the streak. Your teammates continually bring it up in conversation. I tried to forget but it can't be done. It's in your head every time you step to the plate. I know I hit a lot of bad balls, though. I had to. Every pitcher out there was trying to stop me. Some of them would rather have walked me than let me hit. They wouldn't give me a good ball to swing at."

Sisler, though, was gracious enough to acknowledge, "If the record has to go, I hope it goes to a player like DiMaggio. I liked DiMaggio the first time I saw him. He's a natural in everything he does. I'd hate to see my record beaten by some ordinary player who just hits a lucky streak. But if DiMaggio breaks it, fine! I don't know of any player I like more to see do it."

Even the great Ty Cobb, notorious for never giving the modern ballplayer his due, could find little fault with DiMaggio, though he did say, "Some of Joe's friends would like to see him condition himself better through the winter. They insist he takes it too easy. His off-season letdown is too pronounced." Still, Cobb said, "DiMaggio would have been tops in any era of baseball. I like to see records broken. The idea of a fellow having a chance to break a record increases interest in baseball. Of course, like Sisler, I like to see a genuine star break the records and not some fly-by-night sensation."

It wasn't only the famous who were drawn to him, though. The day DiMaggio put Babich in his place—as the Yankees prepared to catch a train for Washington, where the next day some thirty-one thousand people would cram rickety old Griffith Stadium for a doubleheader where DiMaggio could both catch and pass Sisler—a telegram arrived in the visiting clubhouse at Shibe Park and landed on the stool in front of DiMaggio's locker:

PLEASE SEE TONY MORELLA, JEFFERSON HOSPITAL.
SPLEEN REMOVED. LIFE OR DEATH. HE COUNTS ON YOU.
PLEASE SEE HIM BEFORE YOU GO.

(SIGNED) DR. H.E. JONES

DiMaggio grabbed his roommate, Lefty Gomez, and together they decided to take a later train after making a stop at the hospital. There, DiMaggio saw the weak ten-year-old boy from Carbondale, Pennsylvania (whose name was actually Tony Norella), and gave him the thrill of a lifetime by assuring him, "You be listening on your radio tomorrow, Tony, and hear me break that hitting record for you. That's a promise, kid." Alas, there were some miracles even the Great DiMaggio couldn't perform. Though DiMaggio was assured when he arrived at Washington's Shoreham Hotel that young Tony's condition had improved after he left him, that turned out to be bad information. Tony would die early the next morning, before DiMaggio ever took the field against the Senators.

By then, DiMaggio wasn't feeling all that well himself, in truth. Though he tried to downplay the importance of such an individual record, though his allies in the press tried to portray him as icy cool and unfazed by the hoopla consuming him on all sides, Gomez knew differently. He saw how little DiMaggio was sleeping now, a product not only of hotel rooms lacking both air-conditioning and sufficient protection from the meddling eyes of strangers, but of his own desires to catch Sisler, to catch Keeler, to catch his own sixty-one game standard. He saw all those ashtrays and all those dead Camels and all those room-service meals that were left uneaten, because there was no way he could keep a full meal down while he was obsessing over The Streak. He saw all of this. And it only made Gomez shake his head in wonder more than usual.

"All of the craziness," he would say years later, "and the son of gun always came to the park, got his hits, and helped us win baseball games. I've yet to meet the man who could go through what he went through and produce what he produced."

When the Yankees took the field on an unsparingly steamy Sunday afternoon in Washington, they rumbled headlong into an extraordinary baseball extravaganza. Griffith Stadium was always a perfect place for a visiting ballclub to play, years of neglect and years of dreadful baseball having rendered the Senators impotent and their home ballpark virtually neutral. Yet here were 31,008 people jamming the place, filling every aisle, every promenade, every corridor, every concourse, some of them actually spilling onto the field, blocking DiMaggio from the batting cage. They would be only the first of DiMaggio's great worries, though. Pitching for the Senators in the first game was the team's ace, Emil "Dutch" Leonard, a five-time All-Star who would win 191 games playing twenty years for the Dodgers, Senators, Phillies, and Cubs, four of the most woeful teams of the day. Armed with the best knuckleball in baseball, he could make any hitter look foolish if the flutter was working just right. And it was, today. In the second inning, after DiMaggio uncharacteristically disputed a called strike with home plate umpire Johnny Quinn ("Sorry, Joe," Quinn had pleaded, "it was right over"), he'd met a knuckler with the sweet spot of his Louisville Slugger but flied out to center. In the fourth, three knucklers produced a 3-and-0 count, but DiMaggio, taking advantage of his permanent green light and a rare Leonard fastball, swung; he could manage only a pop-up, which was gloved by third baseman George Archie.

One more time, he would push himself ever closer to the abyss. Now, it was the sixth inning, thirty-one thousand people were buzzing nervously, and DiMaggio took a wild hack at a floater for strike one, and stared at a change-up that just missed, evening the count. Even Quinn, doing his best to remain an impartial judge behind his mask, could sense a growing crisis. "Dutch had as much stuff as I've ever seen him have," the umpire would report later. "He was pitching out of a background of white shirts, too." Not only was DiMaggio trying to catch Sisler against a trick pitcher, he was having a hell of a time picking up the ball, too; that was usually never a problem in Washington, where plenty of dark bleacher seats usually provided a splendid backdrop for the batter's eye. "Then," Quinn added, "he threw DiMag a perfect pitch."

It was, too. It was a fastball—looking like it was whistling in at 100 miles an hour, compared to all those slow-motion knucklers—and it was knee-high, on the outside corner, and for an odd, uneasy moment it froze DiMaggio. But only one moment. That wide stance allowed DiMaggio more time to adjust than just about any hitter ever born, and now he adjusted, and found the left-center field gap, the ball splitting left fielder George Case and center fielder Doc Cramer, rolling all the way to the 422-foot sign, igniting a burst of boisterous bedlam. The Yankees exploded. The crowd imploded. And DiMaggio, standing on second base, tied for now with Sisler in the record books, took a deep breath and sighed, no doubt jonesing badly for a smoke.

An hour or so later, he would *really* need one.

It was the bottom of the first of the nightcap. Tommy Henrich, hitting in the three-hole, was about to dig into the batter's box when he heard a screeching voice behind him.

"*Tommy!*"

It was DiMaggio.

"You got my ball bat!"

In later years, players would call their favorite bats "gamers." In the forties, they were "ball bats." By any name, they were more precious to a hitter than pure platinum, because baseball players are more superstitious than witches, and when they get attached to a piece of equipment—bat, hat, glove, socks—they'd sooner part with a week's pay. Even DiMaggio, with more talent coursing through his bloodstream than anyone, was a renowned creature of habit. Back in '33, on the day his minor-league hitting streak began, the Seals' trainer had put a bandage on his hand to cover a stone bruise. He got a hit that day. He got a hit the next day, and the next, and the next, and the bandage stayed right where it was for sixty-one games, long after his hand had fully healed.

Now, he was missing his ball bat, the one he'd named "Betsy Ann," and he was frantic.

"This *is* one of yours," Henrich hurriedly explained, "but it's the one you gave me." It was true. More than a month earlier, on May 21, in the throes of a batting slump, Henrich had borrowed a piece of lumber from DiMaggio's supply of D-29 models, at thirty-six ounces a bit heavier than what Henrich was accustomed to. It had worked wonderfully—Henrich would hit a career-high thirty-one homers in 1941, many of them with DiMaggio's black D-29. DiMaggio grabbed the bat, stared at it, looked at the handle, and realized Henrich was right, this wasn't his Streak bat, whose handle he'd delicately shaved to a perfect fit for his hands. Henrich looked at DiMaggio's face. He was as white as Johnny Babich had been the day before when that line drive had zipped past his jewels.

"Jesus, Tommy," DiMaggio said. "Someone stole my ball bat."

It had happened between games, despite the fact that one of the batboys had been expressly ordered to guard the Yankee bat rack, and it wasn't the only victim of vandalism that day: The same thief had lifted Lefty Gomez's mitt, too. No offense to Lefty, but that little misdemeanor was immediately forgotten. DiMaggio grabbed another bat, and he smoked a scorching line drive off Senators pitcher Sid Hudson, but it soared right into rightfielder Buddy Lewis's glove. It was actually a good piece of hitting for the Yankees, a sacrifice fly that plated Red Rolfe, but DiMaggio muttered on his way out to center in the bottom of the inning: "If that had been my ball bat, it would have dropped in there."

Two innings later, more despair: DiMaggio tried another new bat, and this time pounced on a hanging Hudson curveball, ripping a vicious line drive . . . straight at shortstop Cecil Travis. Two innings later, still more anguish: The Yankees had chased Hudson, and now Red Anderson fed DiMaggio a 2-and-0 fastball that rode in on him; he popped it meekly to short center field, where Cramer gloved it. 0-for-3

Two innings later the Yankee dugout looked and sounded like a funeral parlor, even though they were leading 6-4, even though they were set to leapfrog into first place. DiMaggio was pensive, angry, frustrated, dying inside. So were all 31,008 spectators, and it's a good thing they were unaware of the thief in their midst or else there might have been a public flogging in the 100-degree heat. Henrich, for some reason, felt indirectly responsible for spoiling the day. He walked over to DiMaggio before the two men took their fourth at-bats in the seventh, extended his bat, and said, "You should take this one back and try it, Joe. There's some hits in here." Henrich walked to the plate, popped up to Mickey Vernon at first, then saw DiMaggio approach him unarmed.

"Okay, Tommy," he said. "Let me have it."

Anderson's first pitch nearly rendered the point moot: a high fastball that whistled past DiMaggio's chin and backed him off the plate. But his second couldn't have been more hitter-friendly if he'd rested it on a tee: a fastball, waist-high, outer half of the plate. DiMaggio nearly jumped out of his spikes as the ball jumped off the renegade bat, landing cleanly in an open patch of left field for a single. The Yankees—the staid, corporate, colorless Yankees—all burst out of their dugout and started dancing. DiMaggio tipped his cap. He shook Vernon's hand. He had forty-two. He had the modern record. Only Wee Willie Keeler and his heavily asterisked forty-four lay ahead.

For the first time all day, DiMaggio could exhale.

"How about making it to fifty, Joe?" one of the sportswriters asked in the crowded crush of the postgame clubhouse. Joe's manager intercepted the question.

"Fifty, hell," McCarthy gushed. "Joe's liable to keep it up indefinitely."

DiMaggio himself sounded far more relieved than excited.

"Tickled?" he asked. "What do you think? I'm glad the strain is over. Now I'm going after that forty-four-game mark and I'll keep right on swinging and hitting as long as I can. Yesterday in Philadelphia, I think, was the first time I was really nervous. I was tense out there today, too."

He wasn't the only one. Three thousand miles away, at the DiMaggio family residence at 2150 Beach Street in San Francisco, Giuseppe DiMaggio, the clan's patriarch, had spent much of the afternoon pacing in front of the house "looking like a panther at the zoo," according to his eldest son, Tom. At DiMaggio's Grotto, the family restaurant on Fisherman's Wharf, almost all work had ceased until Joe's favorite niece, Betty, called the sports desk at the *Chronicle* and got the word: *He's done it!*

"Now we can get the waiters and bartenders and busboys at the Grotto to do some work," a relieved Tom DiMaggio said, "and at home we can get the old man to quiet down."

Not quite. Giuseppe had invited *Chronicle* sports editor Will Connolly to the house afterward, and Connolly quoted the old fisherman's unedited exuberance verbatim in the next day's paper: "Joe, he wait-a too long. He waits until-a the seexth inning before he ties-a da record of Seesler. Then he waits until-a da seventh inning before he breaks-a Seesler's record in-a da second game. He makes his papa worry too long. Why cannot my son Joe do it in the first inning?"

All of that pent-up strain found a welcome release on the train ride back to New York's Pennsylvania Station. DiMaggio ordered bottles of beer all around for his teammates in the club car, and after playing eighteen innings in the oppressive Washington humidity he was in a grand mood. Right to the moment when someone brought up his dear departed Betsy Ann. Then the club car turned a shade cloudy.

"Of course the guy had to pick out the best one," he muttered, shaking his head. "I had three of my bats on the ground in front of the dugout, but he got the one I wouldn't take money for. Not only do I need it to get my hits, but I wanted it for my trophy collection. Most of my models are thirty-six inches long and weigh thirty-six ounces, but I had sandpapered the handle of this one to thin it just a trifle and to take off a half-to three-quarters of an ounce in weight. That bat was just right for me. I liked the feel of it. Those times when I went up with my last chance without a hit I used this bat, and you can see why I hate to lose it."

He sighed. Lit another cigarette. Shook his head again. Then ordered another round of beers for the boys. What the hell. Life was still pretty good if you happened to be Joe DiMaggio in the final hours of June 1941, even with Betsy Ann off on her own.

———◆———

It was just a little bit more anxious for everyone else, especially when President Roosevelt announced on the day DiMaggio passed Sisler that the army would add up to 900,000 new men during the next fiscal year, set to begin July 1. All men who'd reached their twenty-first birthday by then would have to register, and sixteen days later a new lottery would be held to send a fresh batch of recruits away from their dears for a year.

Well, *hopefully* it would be a year. Because even though Japanese premier Prince Fumimaro Konoye said during a brief speech that same day, "Japan is very anxious to maintain friendly relations with the United States and we see no reason why our two countries cannot remain friendly," that snippet of hopefulness was buried by the dim dispatches arriving from just about everywhere else.

There was former president Herbert Hoover, for instance, offering a fresh voice to a sizable segment of the country still uneasy with the way the United States had so easily aligned itself with the Soviet Union. "If we go further and join the war and we win," Hoover cautioned, "then we have won for Stalin the grip of Communism on Russia and more opportunity for it to extend over the world. We should at least cease to tell our sons that they would be giving their lives to restore democracy and freedom in the world."

There was Secretary of the Navy Frank Knox, speaking from the opposite side of the aisle, who on June 30 had given voice to the unspoken fears that crawled through the stomachs of so many would-be citizen-soldiers: "The time to use our Navy to clear the Atlantic of the German menace is at hand. Now is the time to put in motion the huge machine we have been building since the war began. We can insure, beyond a shadow of a doubt, the defeat of that pagan force, and insure a victory for Christian civilization."

And, after a few weeks of self-imposed silence, there was Charles Lindbergh, again, emboldened by Hoover's words, declaring in San Francisco: "I would a hundred times rather see my country ally herself with England or even with Germany, with all her faults, than with the cruelty, the Godlessness, and the barbarism that exists in Soviet Russia. An alliance between the United States and Russia should be opposed by every American, by every Christian, and by every humanitarian in the country."

This wicked game of ideological Ping-Pong provided the gloomy daily background against which everything else occurred in American life. No longer was the theater immune to the darkness, either. On July 2, Howard Hawks's long-awaited movie *Sergeant York,* starring Gary Cooper, held its world premiere at the Astor Theater in New York City. The dashing Cooper—one of a handful of Hollywood leading men now being mentioned for the starring role in the next hotly anticipated biopic, this one telling the life story of Lou Gehrig—was in attendance and sat next to Alvin York, the devoutly religious Tennessean who'd been denied a conscientious objector exemption during the Great War and become the most decorated soldier of the entire conflict, killing twenty German soldiers and capturing 132 others during an infantry attack on a German position near the Argonne Forest in October 1918.

When he was introduced following the screening, an appreciative audience stood and gave York a loud ovation, which he accepted on behalf of his fallen comrades in the 328th Infantry Regiment. York expressed the wish that the film would contribute to "national unity in this hour of danger" and rued the fact that "millions of Americans, like myself, must be facing the same questions, the same uncertainties which we faced and I believe resolved for the right some twenty-four years ago." Even the feel-good nationalistic nature of the movie, however, was cause for controversy; some of the leading isolationists, led by Sen. Burton K. Wheeler of Montana, called for congressional hearings investigating the worthiness of "pro-war" motion pictures like *Sergeant York* and *The Great Dictator,* which many had hailed as Charlie Chaplin's masterpiece.

Much as it surely galled him to admit as much, Joseph Stalin recognized how critical to his cause the United States was, and he saw the schism that was growing ever wider in that country, and so on the same day *Sergeant York* held its gala premiere, Stalin made a rare appearance on Soviet radio, delivering a message that he hoped would reach just as many American ears and touch just as many American souls as it would Russian hearts and minds. For the first time, he acknowledged that in just two weeks of war the Nazis had occupied Lithuania, the greater parts of Latvia, and the western parts of White Russia and the Ukraine. He conceded that German troops were clearly on dual collision courses with Leningrad and Moscow.

"A grave danger hangs over our country," Stalin conceded.

"The enemy continues to push ahead, sending fresh forces to the front despite the heroic resistance of the Red Army and despite the fact that the enemy's best divisions and best units of his air force have already been crushed and found their grave on the field of battle."

Addressing his ill-fated truce with Hitler, Stalin said, "No peaceful nation could refuse a peace accord with a neighboring power even if such monsters and cannibals as Hitler and Ribbentrop were found at its head." Justifications complete, he laid out his position for the world to interpret:

"Our cause is just," he said. "The enemy must be crushed. We must win. Because of the war forced upon us, our country has entered into a battle to the death with a most ferocious and perfidious enemy who is cruel and implacable. He is out to seize our lands watered with our sweat. Citizens of the Soviet Union must fight to the last drop of blood."

American polls would soon insist that most had been unmoved by Stalin's pleas, even as they began to accept the fact that entering the conflict at large might be unavoidable. They simply wanted a higher cause to follow than Joe Stalin, and their message was clear: Better your blood than ours, Comrade. For now.

———•———

In barely a month, all of Joe DiMaggio's neighbors on the sports pages had slowly slipped aside, leaving him virtually alone to take the nation's mind off that *other* Joe, and off U-boats, and off the ever-shifting news emanating from Tokyo, and off another looming draft, and off as bitter a political divide as there'd been in the country since the closing hours of Reconstruction.

After capturing the Belmont Stakes, Whirlaway had spent the rest of June in relative peace, emerging briefly at New York's Aqueduct Race Track on June 21 to capture the Dwyer Stakes. The next big race on Whirly's agenda would be July 26, when he'd be in the Chicago suburbs to try to add the Arlington Stakes to his résumé, and to edge a few dollars closer to Seabiscuit on the all-time earnings list.

Billy Conn had an eventful couple of weeks after scaring the hell out of Joe Louis. Greenfield Jimmy Smith may have been dead set against his baby Mary Louise becoming Mrs. Billy Conn, but he was apparently the only one. Billy and Mary Louise quickly became America's new sweethearts, their star-crossed story carried on the front page of every important newspaper in all forty-eight states. Some five thousand people had gathered outside St. Philomena's Church in Pittsburgh on the day after the fight, which is where it was rumored the couple's ceremony was to be held until Greenfield Jimmy put the kibosh on it. Conn not only lost the girl for a time, he also lost his cut of what looked like a sure million-dollar payday when Mike Jacobs announced he'd decided against having a quick Conn-Louis rematch in September and would instead give Lou Nova a long-awaited shot at Louis. "Billy won't be forgotten," Jacobs said. "He'll get a crack at whoever wins that fight sometime in 1942." A few days after that, Conn's misfortune compounded when he somehow lost a $1,200 diamond ring a friend had lent him to show Mary Louise.

"I guess all my luck ran out when Louis nailed me in the thirteenth round," Conn reported glumly. "Mary Louise? She's wonderful. But her father doesn't like prizefighters. I've got to convince him I'm really a gentleman and not a yegg. I'll prove I'm a gentleman yet."

Still, all of these setbacks paled compared to the news Billy received on June 27 in Atlantic City when he learned his mother had finally lost her long, agonizing battle with bone cancer. Billy had been reluctant to leave her side a few days earlier when it looked like the end was near, but she'd rallied, urged him to go to New Jersey where he'd earn a few bucks refereeing a wrestling match, and also made him promise that he wouldn't give up pursuing Mary Louise's hand. Honoring that last wish, Conn and Mary Louise found a sympathetic priest, Father Francis J. Schlindwein, and on July 1, at St. Peter's Church near Philadelphia, they were married at last. George Ryan, a pal of Billy's, was best man, while a maid from the rectory, Mary Byrne, served as maid of honor. When it was done, the happy couple repaired to Mike Jacobs's house in Rumson, New Jersey, where, before commencing their honeymoon, they placed a most difficult call to Pittsburgh, where Mary Louise informed her father that she now had a new last name.

"You wouldn't be able to print what he said," Conn told the reporters.

Actually, what Greenfield Jimmy Smith told the *New York Daily Mirror* was this: "I'll fix him so nobody will want to see him fight." Then he tried to have the couple arrested, but the chief of police of Rumson informed him that since there were no charges pending against his nineteen-year-old and her twenty-three-year-old groom, there was nothing that could be done.

"I'm sorry that Mary's parents are against our wedding, but we're married and happy," Billy said. "We'd like to be on friendly terms with her father and mother, but what can we do?"

The Conns were photographed with broad smiles anyway. In a few weeks they would head out to California, where Billy would star in a movie called *The Pittsburgh Kid,* and in a courageous test of his acting chops he was cast as . . . an upstart boxer from Pittsburgh. He wasn't bitching. It was the easiest fifty grand he'd ever made. "What do I have to complain about," he asked, "other than getting my brains scrambled by Joe Louis?"

———————•———————

Things hadn't gone so well for Louis in the aftermath of his epic victory, either. During the fight he'd pulled the ligaments on both sides of his right wrist, meaning he'd made the most desperate comeback of his life, quite literally, with one hand tied behind his back. That curtailed the effectiveness of his golf game, which was disappointing. On July 2, however, the same day Louis read in his local papers about Billy Conn's marital bliss, he was served with divorce papers by his wife of almost six years, Marva, citing "extreme cruelty."

According to the bill filed by Mrs. Louis in circuit court in Chicago, on January 2, Louis had "struck her a violent blow on the mouth with his hand" and on April 19 "hit her in the face with his hand and stepped on her ankle." She asked for alimony and permission to resume using her maiden name, and claimed Joe owned real estate in Chicago and Detroit valued at $400,000 and had insurance, bonds and stocks, and cash totaling over $400,000. She also estimated his annual income at a staggering $250,000.

Louis, playing one-handed golf when he was told about the suit, murmured, "I don't believe it. I absolutely know nothing about it." He denied he hit her but said he wouldn't contest the suit. "If she doesn't want to live with me, what can I do about it?"

Left unsaid was the critical fact that if Marva decided to pursue her action, not only would Louis's fortune be at risk, but so would his draft status. As a married man he had a Class 3-A deferment. The moment he became single again, that would switch to 1-A, and he'd be in the army five minutes later. The sports pages, chilled at the prospect of a sporting calendar without a half dozen Joe Louis prizefights, reacted in curious ways, mostly demonizing Marva, none more viciously than Dan Parker in the *Mirror* (Whirlaway's erstwhile tormentor), who wrote, quite unbelievably: "Maybe Marva is one of those wives who needs a good punch in the schnozzie to keep her in line." The next week there were more than a few letters to the editor addressing Parker's tasteless observation.

All agreeing with him.

———•———

So DiMaggio wasn't only providing a respite from the real world, but from some of the darker aspects of the sports world, too, a double dose of pressure he would have preferred to share with Ted Williams, who along with his Red Sox teammates was waiting for DiMaggio at Yankee Stadium on July 1, 1941. Williams came into the game hitting .404, and he could commiserate with DiMaggio about the unique challenges he was facing, too. After all, in that day's doubleheader, Williams would go 2-for-6, normally a fine stat line, but with his personal bar set so high it actually *reduced* his average by two points.

DiMaggio could certainly understand. All of the celebration that attended his breaking of Sisler's record had vanished practically overnight. Suddenly all the papers were filled with stories of Mr. Wee Willie Keeler, who had been retired thirty-one years and dead for eighteen but was instantly resurrected as the "real" holder of the hitting-streak record, even if it took some digging to even discover that Keeler had strung together forty-four straight games forty-four years before. None of that seemed to faze Joe. His brother was a different matter.

During batting practice earlier that day, Dominic had kidded Joe: "I think the Yankees and the writers know they have a good thing going and want to keep giving you a moving target to shoot for. I can't wait to see who they'll dig up once you pass Keeler."

"*If* I pass him," Joe said, correcting his kid brother's hubris.

First, he had to tie him, and it looked as if he might actually get an artificial helping hand in the fifth inning of the opener. He'd already batted twice, popping up in the first inning and grounding out in the third, and now the crowd of 52,832, the largest at Yankee Stadium all season, began its regular ritual of switching from excited buzz to nervous hum. They nearly had to downshift again in the fifth, this time to anxious silence, when DiMaggio hit a hard smash right at third baseman Jim Tabor. Tabor knocked the ball down, had difficulty picking it up, hurried the throw, and pulled first baseman Lou Finney off the bag. Just as they'd done back on June 26 during the Elden Auker game, the Yankee dugout emptied at once and looked up to the press box; just as on June 26, it happened to be Dan Daniel's turn to serve as official scorer. One finger meant it was a hit, two fingers an error. Daniel didn't hesitate. He lifted his index finger alone. Hit.

"That was one of the few times I got a break from the scorer on a questionable play," DiMaggio would tell sportswriter Dave Anderson of the *Times* twenty years later. "Instead of giving me the benefit of the doubt— not that I was asking for it—they usually made sure it was a clean hit."

The Streak was going to kill poor Dan Daniel, who endured a few snide comments from his press-box brethren—the fill-in from the *Daily News,* he reported, held his nose for a full minute after the call—and the next week in *The Sporting News,* he would describe the ordeal of adjudicating DiMaggio's streak as "the toughest job of scoring in the history of the major leagues. They can have it! But I seen my duty and I done it, and if anybody ever again asks me to be the scorer, I'll tell him what to do with the job and where to go." The following spring, Daniel would admit to DiMaggio, "There was just as much pressure on me and the other scorers around the league as there was on you not to cheapen The Streak."

DiMaggio was kind enough to take Daniel off the griddle a few innings later by smashing a clean single, and what was most interesting about that was the reaction of the crowd, most of whom still had no idea what Daniel's verdict had been, so the ovation lasted a full five minutes. DiMaggio was a bit more considerate in the nightcap, quickly rapping a first-inning single over Joe Cronin's head at shortstop, which not only spared the weary crowd another few innings of anxiety but also kept him out of danger when storm clouds moved over Yankee Stadium and ultimately shortened the game at five innings.

So now he was tied with Wee Willie Keeler, and even the ever-inventive New York press couldn't find anyone else lurking in the newspaper microfilms who they could throw out there as the next man for DiMaggio to catch. If he could get to forty-five on July 3, he would officially have no one left to chase except for himself. One more time, the crowd—this one a more modest, though still throaty, midweek workday gathering of 8,682— waded through two fruitless times at bat. Some regular DiMaggiophiles had grown so accustomed to the wait that they didn't even bother to make it to the stadium for his first at-bat; prominent among these was Mrs. Joe

DiMaggio, who arrived in the third inning with her parents (as shutterbugs snapped all around her), inquired what Joe had done in his first time up, was told that he'd been robbed of a sure double when Stan Spence made a terrific, leaping catch in right, and sighed, "Too bad." With her own eyes she was able to see Joe nearly crush a home run in the third off Boston's Dick Newsome before the ball hooked just foul, then sighed again when Joe grounded out to third base on the next pitch.

By the fifth inning, DiMaggio himself had grown impatient. He'd already begun complaining privately to his favored scribes that The Streak had caused him to lose all discipline as a hitter, that he now swung at balls he never would have considered just two months ago. Then, on a 2-and-0 pitch, Newsome threw a high fastball that a DiMaggio unburdened by history's calling card would surely have let sail past. Not this time. A walk, most assuredly, was not as good as a hit, and so he swung, and as soon as he hit it he knew what he'd done. So did Ted Williams, playing left field, who suspected he'd be making a fruitless chase of the ball as soon as it made contact with DiMaggio's bat. He was right. The ball disappeared in a tangle of arms beyond the fence, not far from the spot where a seventy-one-year-old stadium usher named Bill Dahlen stood. In 1894, playing for the Chicago Cubs, Dahlen had compiled a forty-two-game hitting streak; it was *his* record that Willie Keeler broke three years later.

"Back in the nineties, nobody paid any attention to a thing like that," Dahlen said. "I didn't remember any remarkable things about my streak except that after I'd been stopped in my forty-third game, I went on for twenty-three more before they stopped me again. That was so long ago that I'd forgotten until DiMaggio's stunt began to get a lot of publicity."

DiMaggio's stunt had now reached forty-five games, and naturally he'd done it with a home run, and Mrs. DiMaggio and the other 8,681 were frantic now, cheering, chanting, singing, tossing straw hats in the air, beside themselves with glee. DiMaggio came out of the dugout and tipped his cap. You could see his smile from the upper deck.

"If it's up to me," DiMaggio said later, in front of his locker, "I will go right on hitting. I'd like to hoist that mark where nobody could reach it. But I don't mind telling you it feels great to have the big excitement over with and the nervousness gone. It's not easy to have everyone ask you, 'Well Joe, will you make it?' It's not a comfortable feeling to come to bat with the idea that if you had to go hitless you would be letting a lot of people down."

DiMaggio still pined for his old bat, but he'd started to move on, started to realize that part of the price of being *Joe DiMaggio* now, in this time, in this summer, was that people wanted a piece of him. Hell, just a few minutes earlier, as he'd left the field after the final out, a glut of fans spilled out of the stands, ostensibly heading for the center-field exit but really heading straight for Joe, who tried to beat them to the dugout. But he didn't quite make it, and one light-fingered kid actually snatched the hat off Joe's head and started running. Mike Ryba, a veteran Red Sox relief pitcher, saw this as it unfolded and tackled the kid, who managed a lateral handoff to a friend, who did some fancy open-field running of his own before a group of panting ushers finally cornered him. DiMaggio got his cap back. *If only Ryba played for the Senators,* DiMaggio sighed. *Maybe Betsy Ann could have been saved after all.*

———————•———————

It was a few days later, with the nation firmly seized by the mania of DiMaggio's Streak, that a twenty-nine-year-old disc jockey named Alan Courtney sat down at a table at Log Cabin Farm, a nightclub in the northern suburbs of New York City. Sitting across the table from Courtney was Les Brown, a bandleader who fronted the "Band of Renown." In years to come, Brown would introduce the world to Doris Day and Tony Bennett, among others, but in the summer of 1941 he was searching for a song that would get his band, featuring singer Betty Bonney, some attention.

Courtney started scribbling something on the tablecloth.

"See if you like this," he told Brown.

> *Who started baseball's famous streak*
> *That's got us all aglow?*
> *He's just a man and not a freak,*
> *Joltin' Joe DiMaggio . . .*

"Not bad," Brown said. "I'll get Ben Homer to do the arrangement."

"That," Courtney said, "is a hell of a name for a guy arranging a DiMaggio song."

They laughed, and Courtney said, "I'll work on it some more, but if we can get it on the market quick, it might sell. Let's hope he keeps hitting."

It did sell. "Joltin' Joe DiMaggio" was precisely the song Les Brown was looking for, and before long it was the most hummed melody anywhere in the country as the Band of Renown played it not only in ballrooms and nightclubs, but over the national NBC radio wire, too. "It was just a simple ditty," Brown would say many years later. "But that was the charm of it."

The song reflected the simpler place that much of America still wanted itself to be, but would likely never be again. Late in the afternoon of the Fourth of July, Roosevelt had provided a sobering reminder of that during a quiet address to the nation from his home in Hyde Park, New York.

"The United States will never survive as a happy and prosperous desert in the middle of a desert of dictatorship," he said. "All of us who lie awake at night—all of us who study and study again—know full well that in these days we cannot save freedom with pitchforks and muskets alone after a dictator combination has gained control of the rest of the world. We know that we cannot save freedom in our own midst, in our own land, if all around us—our neighbor nations—have lost their freedom.

"When we repeat the great pledge to our country and to our flag, it must be our deep conviction that we pledge as well our work, our will, and, if it be necessary, our very lives."

———————●———————

He was simply a courier doing his job and looking for a tip when he walked into the Yankees clubhouse late in the morning of July 5, but the kid found himself in the midst of an immediate stir, for he possessed a most sacred relic in his hands: Betsy Ann. DiMaggio's ball bat was back! The Yankees celebrated as if they'd just won the pennant—which, in essence, they had. That day, they would beat the Philadelphia Athletics 10-5 for their seventh straight victory, and that would turn out to be simply the midpoint of a fourteen-game streak that would be the final catapult the Yankees would need in 1941, launching them from one game behind the Indians at The Streak's beginning to five games ahead by Streak's end. Everything was going right for the Yankees, and for DiMaggio. Even Ed Barrow, the man who'd haggled DiMaggio for that extra three grand in spring training, had to concede as much—though not for public attribution, lest he give his star an extra bit of leverage the next time they had to talk about salary.

"I've been around baseball a long time, but I've never seen anything to equal the change in DiMaggio and the change in that ball club," Barrow told one reporter. "To be frank, DiMaggio's relation to the team has not always been what you might call wholehearted. Joe's a wonderful fellow, but he's also very shy and diffident. Some of the fellows, I know, were convinced he wasn't giving to the club all he had. You know, he always plays so easily and can be a star with so little effort, they thought he was going out there each day and trying to be adequate, rather than outstanding.

"But once his streak got under way, you never saw a gang of men rally around a single figure as much as our team began rooting for Joe. You know the kind of ball club we've got—no pop-off guys, no unnecessary show of emotion. Well, that day in Washington when Joe got a hit late in the game to break Sisler's record, every man on our club was sitting out on the steps, as tense as rabid fans, and when at last he rapped out that hit they went wild, beat their bats on the bat rack, threw their hats in the air and nearly mobbed him when he got back to the dugout. How are you going to beat a team like that?"

Such was the delight when DiMaggio finally gripped Betsy Ann firmly for the first time in nearly a week, smiling as he felt the familiar handle. She hadn't made her way home easily. One of DiMaggio's running mates, a small-time rackets guy named Jimmy "Peanuts" Ceres, who spent a lot of his down time driving DiMaggio's car and running his errands, had spent five full days hunting for the bat once it turned out that the guy who'd taken it in Washington didn't only happen to run a little bit in Newark, Peanuts' home turf, but also had the great misfortune of bragging a little too loudly about his acquisition.

The streets of Newark had ears, and most of those ears funneled back to Peanuts, and one day he and another friend, a funeral director named Jerry Spatola, paid the chatty grifter a visit. Now, this appointment went down one of three ways, depending on whose account you read and how gullible you happened to be. The thief either a) had an attack of conscience after reading how badly Joe missed Betsy Ann, and handed the club back with sincere apologies; b) negotiated with Ceres and Spatola and accepted fair recompense for his booty; c) was "convinced" that it would be best for all involved if he just gave the bat back so everyone could forget the whole thing.

However it went down, DiMaggio was now properly armed again, and he celebrated in two ways. First, he went out and clobbered a 420-foot home run in the bottom of the first inning, allowing the crowd of 19,977 to enjoy the rest of the afternoon in peace after crossing game number forty-six off his to-do list. Then he autographed the bat with which he broke Keeler's record and donated it to the San Francisco chapter of the United Service Organization. Actually, he'd wanted to bestow the ball instead—the new bat might not have been his ball bat, but it had now done the trick four straight games—but once he hit it into the left-field bleachers, that was no longer possible, despite a plea from New York mayor Fiorello LaGuardia that whoever harbored the ball do his civic duty and hand it over. Now that he had Betsy Ann back, parting with the piece of lumber he'd originally lent Henrich was much easier, and he handed it over to flight attendant Polly Ann Carpenter of United Airlines, and off it went for the coast. A week later the bat was raffled off between games of a Seals–Hollywood Stars game after raising some $1,678 (at a quarter a ticket), and the winning ticket holder, James Osborne, gushed, "I couldn't feel luckier if I won a million bucks!"

Neither could DiMaggio. As remarkable as he'd been in building his streak up to forty-six, and now released from the daily grind of trying to surpass someone else's record (and charged instead with the far more agreeable task of merely extending his own), he set out on the hottest stretch of the whole Streak, a push interrupted only by the All-Star Game, in which he managed to get a hit (even A.L. president Will Harridge had to concede that *that* couldn't count toward The Streak), although he wound up ceding the hero's mantle to Ted Williams and his game-winning home run. "I'd have felt terrible if I came within a few games of the record and was stopped," DiMaggio admitted. "But now I don't think much about it. I don't particularly care if I don't reach fifty or sixty straight."

He didn't just reach fifty, he blew past it without even giving a thought to riding the brakes. In the seven games just before and just after the All-Star break, connecting games forty-seven and fifty-three, DiMaggio stepped to the plate for twenty-nine official at-bats and pounded out seventeen hits, an inhuman .586 clip that elevated his batting average to .369 (.401 to that point in The Streak itself) and for the first time allowed him to think he might actually be able to overtake Williams for the batting title. Not only had Ted's average slipped under .400, to .397, but he had reinjured the same ankle that had plagued him all spring, and there was no telling when he'd come back—or how strong he would be when he did.

There seemed no ceiling to what DiMaggio could do, or to the level of adulation he could generate. DiMaggio had always been wildly popular among New York's vast Italian population, but that relationship had never been more vital than it was now, in the awful summer of 1941, with Italy in a lockstep alliance with the Nazis, with Mussolini not only spewing sour bursts of bile every few weeks but also looking very much like Hitler's hand puppet, especially when, early in July, in Rome, a series of decrees for a "final solution" to the Jewish question was reviewed by the Council of Ministers. The law, drafted in three parts, aimed at eliminating all Jews from Italy except those exempted by "favorable discrimination": either families of Aryan stock or those whose "patriotic services" have afforded them a sense of "Aryanization." Those with no Aryan ties would be expelled from Italy over the course of six months to five years, and as long as they remained they'd be forced to wear white distinguishing marks, they'd be excluded from parks, theaters, cinemas, and hospitals, and were forbidden from using radios or telephones or from hiring servants.

In a time such as this, if you had a vowel at the end of your name, you were happy to live in a world where Joe DiMaggio did, too. Of course, DiMaggio's appeal by now superseded ethnic boundaries, or regional ones. Every newspaper in every city now had a DiMaggio Watch box. Every newscast brought up-to-the-at-bat updates. The nightly condensed game-re-creation broadcasts by Don Dunphy on WINS radio became critical links to the New York masses, since prior to the season the Yankees and Giants, negotiating jointly, couldn't find a mutual local sponsor willing to cover the $50,000 cost to carry the teams' play-by-play. If you couldn't get to the park, and you couldn't wait for the next day's newspaper, you had to rely on Dunphy, whose voice had gained instant renown following the Louis-Conn fight.

And every visiting ballpark, as The Streak grew, welcomed DiMaggio as it would a pope or a president, especially after the Yankees opened their post-All-Star schedule with a western swing through St. Louis, Chicago, and Cleveland. On the morning of July 10, as DiMaggio ate breakfast with George Sisler ("I wired congratulations to Joe when he set the new record, but I wanted to meet him personally and tell him how fine I thought he was"), St. Louis Browns employees were all over town hanging up placards and handing out handbills that echoed the same ad that appeared in the morning newspapers:

SENSATIONAL
JOE DIMAGGIO
WILL SEEK TO HIT SAFELY IN HIS
49TH
CONSECUTIVE GAME
THUR. NITE, JULY 10
AT ST. LOUIS
BROWNS VS. YANKEES
SPORTSMAN'S PARK–8:30 P.M.
TICKETS NOW ON SALE AT BROWNS ARCADE TICKET OFFICE
PHONE CHESTNUT 7900.

Over 12,000 people actually came out to the ball yard that night to watch DiMaggio end the suspense with a first-inning hit for the fourth game in a row, and that may sound like a modest attendance until you realize the Browns' average crowd in 1941 was only 2,797.

After reaching his fiftieth game the next night, DiMaggio said, "It's all up to the pitchers to stop me now. The way I feel now, I don't believe I'll be my own undoing. The pressure's completely off now. I go to bat just as relaxed as if there had never been any streak." Not even the ultimate demise of Betsy Ann could flummox him. On July 14, the day the Yankees' fourteen-game winning streak finally ended with a 7-1 loss to the White Sox at Comiskey Park, DiMaggio lifted a lazy pop fly behind second base that plopped in and out of Bill Knickerbocker's glove. It was a no-brainer error, but the worse news for DiMaggio was the sickening *claack* that greeted contact, the age-old sound of a wooden bat being reduced to splinters. DiMaggio was far less upset than he'd been in Washington—breaking a man's bat is a pitcher's sworn duty; stealing one is a petty crime—and he proved as much by legging out a slow roller in the very next inning, a cheap hit that nevertheless pushed The Streak to fifty-four games.

On to Cleveland.

———————●———————

Ken Keltner never forgot what had happened the last time the Yankees were in town, back on June 1, in the second game of a doubleheader at Municipal Stadium. There had been a great, loud crowd that day, 52,081, most of them flocking to this huge Works Project Administration site by Lake Erie because the Indians were in first place, with a chance to bury the Yankees. The Yankees swept both games, though, and were on their way to catching, passing, and lapping the Tribe. That wasn't what stuck out in Keltner's memory, though. In the eighth inning of the nightcap, Joe DiMaggio had hit a rocket just to Keltner's left, and he barely missed snaring the ball; it ticked off his glove instead and rolled away. Keltner was mad at himself; he knew he should have played a hitter like DiMaggio a couple of steps deeper. Keltner, a terrific third baseman who in 1941 was having the second of seven All-Star seasons, was always making mental notes to himself. He did that here: *Never play DiMaggio that shallow again.* At inning's end, as Kelt- ner passed DiMaggio on his way back to the dugout, Joe had muttered something at him, something that sounded like: "One more inch, Ken, and I start all over tomorrow." Keltner had no idea what he was talking about until later, when he read that DiMaggio had extended his modest hitting streak to nineteen games.

Now, the streak had become a Streak of fifty-six games and counting, a month and a half had passed, the Indians were staring up at the Yankees in the standings, and DiMaggio had become a national obsession. In Cleve- land, and everywhere else, many people had their attention focused on the radio, where the second draft lottery in two years yielded number 196 as the first coral-colored capsule retrieved from the oversized goldfish bowl by Staff Sgt. Robert W. Shackleton. But 67,468 people had also found their way to Municipal Stadium this night of July 17, the largest baseball crowd of 1941, the largest to ever view a night game to that point. The night be- fore, at much-tinier League Park across town (where the Indians played a handful of games each year), 15,000 people had crammed into the rickety grandstand to see DiMaggio go 3-for-4, easily pushing his Streak to fifty- six. Now just about anyone who wanted to get a glimpse of DiMaggio try- ing to reach fifty-seven could, thanks to the switch of venue. And just about everyone did.

In the bottom of the first, with two outs and one man on, DiMaggio stepped to the plate to thunderous applause—the first time Keltner could ever remember a visiting player earning such an ovation. Instinctively, Keltner retreated a few steps from where he'd been when Tommy Henrich was hitting, then took an extra step or two back on top of *that,* the heels of his feet now planted on the outfield grass. DiMaggio noticed, thinking to himself: *He's daring me to bunt.* Left-hander Al Smith started DiMaggio with a fastball that was high and outside, then came back with a curveball, a terrible one, that hung invitingly on the inside of the plate. DiMaggio pounced. The moment he made contact, his initial thought was: double or triple? There was a lot of room for a ball to bounce around the spacious outfield, and . . .

Keltner reacted instantly, jerking to his right, gloving the ball as it took a third hop, just as it was about to hug the line all the way to the corner. His momentum carried him to foul territory, but he was able to plant himself, and once he did, the strongest infield arm in the American League took care of the rest. It was a breathtaking play, and as DiMaggio trotted back to the dugout, he shook his head and muttered, "Maybe I should've bunted after all. . . ."

Lefty Gomez, sitting in that dugout, felt his face flush with anger. Earlier that day, just before he and DiMaggio made the short walk from the Cleveland Hotel to the ballpark, Gomez had gotten his shoes shined. DiMaggio, reading a newspaper, was standing by the side, waiting for him, when the shoeshine guy recognized him. "You know," he told Gomez, "you'd better tell Joe to get his hit early tonight. I have a feeling that if he doesn't get it his first time up, he won't get it at all." Gomez, furious, yelled at the guy: "Are you trying to *jinx* him, you son of a bitch?" before storming off. Now, watching Keltner perform this bit of larceny, Gomez couldn't help but remember that warning, buzzing like a fly now in his brain as he grabbed his mitt and headed back out to the pitcher's mound.

In the fourth inning, it grew a little louder. DiMaggio worked the count to 3-and-2, and later admitted he'd have taken a hack at anything that was close to the plate. He did that on Smith's first full-count offering, fouling the ball off, but the next was a slow curve that broke inside and nearly hit him. He reluctantly took the walk, and the crowd hooted loudly. By the seventh, DiMaggio had grown clearly impatient, and so had everyone else. Smith came at him with another big, slow curveball. DiMaggio took another huge swing, and again he made beautiful contact, right on the sweet spot . . . and again, he'd found the most invulnerable spot on the field. The ball might have been hit even harder than the one he'd hit in the first inning, but Keltner, again playing deep, practically playing a short left field, didn't have to range quite as far this time. The crowd wasn't sure whether to cheer its approval for another defensive gem or hum its anxiety that The Streak might be in jeopardy; it tried to do both.

"It was funny," Keltner recalled five decades later. "The fans cheered my plays on Joe. Then they booed me. They didn't know how to react."

The Yankees, one more time, did what they could to give DiMaggio every opportunity to push The Streak a little bit farther. In the eighth, they finally strung together a rally that chased Smith, they scored two runs to extend their lead to 4-1, and they'd loaded the bases with one out for their cleanup hitter.

At shortstop for the Indians was Lou Boudreau, a popular third-year player celebrating his twenty-fourth birthday that night, a milestone commemorated during batting practice when the Al Horwitz Orchestra played "Happy Birthday" and most of the early-arriving crowd sang along. "I remember taking a few small steps to my left, closer to the bag, because I wanted to cheat for the double play," Boudreau would recall exactly sixty years later. "I knew that would leave an enormous hole for Joe between me and Keltner, and as a right-handed hitter he knew how to exploit those things. But I figured it was a win-win. If he hit the ball at me, we get a double play, get out of the inning, and we're still in the game. If he finds the hole, we're gonna lose anyway and at least he's got his hitting streak still alive."

By any reasonable expectation, this would be DiMaggio's final at-bat of the night, and so all 67,468 people rose and applauded as he dug in. The new Cleveland pitcher was Jim Bagby, and he started DiMaggio off with an outside fastball for ball one. DiMaggio fouled off the next pitch, an inside fastball, and then Bagby threw a curveball, which broke wide. The tension inside the ballpark was now unbearable. "You could hear everybody's heart pounding," Boudreau said. "On both sides."

Bagby fired a fastball, a good one, in on DiMaggio's hands. DiMaggio swung. From the start, it didn't look good, a routine grounder heading straight for Boudreau's glove. But then, as if Providence itself was trying to intercede, a most amazing thing happened.

"The ball hit a pebble," Boudreau said in 2001. "All these years later, I can still see the hop it took."

A pebble! Exactly one month earlier, on June 17, DiMaggio had entered the seventh inning hitless, stuck on twenty-nine games, hoping to get one more so he could set the Yankees team record. And a ball exactly like this one had hit a Yankee Stadium pebble just in front of Luke Appling, the White Sox shortstop, bounded up, hit his shoulder, and scooted past.

"Luckily for me," Boudreau said, "I was still pretty young. I had all my reflexes. I made the adjustment, and I picked it up with my bare hand just before it smacked into my ear. And from there it was a routine six-four-three, the same double play I started a million times in my lifetime."

The twin-killing was executed in churchlike silence, Boudreau-to-Ray Mack-to-Oscar Grimes. DiMaggio ran through first base, made a sharp left turn toward centerfield, picked up his glove, and took his position. He didn't kick the dirt. He didn't punch the sky. He didn't betray one ounce of emotion. He knew it had to end sometime. It had just ended now, in Cleveland, in front of all these suddenly silent witnesses.

Or had it?

Incredibly, The Streak had one last death rattle, and it was DiMaggio's roommate who unwittingly tried to resuscitate history. In the ninth inning, with the Yankees guarding a seemingly safe 4-1 lead, the Indians staged a desperate rally. Gomez was pitching a four-hitter but immediately surrendered singles to Gee Walker and Grimes. McCarthy, careful about overtaxing Gomez's thirty-two-year-old arm, summoned Johnny Murphy from the bullpen, and on the first pitch he threw, pinch-hitter Larry Rosenthal smoked a soaring drive between DiMaggio and Henrich to the farthest corner of right-center field for a two-run triple.

Suddenly the crowd was alive again. Not only was the home team suddenly within a run, and not only was the tying run standing ninety feet away with nobody out, but if the Indians could just find a way to bring Rosenthal home, if they extended the game to the tenth inning, DiMaggio might actually get one more shot to make it to fifty-seven. And if that happened, while DiMaggio was only scheduled to hit fourth in the top of the tenth, the three hitters ahead of him would be, in order, Johnny Sturm, Red Rolfe, and Tommy Henrich—the exact same setup during DiMaggio's previous Great Escape, back in the thirty-eighth game against Elden Auker!

Was there any doubt this would happen? That it *had* to happen?

But a funny thing happened next. DiMaggio, who'd been a part of so many miraculous Yankee comebacks and so many late-inning Yankee heroics, and who would see plenty more before he was through, now saw himself burned by that very pinstriped proficiency that made the Yankee engine hum. First, pinch-hitter Hal Trosky bounced a dribbler down the first-base line, which Sturm fielded. One out. Next, another pinch-hitter, Soup Campbell, rapped a sharp grounder right back to Murphy, who knocked the ball down and then—however reluctant he might really have been—threw home to cut down Rosenthal, foolishly trying to score. Two outs. And when Roy Weatherly somewhat anticlimactically grounded out to first, the book was finally, officially closed.

The Streak was finally, officially dead.

"He hit the ball hard, but he had the bad luck to hit them where they could be fielded," was Keltner's immediate reaction to his pair of gems, and fifty years later he was equally modest in describing them: "I was just unconscious. Not just once but twice. That's a pretty good night right there." Not everyone felt that way, though. As Keltner and his wife Evelyn prepared to leave the stadium, a gaggle of uniformed Cleveland police surrounded them and said they'd be escorting the couple to their car.

"There's a lot of angry people here," one of the cops told him. "A lot of DiMaggio fans."

"You've got to be kidding," Keltner said. But the cop's stony silence told him it wasn't a joke. They took the escort. And the next night, when Keltner's name was introduced before the game, he was loudly booed by the Cleveland fans. "They really weren't kidding," Keltner said, laughing. "There really were a lot of angry people."

DiMaggio was philosophical. He gamely posed for pictures, both his hands forming zeros, displaying his goose eggs for the world. "Well," he said, "I guess that's that. But I do feel relieved, now that it's all over. Ending the streak doesn't mean a thing. That seven-game lead we have over the Indians means a lot more. But that Keltner certainly robbed me of at least one hit. That boy can field them. I couldn't get a good piece of the ball out there. But I don't think the lights had anything to do with it. The whole thing was bound to stop sooner or later and it's just as well it happened that way. There's no point alibi-ing that I'd have had a hit if the game was a day game."

That's what he said, anyway.

But much, much later, after everyone had cleared out of the clubhouse, DiMaggio and Phil Rizzuto were the only ones left, and they started to make the short walk back to the Cleveland Hotel. Rizzuto could see that

DiMaggio had a far-off look in his eyes, a melancholy he would never think to share with anyone. They made small talk.

"You know, Phil," DiMaggio said, "there was a guy from Heinz 57 who told me if I'd gotten one more game of the streak, they'd have sent me a check for ten grand."

Rizzuto didn't know if DiMaggio was kidding or not. These things *were* always happening for Joe; recently, there'd been talk of Camel using Joe's face as the centerpiece of the most ambitious ad ever, a huge billboard in Times Square that would blow smoke rings twenty-four hours a day. But he let Joe speak the whole way back, until a block away DiMaggio spotted a saloon, started to walk in, then turned to Rizzuto.

"You want me to come in with you?" Rizzuto asked.

"No, you go back," DiMaggio said. "I want to be alone."

Phil started to do just that. Then DiMaggio called him again.

"Phil, how much money you have on you?"

Rizzuto figured even the solitary DiMaggio realized he needed some company tonight, he reached into his pocket, studied his money clip. "Eighteen dollars," he said.

"Let me have it, will you? I left my wallet in the safe at the ballpark."

Rizzuto did as he was told. He left the great DiMaggio to a roomful of strangers.

———————●———————

Back in New York, Alan Courtney and Les Brown were just as depressed as every other area baseball fan, but they, at least, had some consolation. They finally had the final verse for their song.

And now they speak in whispers low
Of how they stopped our Joe
One night in Cleveland Oh Oh Oh
Goodbye streak DiMaggio . . .

Joe, Joe, DiMaggio . . .
We want you on our side!

9

"WASN'T IT A PIP?"

TERRIBLE TED, THE SPLENDID SPLINTER, THE KID, AND THE PURSUIT OF .400

Hall of Fame pitcher Grover Cleveland Alexander watches Satchel Paige warm up before a Negro League game at Yankee Stadium on May 11. Years later, Paige's own candidacy to the Hall of Fame would be loudly championed by Ted Williams.

Fast fire engines painted red
Once meant a lot to Red Sox Ted
And once a midnight fourth alarm
Compared to baseball held more charm
But now he's overcome this craze
That he must put out every blaze
Instead he makes all pitchers doubt
That they can even put him out.

—Tim Cohane, *New York World-Telegram,*
June 29, 1941

———————●———————

Right from the start he'd been a real piece of work, a fresh, scrawny kid who didn't know his place and honestly didn't care that he had a rare gift for pissing people off. All Ted Williams knew was that he was worth the trouble, because he could do one thing in this world better than just about any other man. He could hit a baseball. He could hit a fastball, a forkball, a screwball, or a slider. He could clobber a knuckleball, a palmball, a change-up, or a sinker. Could he hit a spitball? Hell, yes, he could hit a spitball. "They tell me it's supposed to be illegal, but there's some balls you see coming at you that'll drench you if you don't hit 'em first," he'd said during his rookie year.

He had a nickname for all occasions. When he first came up, skinny as a stringbean, he was "Kid," and he'd retain that one his whole career, well into his forties when it sounded more ironic than iconic. When the writers wanted to glorify him, he could be "the Splendid Splinter" or "the Thumper" or "the Willowy Walloper" or, later on, "Teddy Ballgame." When they wanted to rip him, he was "Terrible Ted" or "Ted the Tyrant" or "Tempestuous Ted" or any other alliterative cleverness they could come up with on deadline.

Sometimes, he could be several variations at once.

Mostly, in 1940, he'd been a pain in the ass. Oh, he'd had a great season, no one questioned that. In only his second full year, he'd hit .344, good for third in the league. He'd collected 193 hits. He'd led the league in runs (134), led the league in on-base percentage (.442), finished fifth in RBIs (113), fourth in triples (14), fourth in doubles (43). And yet he'd been miserable most of the year. He'd hit only twenty-three home runs, a disappointing enough total that was compounded by the fact that the Red Sox had actually moved the right-field fence at Fenway Park in some twenty-three feet before the season to make their home park more user-friendly for their young lefty-swinging star. Right field was derisively dubbed "Williamsburg."

Williams wasn't happy. And when he wasn't happy, he wasn't afraid to share his opinions. In mid-August, his frustration had bubbled to the surface when he popped off to Austen Lake, a writer for the *Boston Evening American,* saying, "I've asked [Sox owner Tom] Yawkey and [Boston manager Joe] Cronin to trade me away from Boston many times this summer. I don't like the town, I don't like the people, and the newspapermen have been on my ass all year long. You can print the whole rotten mess just as I said it." Then, during a trip to New York to play the Yankees late that season, Williams visited an uncle who was a firefighter in Westchester County, located just north of the Bronx line. The two of them spent most of an off-day at the firehouse, playing checkers and chatting about baseball and fighting fires and the relative adventures available in both professions. It was a glorious day, especially since Ted wasn't hitting all that well, and his frustrations were beginning to simmer, and boil, and a few days later, talking to a wire-service reporter, Ted fondly retold the story of his day at the engine company, and he said, "Now that's the life, being a fireman. It sure beats hell out of being a ballplayer. I'd rather be a fireman."

If Williams had tattooed "Bash Me" on his forehead, he wouldn't have been asking louder for the abuse that followed. When the Red Sox reached Chicago, where the White Sox were stocked with some of the best needlers in the game, led by manager Jimmy Dykes, the more boisterous bench jockeys were waiting for him wearing fire hats and clutching fire bells, and every time Williams walked to the plate they released a screaming siren from the dugout. Wherever he went, he was greeted by mocking opponents yelling from the enemy dugouts, "Fireman, save my child!"

And the press . . . well, they had a lot of fun with this stuff, too.

At first, Williams seethed. But as the memory of 1940 started to dim over the winter, as he lost himself hunting in the wilds of Minnesota and started thinking about what he wanted to accomplish in 1941, he realized something: Maybe it wasn't always the world that was to blame for the fixes he regularly found himself in. Maybe it really *wasn't* the press's fault, or the fans', or the Red Sox front office, or his teammates. Maybe it really *was* something he could change with a slight attitude adjustment. Maybe he really *didn't* have all the answers at the advanced age of twenty-two.

"I'm turning over a new leaf," he announced early in spring training. "The old Ted, you won't see him around these parts any more. I want to start fresh with everybody."

Naturally, someone asked him the obvious question.

"So does this mean the fire department is out, Ted?"

In 1940, Ted Williams might have taken a swing at the smart-ass. In truth, within a few years, Williams almost surely would have, after he'd tired of playing polite games with everyone. But in the spring of 1941, perched on his freshly turned leaf, eager to start anew, Ted was delighted to entertain such an insightful interrogation.

"You don't believe I ever said that in seriousness, do you?" he said, slapping his knee, roaring with laughter. "Not that being a fireman isn't a soft touch. My uncle belongs to the department in Mount Vernon, and as a kid I hung around firehouses back home [in San Diego]. You get a good salary, sit around waiting for something to burn, and after twenty years go on a pension. While this picture is attractive enough, I have loved baseball ever since I was old enough to swing a bat. Funny how that fireman gag keeps following me around. In Chicago one day a dozen firemen showed up at Comiskey Park in uniforms and helmets. They gave me a mock reception. When we showed up at Cooperstown last year they made me an honorary chief of their force."

The boys in the press—the same men he would later bitterly dub the "knights of the keyboard"—gleefully wrote down every syllable. Maybe the Kid really was ready to spend a full year as the Splendid Splinter. Maybe Terrible Ted really *was* dead.

"I can't wait for the season to start," he announced.

Of course, that didn't necessarily mean he was going to show up early for spring training at Sarasota, Florida. Or, for that matter, even on time. Throughout 1940, Williams vowed he would make the Red Sox pay him "real money" in 1941 and predicted he would be a holdout, and when the rest of the Sox began to trickle in to their winter headquarters in the middle of February, no one had yet heard from Williams—not manager Cronin, not general manager Eddie Collins, not owner Yawkey, not any of his teammates. The only sign any of them had that Williams hadn't gone completely underground was during the obligatory draft-number stories that popped up in late January, when the Hank Greenberg fiasco started to fester. Williams's number was 648, which wasn't terribly high, and while one draft board source said it was "highly likely" that Williams would get his call "midway through the summer" and another said it was "most doubtful" that he'd be summoned before mid-1942 at the earliest, a quote attributed to Williams himself said simply, "I am the sole supporter of my mother, and I expect the draft board will want to know that when I fill out my questionnaire."

That was it. Collins mailed Williams a contract for $18,000, a $5,500 increase from Ted's 1940 salary, and while he hadn't received an acceptance yet, he also hadn't received the unsigned contract in the mail, either. The Boston papers renewed the belief that Williams wasn't unhappy with the money but with Boston; there were whispers that he wanted to play in New York, with its outfield dimensions custom-made for a powerful lefty stroke like Williams's, or Detroit, where Teddy had always raked the ball, where they would soon need all the drawing power they could muster with Hank Greenberg on his way to work for Uncle Sam. That was the last thing the city of Boston needed to hear in the middle of this February, for although the National Hockey League Bruins were in the midst of a league-record twenty-three-game unbeaten streak (and would win the Stanley Cup a few months later), the city's sporting self-image was at an all-time low. The Red Sox hadn't won a pennant in twenty-three years, the Braves in twenty-seven. The National Football League, growing in popularity by the year, kept refusing to plant a franchise in a city that had lost the Redskins to Washington following the 1935 season. Worst of all, on February 14, after days of denying he was even interested in the job, football coach Frank Leahy had abandoned Boston College after one year to bolt for Notre Dame, his alma mater, a devastating blow to one of the city's marquee sporting programs.

Now Williams wanted out, too?

On the last day of February, a distressed and clearly annoyed Cronin reported after a morning workout, "Yes, sure enough, Williams is not here. We will carry on without him. I cannot tell you a thing about Williams because I don't know anything. My last information was that Teddy and Eddie Collins had started a one-sided correspondence and that the last shot was fired by our business manager. I also believe this was some weeks ago."

Within hours, though, Williams finally resurfaced, distressed that all his careful image-building had apparently taken a broadside hit. He wasn't playing games, he said, he'd simply lost track of the days while he was off hunting wolves in Minnesota.

"I am not a holdout," he told an Associated Press reporter who reached him in Princeton, Minnesota. "I expect to sign up at any time now. Chances are I'll be heading for Sarasota the first of next week. The Red Sox and I haven't agreed yet on the size of the paycheck but we will. I expect to get in touch with Collins soon, maybe tonight."

Surprisingly, that really was all there was to the story. Williams and Collins talked about the contract for about five minutes, Ted said he'd sign it and bring it with him to Florida, he'd play for eighteen grand and do it with a smile, and Collins said that would be fine with him. When Williams finally showed up at camp on March 8, he was still effervescent, still bubbly, still vowing to keep his leaf properly turned.

"What a ride!" he exclaimed. "I thought I'd never get here. I'm glad the club's in Miami because I feel in the mood for some batting practice. I haven't had a bat in my hands all winter, nor a ball either."

"Ted," someone asked. "What about your contract?"

"I am perfectly satisfied and am well pleased to get back to work," he said. "You may be sure I will do my best to show my appreciation and that's all I can do."

The writers looked at each other. Was this for real? They watched Williams run out to a back field, where pitchers Johnny Wilson and Lefty

Grove agreed to throw him batting practice. Even as a rookie Ted had never looked this eager. Wilson threw for fifteen minutes, and Grove for fifteen minutes, and Williams sprayed line drives all over the field, ball after ball, bucket after bucket, and when Grove finally walked off the mound with his arm hanging, Williams roared, "Come on, one more! One more!"

"Kid," Grove snorted. "I'm forty years old. Let's see how much vim and vinegar *you* got left when you're forty."

He was like that all week. One morning he actually shook hands with each writer and told them, "I want to officially bury the hatchet and start over with every one of you, is that a deal?" He took batting practice until his hands bled, then took outfield practice even though he'd said more than once, "I don't give a shit about playing defense, I really don't, just let me swing the fuckin' bat." By March 12 he was itching for game action, and Cronin told him he'd be in the lineup the next day against the Reds, so in the meantime he continued to regale the writers with tales of his winter exploits in the Minnesota woods ("The hunters up there are so good, they get tired of shooting ducks and pheasants, so they go after wolves instead and the state pays them a bounty for each one. That's *serious* hunting.") and for the first time gave an indirect hint that one of his goals was to join the elite club of six men who'd hit .400 in the modern era: Rogers Hornsby (three times), Ty Cobb (twice), George Sisler (twice), Nap Lajoie, Harry Heilmann (the last American Leaguer to do it, in 1923), and Bill Terry (the last man in either league to get there, in 1930).

"Gee, I wish I could hit the ball like Hugh Duffy did," Williams said, referring to the nineteenth-century outfielder who'd hit .440 for the Boston Beaneaters in 1894 (benefiting from a rule change that counted walks as hits), still the highest average in baseball history. "I'd rather play ball than eat, sleep or hunt. The fans want a ballplayer to give everything he has. That's my aim not only this year but every year. That's my greeting to Boston baseball fans."

For all his polite promises and ambitions, the 1941 season's greeting to Williams would be a tad rude. It started in that very first exhibition appearance against the Reds, when he chased a fly ball off the bat of Harry Craft all the way to the left-field fence and stepped in a gulley at the base of the wall. His ankle screamed in pain and he crumpled to the ground; it was diagnosed as a slight sprain and he remained in the game and tried to walk it off. He was shaken, but okay. Two days later he connected for his first hit of the spring, a triple that, he admitted, "would have been an inside-the-parker if I had a full set of feet under me. But I will soon."

No, he wouldn't. On March 19 the Red Sox were playing the Newark Bears, a Yankees' affiliate, and Williams was on first base in the third inning when Cronin flashed a hit-and-run signal. Al Flair, the hitter, swung and missed, and Ted tried to hurry his stride to second ahead of the catcher's throw, but in his haste he caught his spikes in the clay soil just as he started his slide. He never did reach the bag and was tagged out a full three feet shy of second base, not giving even one good goddamn about it because it felt like his right foot had been ripped off. Trainer Win Green looked at the swollen ankle and decided it wasn't anything that some tape, some ice, and some hot compresses couldn't solve—"He should be all right to resume play within a very few days," he said—but Cronin decided he'd take it slowly with his best player. He wouldn't bring him to Havana for the Red Sox–Cuban exhibition series; instead, he'd allow him to recuperate fully with Louisville, the Red Sox's top farm club.

"It's better to get those ankles thoroughly rested and cured before you give them any business pressure, and I don't intend to handicap Williams further by making him play before the ankle ceases to bother him," Cronin said. "To do so might give him a really bad charley horse. He tells me the ankle is much better today but he's not going to Havana, where I understand the playing surface is quite hard."

So Williams's days were filled with batting practice and little else, which would normally have been nothing short of paradise for him. But the ankle wouldn't let him enjoy himself. It kept barking at him, wouldn't heal properly, wouldn't respond to treatments. Williams was worried. He'd twisted his ankle before, sprained it before, and it hurt like hell, sometimes worse than this, but this was a different kind of pain. When the Sox returned from Cuba, he tried pinch-hitting a couple of times but still didn't feel right, and by the first of April, with the ankle still causing him misery, Yawkey decided to take matters into his own hands.

The owner's brother-in-law, Dr. L. E. Sorrell, operated Norwood Hospital in Birmingham, Alabama, which is where the Sox happened to be on April 5 as they made their way north after breaking camp at Sarasota. It was there that X rays revealed the dreadful news that Williams actually had a broken ankle and would probably be lost to the Red Sox for a month, maybe more, depending on what Sox team doctor T. K. Richards thought once he was able to examine Williams's foot back home in Boston. Sorrell said the injury could have been a lot worse but there was no displacement, just a small separation in one of the small bones beneath the large bone of the right ankle. He wouldn't need a cast and he wouldn't need crutches, but Williams nearly did need a straitjacket when he first heard the initial diagnosis, especially since that very afternoon, taking batting practice at Rickwood Park, he had hit five straight home runs, two of them estimated to be the longest balls ever hit within the Birmingham city limits. How could he be *that* hurt and hit a baseball *that* hard?

"Four or six weeks is bullshit," Williams said, standing on the ankle in the lobby of Birmingham's Tutwiler Hotel, practicing his swing with a rolled-up newspaper. "I'll be back in there in a couple of weeks. At least I hope so. I had hoped the ankle would improve steadily. It doesn't hurt when I walk or stand or even when I hit and pivot. But when I twist the ankle around it catches me a bit, not much, and it's uncomfortable. And the muscles of my lower leg are sore, but they tell me that's the natural result of trying to favor the ankle. Bet you Dr. Richards will have me back in there in ten days or a couple of weeks, tops."

By now, all of Boston had been swept up in the calamity of the Kid's bad wheel, and so when Williams's train arrived at Back Bay Station at seven o'clock on the evening of April 7, a thick crowd of well-wishers and curiosity seekers greeted him as he stepped off the *Colonial Express*. Mobbed by fans, by media, by Red Sox office workers, Williams said, "The ankle doesn't bother me when I hit, it's only when I run. I can't run on the damn thing. You can see I'm walking now with practically no limp and I haven't even got a hunk of adhesive tape on the ankle. I saw the X-ray pictures myself. The chip isn't any bigger than a half a pea."

Dr. Richards examined Ted the next day and nearly got a standing ovation himself when he declared that the ankle seemed to be mending nicely and should be fully healed in a week's time, which just so happened to be Opening Day for the Red Sox, at home against the Senators. But the good doctor turned out to be too much of an optimist; each day Williams would rise, he would shake out the ankle, he would get taped, and he would take a full round of batting practice, and all would be well with the ankle. And then he would try to run on it, and the pain would reach up and bite him. Williams sullenly announced he'd have to sit out the opener, saying, "I've never before wanted to play all 154 games more than I do this year."

Privately, however, he wasn't broken up. At one point he confided to Dominic DiMaggio, "Dommie, you know I'm never worth an ounce of shit when the weather's cold. Maybe this way I can start out on fire for a change."

He did have a moment, though, a happy harbinger of what the summer would hold for him once he got healthy. The Sox went into the bottom of the ninth on Opening Day trailing the Senators 6-4, when Frank Pytlak led off with a double off the left-centerfield wall. The sun was already gone, it was past six o'clock, and many of the 17,500 who'd watched the game had started to inch toward the exits, but Pytlak's hit stopped them cold in their tracks; the next thing they saw made them scramble back to their seats as quickly as they could. For here came Ted Williams, sauntering to the on-deck circle—*Is he limping?* the people asked. *Does he look hurt?*—and he dug into the batter's box. Sidney Hudson's first pitch was wild and in the dirt, allowing Pytlak to move up to third. The next pitch was straight and true and fat and inviting, and Williams clobbered it to right field, an RBI single that drew the Sox to within 6-5, and the fans were in a frenzy. Ted eased slowly into first, gave way to pinch-runner Tommy Carey, and ducked into the dugout with cheers still ringing in his ears.

"That guy," teammate Jim Tabor marveled later, "could hit with one leg cut off."

"My legs aren't so good," Williams said. "But the eye still works."

The Red Sox rallied and won the game. The next day's papers were all about Ted Williams. Life was good. And about to get much, much better for the Splendid Splinter, Ted the Terrible no more.

———————•———————

From the beginning, there was a distance to the violence in the Pacific that made it seem surreal, unrelated to the rest of the world. In 1941 it was still possible to believe that the Empire of Japan existed on another planet, in another realm, frightening in its philosophies and mad, perhaps, in its methods, but detached from the United States in a way that the dictators of Europe could never be again. So it was with relative indifference that a veteran diplomat named Yosuke Matsuoka initiated a fateful world tour in the spring of 1941 that would quietly edge the world closer to the familiar infernos of war.

Japan had fought on the side of the angels in the Great War, declaring war on Germany on August 23, 1914, but its interests in the conflict had little to do with the principles for which thousands of Allied soldiers were falling in the forests of France and the trenches of the Western Front and far more to do with its own growing international profile. Japan had emerged within the last quarter century as a military force to be reckoned with, defeating its Asiatic neighbors in Russia and China in separate wars and steadily increasing both its boundaries and its ambitions. Japan acquired formerly German holdings in Micronesia following the Great War, won a spot sitting among the Big Five Powers at the Treaty of Versailles Conference, and set its sights on dominating its quiet corner of the world once the rest of the world retreated safely within its borders.

Yet while the other Allies were content to breathe deeply and forswear the mere thought of spilling more blood, Japan continued to flex its muscles. With little resistance, Japan invaded Manchuria in 1931, and Jehol, a Chinese territory bordering Manchuria, two years later. All of this was mere prelude to 1937, when Japan officially set its eyes on its most coveted prize, China, hoping to seize on the split between Chiang Kai-shek's Nationalists and Mao Tse-tung's Communists. When Japan successfully captured Nanking, the Nationalist capital, its soldiers killed some three hundred thousand people in the process, mostly civilians.

If these rapid bursts of expansion failed to incite the passions of the American public at large, especially since the atrocities taking place on the European continent seemed so much more imminent, and relevant, they certainly gained the attention of Franklin Roosevelt, who understood that allowing a belligerent nation to rampage unchecked in Asia would be suicidal to America's own self-interest. It was obvious that Japan was no longer interested in maintaining even the tenuous shared philosophies that had allowed the two nations to fight on the same side of the Great War just twenty years earlier; nothing emphasized this more than when Japan signed the Tripartite Pact in Berlin on September 27, 1940, formalizing its alliance with Germany and Italy, and essentially sending a message directly to Roosevelt: Either maintain America's neutrality or suffer the consequences of a two-front war.

From that moment, Roosevelt understood that the possibility of remaining completely nonaligned was growing slimmer and slimmer by the day. He eyed warily Matsuoka's tour of his partner countries. Matsuoka, sixty-one, had been named Japan's foreign minister in 1940, capping a long and meritorious rise through Japan's diplomatic corps. In 1893, at age thirteen, he had been sent to live with relatives in the United States, then graduated from the University of Oregon in 1900. He was as well versed as anyone in Japan about American values and mores, and was well tuned in to American attitudes toward joining another world war. Upon his arrival in Berlin on March 26, he was given a hero's reception and granted a two-and-a-half-hour meeting with Hitler, to whom he wished a speedy victory and said, "The Japanese nation is with you in joy or in sorrow, and it will not lag behind you in fidelity, courage and firm determination to arrange the world on the basis of the new order. We must live in the future, not in the past."

In Rome four days later, Matsuoka insisted his visit was to "exchange greetings," and not to make war commitments, insisting, "I would like very much to go to the United States, but my time will not permit it." He met with Mussolini, and then with Pope Pius in Vatican City, and then headed off to Russia, which was still six weeks away from watching the German army overrun its borders and so was still very much interested in signing a neutrality pact with Japan, hoping to hedge its bets. It was in Moscow, on April 22, when Matsuoka first strayed from his relentlessly bland rhetoric with regard to the United States and hinted at his country's true agenda.

"As I understand it," he said, "America considers herself the champion of world peace. If that is so, and if America looks to deeds and not words, she should have no objection to Japan's course. And if she understands Japan's real intentions, she will applaud what Japan has done."

Asked if he entertained any plan for negotiating with the United States, he said, "I have no idea," but added: "Japan earnestly wishes to contribute to the welfare of mankind and to the preservation of world peace. But if there are people or countries who purposely close their eyes to the real intentions of Japan, it is impossible to talk with them."

Then he repaired to Stalin's study, where the two men shared a bottle of vodka.

———————●———————

That same day, in Boston, news accounts of the Matsuoka-Stalin summit were buried deep beneath bold headlines announcing a little good news for a change: Ted Williams would finally be in the starting lineup, at Washington's Griffith Stadium. After his Opening Day heroics, Williams had appeared as a pinch-hitter in four other games, scratching out one hit (meaning that he started the season 2-for-5, a .400 clip), and the Sox had broken well, winning their first five games, matching their fastest start in twenty-one years. They knew they couldn't maintain anywhere near that pace without their best hitter, and Williams knew it, too, but he also couldn't will the pain out of his foot. He expected to remain a pinch-hitter for a little while longer, but when Pete Fox wound up in a dentist's chair with an ulcerated tooth, Williams grabbed a glove and limped out to left field. He was painful to watch. Twice he failed to reach catchable balls, and once he ended a rally when he was unable to leg out a base hit on a slow-rolling ball up the third-base line, but he did add a double and a single (maybe he really *could* hit with one of his legs cut off) and announced, "I've never felt more comfortable with a bat in my hands than I do right now. Once I get the damned foot taken care of, I can't wait to see what I can do. I just don't know how long that'll be."

It turned out to be six days. On an off-day in Boston before heading to Detroit (his favorite road venue in the whole American League), with Cronin watching his every move for a limp, for a wince, for a sign of weakness, Williams ran, he did sliding drills, he took fungos in the outfield and then he took a half hour of batting practice, and it was a jubilant Cronin who announced, "The Kid'll be in there tomorrow in left field. Judging by the way Williams hit and ran and even slid into bases at Fenway Park this noon, I'm thinking he'll be a real addition to our ball club. Today's the first time since he was hurt in Sarasota that he tried sliding again and it didn't hurt him and he showed no limp."

Williams celebrated his return to the lineup with a double and a home run into the upper deck at Briggs Stadium, and over the course of the next two weeks he finally eased his way into the rhythms of the baseball season. He kept tabs on Joe DiMaggio through the newspapers and through his friend Dominic, noticing Joe's red-hot start as well as the elongated funk that started to shrink his batting average practically in half. Williams had always stated that his life's ambition was to be able to walk down a street anywhere in the country and hear people whisper, "There goes the best damned hitter who ever lived," but he knew that at this stage in their careers, if Ted and Joe walked down that street together, nobody would be whispering Williams's name.

Still, he hadn't changed his mind: He *was* feeling as good as he'd ever felt before at the plate, he was seeing the ball great, he was swinging the bat well. His batting average really wasn't reflecting that; after going 0-for-5 against the White Sox on May 14, he was down to a season-low .339, but even that didn't worry him that much. He was still hitting the ball hard, he was just hitting into bad luck. Eventually, he figured, he'd start finding holes.

The next day, he started finding them. It was only a single off the Indians' Al Milnar, his lone hit in three at-bats in a 6-4 loss, and there was no way of knowing how significant that was, or how meaningful it would also turn out to be that 250 miles away, at Yankee Stadium, Joe DiMaggio would line an RBI single in the bottom of the first inning off the White Sox's Eddie Smith. To that point, May 15, 1941, the baseball season had belonged to Bob Feller, who had already won six games and looked like a good bet to reach thirty; to Pvt. Hank Greenberg, who'd bid farewell to baseball with two home runs against the Yankees; even to the ragtag Brooklyn Dodgers, lovable losers no more, who, sparked by fiery manager Leo Durocher and fireplug catcher Mickey Owen, actually looked like pennant contenders for a change. From that moment forward, however, all those other stories faded into background music. From May 15 through the end of September, and on through the limitless corridors of time and memory, 1941 would be about two men only. Both of whom started hitting that day and, for all practical purposes, never stopped.

It took a while for people to pair them up. DiMaggio seemed to get only a hit a day, Williams two and three and four of them at a time. Suddenly all those balls he'd hit right at people were finding wide swatches of grass, or bouncing off outfield walls, or clearing those walls altogether. On May 24, when they faced off against one another in front of twenty-one thousand people at Yankee Stadium, both hitting streaks reached ten. DiMaggio's one hit was a two-run single off Earl Johnson that capped a four-run rally in the seventh inning, nudging his average to .318, while Williams socked two hits off Lefty Gomez (including an infield single, one of only five "leg hits" he would collect all season), inflating his average to .381. The next day, while DiMaggio dutifully scratched out a single, Williams went 4-for-5, sending his batting average soaring over the magic barrier to .404, inspiring the next morning's *Boston Herald* to run a three-picture montage of the Thumper, with the caption: "The .404 eyes, swing and grip of Ted Williams are presented today, for yesterday the Red Sox outfielder collected three singles and one double against the Yankees to send his batting average over the charmed .400 mark."

It was a rarefied piece of real estate Williams now occupied, and he enjoyed the neighborhood immensely, and he was determined to stay there awhile. In the four games after reaching .400, he went 11-for-20, fattening the average even more, to .424. Four more hits in a June 1 doubleheader against the Tigers and it climbed to .430. By June 7 the number was .431, the hitting streak was at twenty-three games (in which he'd hit .481; that same day, DiMaggio's streak reached twenty-two, and during *his* hot stretch his average was a mere .368), and Ted had to admit that as optimistic as he'd been when he reported to Sarasota, the season had thus far exceeded even his craziest fantasies.

"They used to say I was a handful," Williams told a small group of writers that afternoon. "I'll admit I had a lousy attitude. But I don't think I deserved all they wrote about me, even though I have to admit the start of it all was probably my fault. When they moved right field closer in Fenway Park, I really got it bad in Boston. Everyone thought I'd hit eighty homers and I guess I thought I would, too. When I only hit twenty-three last season, I got mad about it myself. And a few of the boys got sore at me.

"Boy, it got so bad I hated to go out and meet people. But when I did a lot of them would say, 'You aren't as bad as I thought you were.' But that's all over now. I'm just trying to get along. It's a dream I've always had—the way I'm hitting now. Boy, I'm just busting the cover off the ball. I'm lucky because a lot of my drives are going where they ain't. And hell, it's only June. I may be down to .360 in another month."

He didn't really believe that, though. Even after the White Sox's Ted Lyons and Thornton Lee combined to keep Williams hitless in a doubleheader on June 8, finally ending the streak at twenty-three (on the same day DiMaggio went 4-for-8 in a doubleheader against the Browns, reaching games twenty-three and twenty-four), he kept hitting: 2-for-7 in a doubleheader against the Browns; 7-for-11 in a three-game series against the White Sox, whose manager, Jimmy Dykes, was beside himself at how easy Ted Williams made the act of hitting a baseball look, and who'd stopped needling the erstwhile firehouse apprentice and started fretting over how to get him out.

"Why, that fellow's hardly human up there at bat, there's no question of what you ought to do to him in a close game: Just walk him no matter what the conditions are regarding men on base," said Dykes, who in a few weeks would invent a more original plan to try to muffle his bat. "He's murder out there. He whacked a 3-and-2 pitch that was as hard as any ball I've ever seen hit. That Williams is one of the great hitters of all time, all right. What wrist action! What an eye! You never see him get out of form by making a lunge after a bad pitch. He makes the pitcher come in there, over the plate, and of course that makes his hitting work easier.

"How about his disposition? Well, you must remember that he's hitting like a couple of furies right now, and the test of his disposition is whether he still can laugh and be genial when his hits aren't coming so regularly. If he hits a slump he may drop back and become unreasonable."

But as the days passed, it started to look as though Williams might well be slump-proof. Oh, he'd take the occasional collar, but even then he was getting his money's worth with his hacks, and he was mystifying opposing managers and coaches. How do you pitch to a guy like this? "All you can do is pitch low and inside to him," Tigers coach Bing Miller reasoned, "and hope he'll pull the ball foul." Even the pain that started to resurface in Williams's ankle couldn't halt him; scheduled to take a follow-up X-ray toward the end of June, Williams never showed up, figuring, "All they'll tell me is bad news, and I don't need to hear any bad news."

It was at this point of the summer that Williams's pursuit became something of a lonely mission. June's hectic sporting landscape was one reason. But even once Whirlaway dashed off with the Triple Crown, even after Joe Louis and Billy Conn ended their epic battle, Williams became something of a forgotten man thanks to his closest rival. By the end of June, DiMaggio's hitting streak had already entwined itself in the national conscience, had become a national obsession, and there simply wasn't room in most imaginations to ponder Ted's daily brushes with excellence, too. There were two reasons for this. For one, DiMaggio's streak was unique, promising to take baseball to a place it had possibly never seen before, while six other men had already reached .400 for a season. But there was something else, too. At a time when selflessness had become the quintessential American value, DiMaggio's daily feats embodied that principle to its core. Hadn't the Yankees turned their season around by rallying behind the Clipper? Weren't they steaming toward first place now? And wasn't that the ultimate goal? The Red Sox, meanwhile, had failed to put Williams's heroics to similar good use, and as amazing as Ted's offensive feats were, he was performing them in a vacuum. Incredibly, during the first 16 games of his 23-game hitting steak, the Red Sox went 5-10 with a tie, tumbling into sixth place. What did that tell you?

Williams didn't let these questions flummox him, he simply immersed himself in hitting. He sought out Hugh Duffy, he of that .440 batting average in 1894, now seventy-four and still coaching for the Red Sox, a regular reminder of the impossible standards Williams set for himself.

"I think he has a wonderful chance to top my record," Duffy said. "I can say this about Teddy—I have never seen a better hitter than Williams in all my life, and that goes for Cobb, Ruth, Hornsby, and all the rest. The boys have been kidding him about my record, and Teddy comes to me quite often for a checkup, but there's little I can tell him about it. I have one bit of advice and that is not to start thinking about making any records because the minute you do, you tighten up and lose rhythm in your swing. That's one thing Teddy has, wonderful rhythm.

"You've got to be lucky. The year before I hit .440, I had an average of something like .380 [actually .362], and I'm sure that I hit the ball better that year than the next one when I made the record. I tell that to some people and they think I'm daffy, but honest, it's the truth. All Teddy has to do is to keep swinging in that lazy natural way of his and he'll hit a million. I hope he doesn't start to think that he's in a slump. That's when you begin to slump, when you start worrying about it. You have to be relaxed at all times up at the plate, and you can't be if you have something on your mind that you shouldn't be thinking of."

Williams had other obstacles Duffy didn't have to worry about. Not only did he have to deal with modern fixes to the rules—walks no longer counted as hits, foul balls now *did* count as strikes—he was playing at a unique time in the history of the sacrifice fly rule, in which a runner on third base was permitted to "tag up" and score following a fly ball out to an outfielder. From 1908 until 1931, and then again in 1939, a hitter credited with a sac fly wasn't charged with a time at-bat, in the same way a hitter who gave himself up via sacrifice bunt wasn't charged with one. But starting in 1940, and extending until 1954, that little hitter's boon was eliminated. A sac fly counted as a regular out. For a fly-ball hitter like Ted

Williams, there's no telling how many batting average points that cost him. Joe Cronin always figured Ted had "at least twelve, maybe fifteen of them" in 1941.

That would be an issue only, however, if Ted fell short of .400. And as baseball cruised into the All-Star break, that didn't seem likely. He'd make it to Detroit for the midsummer classic hitting .405, still overshadowed by DiMaggio and his Streak (which now sat at forty-eight), but comfortable with his own splendid summer. He made little secret of his second-half ambitions. "I admit it," he said, "I love to hit. One of these years I aim to finish over .400. After all, I'm only twenty-three now and I ought to have a lot of chances before I'm done. I'm looking forward to the All-Star Game. Only the best of the best are allowed to play in it. It's an honor to be in that group."

———————●———————

Twenty-five summers later, fortified by the twin blessings of age and perspective, an older, wiser Ted Williams would acknowledge just how naïve those sentiments were, that for all the star power that All-Star Game might have possessed, there was an entire segment of the population that went unrepresented in Detroit, where the "best of the best" were also the whitest of the white. On July 25, 1966, on the steps of the Baseball Hall of Fame at Cooperstown, New York, Ted Williams would acknowledge that cheerless truth, delivering one of the most eloquent, unforgettable induction speeches the Hall has ever heard, the cornerstone of which was this:

"Baseball gives every American boy a chance to excel," Williams said. "Not just to be as good as anybody else, but to be better. This is the nature of man and the name of the game. I hope someday Satchel Paige and Josh Gibson will be voted into the Hall of Fame as symbols of the great Negro players who are not here only because they weren't given the chance."

In 1941, this was a subject that white baseball players never touched, mostly because it was a subject that was rarely mentioned by anyone with whom they would interact in their daily baseball lives: white owners, white general managers, white managers, white sportswriters. In 1941, facts were facts: Major League Baseball was a stubborn bastion of Caucasian faces, as were all of the affiliates linked to those sixteen big-league ballclubs. It had been that way since the turn of the century. It would remain that way for six more years. Sometimes, the simplest way to rationalize the treatment of African Americans in those years is to falsely label it a product of "Jim Crow America," and while it's true that segregation in the Deep South was as pronounced in the early 1940s as it ever had been, and would remain that way for the better part of another quarter century, Major League Baseball had no regional excuse to fall back on.

Fifteen of the sixteen clubs played north of the Mason-Dixon Line. There were two teams in Philadelphia, two in Boston, three in New York City, all three cities bastions of New Deal liberalism. There were two teams in Chicago, a more conservative town than the others but still vibrant with black faces, black culture, and black athletes who shared athletic fields with whites at almost every other level. There was one team in Detroit and one in Pittsburgh and one in Cleveland, cities of blue-collar opportunity that had each drawn thousands of migrating African Americans from the South in search of jobs in factories and plants and mills. The troublesome spots were in St. Louis, whose geography insisted it was Midwestern but whose mores were very much Southern; Cincinnati, located just across the river from Kentucky; and Washington, the one truly Southern town in baseball that remained very much a segregated city in 1941.

White players barnstormed with black players all the time in the offseason, and it was during these hastily formed alliances that the game's white stars had their eyes opened to the vast injustices the system perpetuated. That's where Williams first laid eyes on Paige, perhaps the greatest pitcher ever born; and on Josh Gibson, the only man, white or black, who ever hit a fair ball completely out of Yankee Stadium; and on Cool Papa Bell, maybe the fastest man to ever play baseball; and on Buck Leonard, maybe the most complete player anywhere on the planet. Joe DiMaggio saw the same things. Bob Feller, young and brash, wasn't afraid to proclaim after one barnstorming season, "If Satchel Paige played in the American League, he'd win thirty games." But few listened. Mostly, white America justified the separation of white baseball and black baseball by simply dismissing the quality of the "shadowball," saying most black players would be lucky to be competitive in the Double-A minors.

This ran contrary to what people saw with their own eyes, of course, and the summer of 1941 was when those eyes began to open ever wider to the truth of this. White America may have celebrated the gathering of National League and American League All-Stars in Detroit on July 8, but there were

fifty-two thousand people who crammed into every nook, cranny, and cre-
vasse of Chicago's Comiskey Park on the scorching-hot afternoon of July
27 to watch the ninth-annual East-West Classic, the Negro Leagues' all-star
game. Count Basie had written a song called the "Goin' to Chicago Blues,"
and a singer named Jimmy Rushing had a hit with it that summer, and that
tune was on the lips of just about everyone packed inside the stadium that
day, or staying back at the Grand Hotel, where most of the ballplayers were
lodged, a welcome first-class accommodation for men accustomed to dealing with much less. Ella Fitzgerald was at the Grand, and at the game. So
was Billie Holiday. So was just about every recognizable black face in the
United States, and if they weren't at the ballpark, or at the hotel, they were
in one of the dozens of jazz and blues clubs that covered downtown
Chicago like dust.

"You didn't go to Chicago to sleep," Monte Irvin, a young ballplayer for
the Newark Eagles playing in his first Classic that July, would write sixty
years later. "I found out later that the big-league All-Star Game wasn't
nearly as much fun."

Irvin had been a four-sport star at East Orange High School, probably
the finest athlete ever produced in the state of New Jersey. One day in 1938,
unbeknownst to him, the owner of the New York Giants, Horace Stoneham, had sent one of his scouts to watch him play baseball, after one of
Irvin's teachers had told Stoneham, "We have a player here you have to see
to believe." The scout agreed completely with that raw assessment. On a
form that only Stoneham's eyes would ever see, he had written, "Could be
the next Joe DiMaggio" and "Could be one of the greatest players I've ever
seen." Years later, long after Irvin had finally joined the Giants (at age thirty,
in 1949), won a World Series there, and moved on to a career in the commissioner's office (and a spot in Cooperstown, inducted in 1973), long after Stoneham had moved the Giants to San Francisco, Stoneham shared
that story with Irvin.

"What did you tell the scout?" Irvin asked.

"I said it was too soon," Stoneham said, sadly dropping his head. "I wish
I'd been braver than that."

It was in 1941, at age twenty-two, that Monte Irvin fully blossomed into
the most remarkable, and busiest, player in all of baseball. Buck O'Neil, the
unofficial poet laureate of the Negro Leagues, would describe Irvin in later
years in a simple but eloquent way—"He was Willie Mays before Willie

Mays"—and that was never truer than in this summer. A year earlier he'd hit a gaudy .422 (explained away by the white press as being a by-product "of inferior Negro pitching"), and he followed that by hitting .386 with forty homers in '41, winning most valuable player honors, and defiantly jumping the Eagles in a salary dispute at season's end. He landed in Mexico, where he simply kept cruising, winning the Mexican League's Triple Crown, hitting .398 with thirty-eight homers in sixty games before the army finally summoned him.

He was wide-eyed in Chicago the day of the East-West Classic, taking in everything, taking mental snapshots that would last a lifetime. The stands were covered with red, white, and blue banners. Jazz bands entertained the crowd between innings, but it was the great Satchel Paige, who was at least thirty-five years old that summer, if not closer to forty, who entertained the players before the game.

"Fellas," Paige crowed, "the East-West Game belongs to me. I don't have to pitch but two or three innings, so I'm gonna be very stingy today. In fact, I'm givin' up nothin'! When I get around to the Grand Hotel tonight, I'll buy you all a beer. But today, nothin'! Zero!"

Paige was true to his word, too, as he usually was. By the time Paige entered the game for the West in the eighth inning, his team was already behind by seven runs, but that didn't matter to the fans, many of whom climbed over the lower railings so they could point their Kodaks at the great pitcher. Paige, ever the patient showman, waited until everyone had their shots, he doffed his cap, and he went to work. Paige's reputation preceded him, and some of the younger players had never actually faced him in person. East first baseman Lennie Pearson, for instance, took three straight strikes and returned to the dugout, looking like a man who'd just cheated an executioner.

"Len," Irvin asked, "what kind of stuff does he have?"

"I don't know," Pearson said. "I didn't see it."

"He was telling the truth," Irvin recalled years later. "Satch was throwing so hard you could hardly see the ball."

Even the white press couldn't explain Paige's dominance away as the by-product of inferior Negro hitting, however. Engaging, nonthreatening, and given the stamp of approval by most of America's great white stars, Satch was featured in a two-page *Life* magazine spread in May, photographs of Paige pitching in Yankee Stadium with some jarringly frank observations:

"Barred from organized professional baseball because he is a Negro, Paige has played against many of the major-league stars in exhibition games. According to them he has more than proved his ability to play in the big leagues. He won four out of six games from Dizzy Dean in a series and Joe DiMaggio says Paige is the greatest pitcher he has ever batted against."

When Paige returned to New York in July, as a member of the Kansas City Monarchs, it was a big enough event to draw nearly thirty thousand fans of all colors, creeds, and rooting interests to the Stadium to watch the Monarchs play the New York Cuban Stars. Only two of the city's two hundred or so sportswriters saw fit to attend, however. One was the iconoclastic Stanley Frank of the *New York Post,* a longtime baseball writer and newly christened columnist who was never afraid to wander contrary to the public tide. Three years later, in the heady months after D-day, Frank would be one of four journalists expelled from France by the 9th Air Force's public relations chief, Col. Robert Parham (who'd worked for United Press prior to the war), for writing news articles and human interest stories other than the PR pap the army wanted written about the 9th. For now, he was content with challenging his fellow baseball partisans to take advantage of the treat that would soon be in their midst.

"One of the greatest pitchers of our time performs in the Yankee Stadium tomorrow," Frank wrote on July 19. "The natural artist—that's the word—in question is not Charley Ruffing, who will be engaged in Detroit, or Bob Feller, who has previous commitments in Cleveland. Their professional peer is Satchel Paige. The name doesn't register, perhaps. Because not one baseball fan in a thousand has ever seen Satchel pitch, and more's the pity.

"Satchel Paige is a Negro, but the little white ball draws no color line in the hands of an artist. It will take off like something shot from a gun and it will dip and swerve for a Negro as artfully as it ever did for a white man. These things, and more, it does for Satchel Paige, as great a pitcher as baseball has seen in the last decade. The trouble is, organized baseball hasn't seen him."

Frank asked Paige, "What would a team of Negro Leaguers do if they were allowed to sub for the Phillies or the Browns?"

"We'd win or finish second every year."

"And how many games would *you* win?"

"Well," Paige said, stroking his chin, "I could start twice a week and re-lieve two other times a week. I figure thirty-five, give or take a few."

Not everyone was as convinced as Frank. Nationally syndicated colum-nist Bob Considine, to his credit, was the only recognizable writer who not only went to see Paige pitch the next day, but also descended to the club-house after the fifth inning when Satch, pitching a one-hitter, had to leave the game after being hit by a pitch. Considine was considered one of the more progressive journalists at the time, but even he was not immune to falling lazily into prevalent racial stereotypes of the day. Just a week earlier, in a column, he'd written about Joe Louis's "double-barrel shotgun nose," and he was one of many white writers who liked to phonetically spell Louis quotes so that they took on a demeaning Step'n Fetchit quality, such as turning the sentence "I sure asked him to" into "I sho' axed him to." Con-sidine caught Paige in an especially chatty—and catty—mood.

"I can't even guess how many games I pitched in my life. I've been mak-ing my living from this game since I was fifteen or sixteen. One of them fel-lows who didn't want to follow me today, and made me pitch another inning, he ain't pitched in four days. Man, I ain't had four days rest since I been playing baseball. I figure I pitch about 125 games a year, summer and winter. I've had sore arms before, plenty of them, but I never do anything about them. We don't carry no trainer with us, nobody to baby us like those big league fellows got. We rub each others arms when they're sore, and pour hot water on sore arms. We don't get no babying. We work, drive in a car all night and work the next day. And play more baseball in two days than those big league fellows play in a month."

Considine said, "What about playing in the white leagues? I think you could have made it about five years ago, but not anymore."

Now he had Paige's attention.

"If the Jim Crow law in baseball say 'No Colored boys playing on white teams,' I think there ought to be a full Colored team in each big league," he snapped. "Don't think they wouldn't show those boys some serious base-ball, too. We could get up one great team, I know that for sure." Paige men-tioned a few contemporary names, then said, "And I'll tell you what, Cool Papa Bell is even older than me, but he could still play with those white boys."

"Bell?" Considine asked. "I've never heard of him."

Paige shook his head sadly. This was the world he had lived in his whole life, a world where one of the best-known white sports columnists had never even heard of one of the best-known black baseball players, and in July 1941 there was no reason to believe it would change anytime soon.

———————————●———————————

Ted Williams knew he would drown if he tried to rail against all the attention Joe DiMaggio was getting. It was a war he'd never win. So he joined the loyal opposition early in his career and never really wavered. "I'm lucky to be playing against two of the great ballplayers of all time. DiMaggio is the greatest hitter I ever saw and probably will see during my career. And Feller is the best pitcher. I have to tie into a pitch to get power. DiMaggio is stronger. He hits the ball hard in any direction. And then there's the matter of temperament. I've been down on myself, but I never heard of Joe getting unsettled."

Ted even brought a movie camera with him to the dugout the day of the All-Star Game, which he trained on DiMaggio whenever he could. "I want to study his style," he explained. "It might help me."

In the game, the American League boasted one of the most formidable one-two punches ever penciled into the three and four slots in a batting order, Joe DiMaggio just ahead of Ted Williams, and they'd had a fine day, collecting a hit each and an RBI apiece, but as the A.L. came to bat in the bottom of the ninth they still trailed 5-3. But they loaded the bases with one out, and up stepped Joe DiMaggio, walking into a fairy-tale ending that even he wouldn't have been so audacious to write. Only the best DiMaggio could do was pound the ball on the ground toward shortstop Eddie Miller, who fielded it cleanly and flipped to second baseman Bill Herman. But Herman rushed his relay throw, the ball was a bit wide of first, and DiMaggio barely escaped grounding into a game-ending double play.

Now it was up to Williams, with the score now 5-4 and runners at the corners. "Let me tell you something," said Claude Passeau, the Cubs pitcher now trying to nail down the last out for the National League, "it is kind of tough to get rid of a .360 hitter and then have to pitch to a .400 hitter."

Williams worked the count to 2-and-1. Now Passeau came after him with a slider, waist high. "The instant it left my hand," he would say, "I knew I was a dead duck. I'd struck Ted out on a low outside fastball and that's what I intended to give him, but the ball got away from me and I knew where it was going the second I released it."

It wound up hitting the facing of the upper deck, got tangled up for a second in a large piece of bunting, then fell back to earth, just a few steps away from where Cardinals outfielder Enos Slaughter was standing. Slaughter left the ball where it sat, easy prey for the souvenir hounds descending from the stands. A shower of straw hats, maybe ten thousand of them, fluttered down to the field from the grandstand as well. Williams? He started clapping as soon as he realized the ball was going to stay fair, and he kept clapping as he galloped around the bases, as he stepped on home plate, as he was mobbed by his American League teammates, as he received greetings and kisses from manager Del Baker and the other coaches.

For one blessed day in the summer of 1941, there was little question who the best damned hitter was, and you couldn't blast the smile off Ted Williams's face with a gross of dynamite.

"I just shut my eyes and swung," he said. "I had a feeling if I got up there in the ninth I'd go for the downs. There ain't nothing like hitting a home run. I just let go on an inside slider. Boy, wasn't it a pip? I want to be the most popular player who ever played in Boston. I guess I just can't be a yes-man all the time like a lot of people. . . ."

No one cared about that anymore. The fresh, scrawny kid was still a piece of work. But he was also hitting .405. Sometimes, he really was worth the trouble.

10

"BUD, I'M A HITTER."

HOW TEDDY BALLGAME BECAME THE BEST
DAMNED HITTER WHO EVER LIVED

Ted Williams is greeted by Joe DiMaggio after hitting the game-winning home run in the All-Star game in Detroit on July 9.

Joe's not as tough as Ted Williams, at least not for me. Ted's a left-hander, of course, which means he should do a little better against me than a right-hander like Joe. But honestly, I just can't get that guy out. I can't throw my fastball past him, and I haven't got enough curve to fool him. I'm not kidding when I tell you that I fell pretty lucky when he hits a single off my curve. If I give him a fast one, he'll triple.

—Bob Feller, July 24, 1941

———————●———————

For the first time in his career, Ted Williams was the primary player on baseball's lips, the first name on the tip of its tongue. In those heady forty-eight hours after he'd clobbered Claude Passeau's buckle-high fastball for the three-run home run that won the All-Star Game, Joe DiMaggio's Streak was temporarily forgotten, Bob Feller's pursuit of thirty victories was completely overwhelmed, and the glare of baseball's blinding spotlight fixed exclusively on the man wearing number 9 for the Boston Red Sox, the Kid with the .405 batting average, whose transformation from surly, selfish star to gregarious team man seemed almost complete. Almost being the key word.

"Oh, hell, I don't give a damn about fielding anyway," he told a reporter the day after the All-Star Game as he lounged in a room at the Book-Cadillac Hotel in Detroit, where the Red Sox would resume the season.

"They say I'm a bonehead fielder and maybe they're right. But, bud, I'm a hitter. And I can blast 'em."

"How do you explain your average?" he was asked. "Babe Ruth never hit .400. Lou Gehrig never did it. Joe DiMaggio tried a couple of years ago and had to settle for .381. Why have you been able to keep yours so high?"

"Luck, I guess," Williams said, before laughing at how disingenuous that sounded. "Aw, hell, it's not all luck. You know, you have to be swinging good. But I'm hitting just as I did last year, same grip, same stance, same swing. More of 'em are falling safe. After a few years in the league, I know the pitchers better and I guess that helps. But, shit, a fellow can be hitting the ball fine and lose twenty points in his average in a week or so. It's just a matter of what the old fellow, Keeler, used to say: Hitting 'em where they ain't."

He knew the odds against him finishing north of .400 were still stacked.

"It's been eighteen years since an American Leaguer did that, and we've had some pretty fair punchers up here during that time, so that tells you how hard it is," he said. "I guess the odds against me are twenty-five-to-one, maybe fifty-to-one. Especially since Joe Cronin's got me hitting third, which is a handicap. It's better to be hitting fourth or fifth. You've got more men on base. [Charlie] Keller [the Yankee slugger who Williams was chasing along with DiMaggio for the home run and RBI leadership] has got somebody on base almost every time he comes up and he's liable to push somebody across every time he hits one. Hell, I haven't had but one chance this year to hit with the bases loaded. That was against the White Sox, and [Ted] Lyons walked me. Tension? Nah, there's no tension for me hitting in the clutch. Why should I tighten up? Jesus, I'd like to have the bases loaded every time I get up. And don't forget, there's some tension in the pitcher, too, especially when he's facing me."

He laughed again. Williams could have said it a little better, a little more modestly, but what the hell was the point? He was right. And he knew—absolutely *knew*—that he was going to push that .405 higher almost immediately, because the schedule maker had been kind enough to let him start his second-half pursuit of .400 at Briggs Stadium, which was his favorite ballpark in the world and always had been. The story was, the very first time Williams stood in the batter's box at Briggs, on May 4, 1939, he watched three balls sail by him, well out of the strike zone. Tigers catcher Rudy York, a renowned chatterbox, knew this rook was a little too brash for his own good, but also knew that in 1939, nobody was given the green light to swing away on 3-and-0, least of all a twenty-year-old infant.

"You wouldn't swing at the next one, would you, kid?" York asked.

"I would," Williams replied, "and I will."

York, cackling, stuck out one finger, fastball, right down the pipe. Williams always did like fastballs down the pipe, and this one he delivered onto the roof of the rightfield stands, the longest home run in the history of this stadium that Hank Greenberg had called home for seven years. Three innings later, he hit another prodigious blast.

"I think," the Kid crowed later on, "that I might just move my things from my apartment in Boston into the visitor's clubhouse here."

Whatever kindnesses Detroit had bestowed on him in the past didn't help him much now, however. After rain washed out a game on July 10, the Tigers' Bobo Newsom handcuffed Williams, retiring him four times in four at-bats the next day, and in an eyeblink—like *that*—Williams lost seven points on his average and woke up the next morning at .398. It was just another reminder of what a relentless pursuit .400 really was. No matter how you cut up the season, the simple arithmetic of the mission was this: To get to .400, you had to hit safely two out of every five times you walked to the plate, on average. Even the greatest players in history would have gladly settled for two-for-every-six, which would yield a .333 average, good enough to win a batting title some years. There were plenty of All-Stars who spent their entire careers plenty pleased to go two-for-every-seven (a more-than-respectable .287 average), and every year there were dozens of regulars forced to settle for two-for-every-eight (and while .250 might not sound like a very good batting average, sixty-five years later a player named Jose Valentin would earn more than $33 million in a fourteen-year baseball career in which his career mark was .241).

But even the complexities of maintaining a .400 average weren't nearly as fragile as other things, such as a bum ankle. The discomfort hadn't ever really gone away. In fact, just ten days earlier, Red Sox trainer Win Green had said, "Ted still has trouble getting up on his toes. I have to wrap that ankle in a vise every day. It's lucky it's the right ankle and not the left. I don't think he'd be able to get any power into his swing if the chipped bone was in his other ankle."

Still, Ted had learned to play with pain, and play well, and when he was hitting he could have had a javelin sticking out of his back and he wouldn't

have noticed. But on July 12, in the third inning of the first game of a doubleheader, after drawing his second walk of the day, Tigers catcher Birdie
Tebbetts somehow surmised that Williams—who stole exactly twenty-four
bases in his nineteen-year career—might be itching to run. He called for a
pitchout, and pitcher Al Benton obliged, and even though Williams barely
budged off first base, Tebbetts, figuring he might as well throw *somewhere*,
made a snap throw to first, trying to pick him off. Williams was stunned,
but he was also so close to the bag that he barely needed to slide. But he did
anyway, he led with the bad foot, and it jammed into the bag, and the pain
was instant and it was crippling.

"Jesus God, I think I *really* broke it this time!" Williams screamed as
trainer Green raced out to tend to the ankle. After a few minutes, the pain
dulling slightly, Williams decided to stay in the game. He walked again in
the fifth and fouled out in the sixth (lowering the average to .397), and then
agreed it was time to call it a day. It was hard to believe that only four days
had passed since his blast off Passeau, since he'd been the toast of baseball,
since he'd felt bulletproof in a batter's box. By the time he showed up in the
press box at Cleveland's Municipal Stadium on July 13, sitting next to Sox
owner Tom Yawkey and traveling secretary Phil Troy, Williams seemed resigned to having to wait for another year to set his sights on the magic
number again.

"I have no illusions of hitting .400 for the season," he admitted. "Each
morning I take a quick look in the newspapers to see if I'm still up there. I
just don't think I'm lucky enough to be a .400 hitter."

But the next day, after sitting for X rays at the Cleveland Clinic, Dr.
Richards informed him that there was no new break; the pictures looked
just as they did the last time, there was no reason he couldn't return once
the swelling went down. "Maybe I can start pinch-hitting," Williams said.
"All I know is, watching the boys lose while I'm in street clothes hurts
worse than if they cut my ankle off entirely."

He tried on July 16, with the Red Sox in Chicago, stepping in for Skeeter
Newsome in the eighth inning of a 1-1 tie. Comiskey Park was notoriously
tough on anyone not wearing a White Sox uniform—the very next night,
in fact, when it was announced that Joe DiMaggio's hitting streak had finally been stopped 350 miles away, 27,437 people would loudly cheer the
news—but this was different, a much smaller gathering of about 4,000
greeting Ted warmly, American League fans giving him thanks for his

game-winning All-Star homer. He responded with a long fly ball, a sacrifice fly that scored a run but did nothing to help his batting average, shaving another two points. On June 19, with the Red Sox in the process of dropping two games to the dreadful Browns in St. Louis (where there were no handbills distributed touting "the sensational Ted Williams"; DiMaggio had clearly recaptured the national imagination), he pinch-hit twice, failed both times, and now was down to .393, the lowest his average had been since May 24.

A pinch-hit homer against the Browns the next day, however, not only set the average in the right direction one more time, back up to .396, it also infused a little feistiness back into Williams, who'd mostly suffered in silence as his ankle and his average both kept killing him. On the train back to Boston, Williams entered the club car, saw Joe Cronin, and asked if he could have a word with the skipper.

"I feel so much better I may be able to get back in there tomorrow," Williams said. "I'll give the leg a workout, and I hope it feels good enough for me to get back in there regularly."

Cronin wasn't totally sold. "From watching you in practice, I'd say you still can't shift on that ankle in the outfield, and I don't see how I can risk aggravating it further by having you play regularly again just yet."

"I really didn't have to limp as much as I did when trotting out that home run," he said. "I favored the ankle more than I really had to because I wasn't warmed up and didn't want to risk turning on it. I certainly would like to play tomorrow."

Cronin, of course, wanted his best player in the lineup more than anything, but he was also trying to be responsible. Everyone in the game knew how Dizzy Dean had ruined his career four years earlier when he broke his toe in the 1937 All-Star Game, kept pitching through the pain, altered his pitching motion, and wound up shredding his arm. Ol' Diz was essentially done at age twenty-seven, though he'd actually held on until May 15, 1941, when he formally retired at thirty-one. Fooling with a bad wheel had cost Dean maybe two hundred more victories and untold thousands of dollars. Cronin didn't want the same thing to cost Williams two thousand or more base hits. "Talk to the doctor when we get back," Cronin finally said. "If he says you should get back in there, then it's fine with me."

Ted tried to do the right thing. On the morning of July 22 he went to get the all-clear from Dr. Richards, but when he showed up at the office he was told the doctor was performing an operation and would be tied up for several hours. *Well*, Williams figured, *I tried*. He rushed back to Fenway Park, took batting practice, took great care not to wince or to limp or to show any physical weakness whatsoever, and Cronin penciled his name in the lineup. In his first at-bat, after receiving a standing ovation from the 8,100 people inside Fenway Park (and steadfastly refusing to tip his cap to them, a stubborn retort for their betrayals of 1940, which he would cling to the rest of his career), he promptly slammed his eighteenth home run of the season off John Rigney, who by now wished he could have honored his draft notice, at least on those days he had to face the Red Sox. "DiMaggio's a great hitter," he muttered afterward, "but he doesn't hit like that with one leg. I can't get Williams out no matter how hurt he is."

Now Williams was back in that rarefied and impossible-to-achieve place that only a select few hitters have ever occupied, and even at the tender age of twenty-three he knew that he might never see this summit again. "The art of hitting," Williams would say much later in his life, "is all about balancing what is usually a series of failures with the belief that you are good enough to make it all about a series of successes instead. Sometimes you might even do that for a week or two at a clip. Rare is the time you can stay in that zone longer than that. I was lucky enough to have an extended stay."

There were impediments, of course. On July 23, Williams's old nemesis Jimmy Dykes, the White Sox manager, briefly unveiled a gimmick that drew snickers and laughter in that summer of 1941, but was really several years ahead of its time. When Williams came to the plate in the bottom of the first inning that afternoon, Dykes motioned from the dugout and suddenly his infielders abandoned their usual posts. Third baseman Bob Kennedy left the line completely wide open, positioning himself where the shortstop usually played. Luke Appling, the shortstop, was now standing on the outfield grass on the first-base side of second. And second baseman Bill Knickerbocker and first baseman Joe Kuhel had also left the infield dirt, standing almost next to each other on the grass, Kuhel hugging the right-field line and Knickerbocker all but hugging Kuhel.

Williams saw the shift and started laughing out loud.

"Dykes, you crazy son of a bitch," he yelled, "what the hell are you doing?"

What he was doing was inventing the "Williams shift," and it was supposed to act as a Maginot Line of sorts, depriving Williams, a dead-pull hitter, of his favorite holes along the right side of the infield, a strategy that would later be credited almost entirely to Lou Boudreau after he became manager of the Indians. Unfortunately for Dykes, his invention worked almost as well as the real Maginot Line had, since Williams had no problem shooting a line drive down the evacuated left-field line, and he collected four hits in ten times up against the Shift, numbers that hardly inspired any other managers to copycat Dykes.

Not that it really mattered. Williams was back, and he was smoking hot, and he went 2-for-3 against the Indians on July 25, and when he woke up the next day, most of the morning's copy was devoted to Red Sox pitcher Lefty Grove, who'd won his three hundredth (and, it would turn out, final) game. But Williams, as was his custom, had something else to check out. Next to the stories detailing Grove's glories was the listing of the top American League hitters. Williams knew where to find his name, in the same spot atop that register it had occupied since mid-May. And this is what he saw:

	AB	Hits	Avg.
TWilliams (Bos)	260	104	.400
JDiMaggio (NY)	369	139	.377
Travis (Wash)	342	129	.369

He was back where he'd always wanted to be. And he was damned if he was going to leave anytime soon.

———————●———————

They were called the Neutrality Acts, and they reflected just how wary most of the American public was of war, how long the national memory was, and how devastating the Great War had been. The United States had been a part of that conflict for only seventeen months yet had suffered 116,516 combat deaths. And the over 200,000 wounded veterans walking in the midst of their fellow citizens served as a visible and unyielding reminder of war's terrible cost. Mostly, they kept Franklin Roosevelt's hands tied from intervening too completely even as the Nazi war machine had been born, then nurtured, and then cranked into overdrive across the 1930s, but he had succeeded in getting them modified just enough to where he was able to push through the Lend-Lease Bill early in 1941, after France had fallen and it appeared England might soon follow. And it made for a nervous daily drama as the summer of '41 sped along. Because the isolationists, a sizable group despite what the polls might say, firmly believed it was Roosevelt's chief intention to have those acts repealed. And once repealed, it was a short step toward war.

Twice in the spring of '41, German ships had sunk liners on which a sizable number of the passengers were American, even if the ships themselves weren't sailing under the American flag. The *Robin Moor* was the most celebrated; also in May, the Egyptian ship SS *ZamZam*, with 202 passengers (138 of them American), had been sunk by German U-boats, whose captains wrongly assumed there was war cargo on board. As with the *Moor*, there were, remarkably, no casualities on the *ZamZam*, just the usual follow-up rhetoric between American and German spokesmen.

Still, as the summer progressed, as tensions began to mount and anxieties began to climb, every cross word fired from the United States across either ocean started to look like another volley intended to pierce the veneer of the Neutrality Acts. Adolf Hitler, on June 5, had tried to convince the world that Germany's "invasion of the western hemisphere is as fantastic as the idea of invading the moon," but if Hitler's intention was to soothe American nerves, he sabotaged himself by adding a brief coda at the end of his speech: "Convoy," he warned, "means war."

Henry L. Stimson, Roosevelt's secretary of war, certainly saw this as no idle boast, and a week later, while delivering a commencement address to graduates of the U.S Naval Academy at Annapolis, he said, "I would be remiss if I did not try to help you understand the nature of the crisis which confronts all of us today and to give you the encouragement in meeting it. The duty of meeting it may fall in large measure upon your shoulders."

And lest anyone forget that the growing national migraine included another outspoken nation across another vast ocean, there came on June 14 this official pronouncement from the Japanese government: "The United States is violating the provisions of the Neutrality Articles of international law right and left, yet insists on Japanese observance of the nine-power pact, which is a dead letter. It is an inconsistency we cannot accept."

Such raw defiance spurred Roosevelt to push to increase soldiers' service time beyond the standard one-year tour, especially since there was an almost daily need to increase and fortify the size of the American army. On July 7, U.S. forces occupied Iceland, right in the middle of the Nazi blockade zone (seven hundred miles from Scotland, nine hundred miles away from German-occupied Norway) at the invitation of the island's government, the most direct role the Americans had yet played in the European troubles, which prompted Republicans to charge that the occupation was an illegal step toward undeclared war.

"The United States cannot permit the occupation by Germany of strategic outposts in the Atlantic to be used as air or naval bases for the eventual attack against the Western Hemisphere," Roosevelt said in addressing Congress, later reiterating his intention to use U.S. forces outside the strictly defined borders of the "Western Hemisphere" whenever the interests of national defense demanded it. Knox praised the decision, saying, "This will allow the Navy to use its guns as well as its eyes in patrolling the ocean."

Roosevelt understood the nation's reluctance to mobilize, realized how distasteful another war would be less than a quarter of a century after the conclusion of the last one—the one that was supposed to end all wars—and remembered that one of the key elements of the platform that earned him a third term was his pledge to keep American guns silent at any reasonable cost. But he was also well aware of the price already being paid for seeking that unconditional peace, and if he hadn't been, July 14 would have provided all the testimony he needed. For in Paris, where the fallen Republic once hired jazz bands for Bastille Day celebrations that often lasted uninterrupted for three days, its occupied streets were filled with an odd, eerie silence this holiday.

Thousands of Parisians walked silently past the monument marking the site of the prison where the French Revolution had been born 152 years earlier. There was no drinking, because of the wine famine. There was no street dancing, for the Nazis had outlawed it, breaking 150 years of tradition. Flags were displayed in some private homes, and representatives of a youth organization in Lyon climbed four-thousand-foot Mount Pilat to hoist the French tricolor at sunrise, but otherwise the day passed mainly in silence and in sadness.

"The spirit of the French people will rise again," Churchill said that day. "Purified and rejuvenated by what it has undergone. Hard, stern years lie before us. But the end is certain, and the end will make amends for it all. The soul of France can never die."

But its voice, its spirit, and its feisty soul had been stilled for the time be-ing, and even the most fervent isolationist had to concede the tragedy in that.

———————•———————

By the end of July, slowly, steadily, Ted Williams's pursuit of .400 stopped being a curiosity and started to enter the realm of national fascination. Joe DiMaggio's Streak was over, and he'd begun a new one which, on July 26, reached nine games. Whirlaway, in his first major race since his Belmont Stakes coronation seven weeks before, stunned an overflow crowd of fifty thousand at Arlington Park racetrack in the northwestern suburbs of Chicago that same day by losing the Arlington Classic to Attention, a ten-to-one underdog, who matched him stride-for-stride down the stretch. Little noticed in the swirl of more pressing news was Franklin Roosevelt's announcement that the U.S. Army would oversee responsibility for Fil-ipino armed forces, and the man he chose to lead that new mission was a fifty-seven-year-old former army chief of staff named Douglas MacArthur, lured out of retirement with the new rank of lieutenant general, overseeing a new army component, the United States Armed Forces in the Far East.

Ted Williams meanwhile went to bat four times against Bob Feller, al-ready seeking his twentieth win of the season, and he slammed out three hits, and later he would say, "As hard as it is to think about facing a guy who's as great as Feller, I prefer taking on the better pitchers because you know they have the guts and the talent to challenge you, even if most days they'll get the better of you. I feel a lot more comfortable going against Feller or Lefty Gomez or Red Ruffing than I do against a rookie I know nothing about, even if the kid's throwing nothing special." Williams was hitting the ball hard almost every time up, and it couldn't have come at a better time because for the first time in weeks, people were speculating that DiMaggio's new streak might be the thing that propelled him to challenge Williams for the batting title. DiMaggio's average now stood at .377, a sea-son high, and though Williams's big day nudged him up to .405, DiMaggio was now well within striking distance.

Only, he'd need Williams's bat to cool off. And as July melted into Au-gust, there was no sign that Williams's bat had any interest in betraying him. In later years, whenever someone would try to scale the same mountaintop

Williams climbed in that summer of 1941, the same modern-day obstacles
would be cited as reasons why it's so difficult to hit .400—more air travel,
more night games, more media scrutiny. And it's true that Williams had
none of those things conspiring against him. But what he did have to overcome was the most difficult impediment of all, shared by anyone who's ever
tried to reach .400: the wearying grind of a six-month season.

Just two years earlier, DiMaggio himself had learned all about that. He'd
spent the summer of 1939 on one long, extended hot streak, entering September at .411 and still hitting as high as .409 on the morning of September 10. But that day he went 0-for-8 in a doubleheader, the start of an
0-for-14 minislump that knocked him south of .400 for good. DiMaggio
always claimed in later years that Joe McCarthy had advised him to keep
playing in September despite an infection that nearly closed his left eye
shut, explaining that he didn't want DiMaggio to be viewed as a "cheese
champion," maintaining .400 by sitting on the bench. However it worked
out, DiMaggio's pursuit was finally sabotaged by his own body breaking
down.

The remarkable thing about Williams, two years later, was that he got
stronger as the summer grew hotter; he seemed drawn to the attention,
drawn to the spotlight, drawn to the scrutiny each at-bat would generate
from here on in. By the end of July his average was back up to .409. He flew
to New York on an off day to pose for the cover of *Life* magazine. The
Boston Globe began running daily comparisons between Williams and Bill
Terry's 1930 season (July 29: Williams, .407; Terry, .395). He hit his first
grand slam of the season July 31, crowing, "I finally got a chance to clean
'em up! *That's* what you call a fun day!" He amazed opponent after opponent, frustrated pitcher after pitcher, moved Browns catcher Rick Ferrell to
shake his head in wonder and say, in almost reverent tones, "I've heard
pitchers say that he takes a fine look at their stuff the first time he faces
them and then seems to be able to almost call the turn on what they're going to throw thereafter. *Who can do that?*"

He even managed to land on the front page of every newspaper in New
England on an *off day,* the first of August, when he landed a 374-pound
tuna after ninety minutes of battling off Plum Island, in Newburyport,
Massachusetts, from his friend Malcolm Hudson's boat *Nancy II.* Williams
explained that he used a thirty-seven-thread-line on his reel. The area had
been suffering through a two-week "catchless" streak—"Even the men who

fish this area for a living have been shut out," one resident marveled—but by now, this didn't startle anyone, because it was clear there was very little Ted Williams *couldn't* do.

And, goddamn, that sure meant hitting a baseball as hard and consistently as anyone who ever lived. Williams returned from his one-day fishing adventure and banged out two more hits against the Tigers at Fenway Park, and now he was up to .412. That was a good thing, because in New York Joe DiMaggio was also going 2-for-3 against the Browns to elevate his average to a season-high .381 and extend his latest streak to sixteen (giving him an otherworldly stretch of hitting in 72 out of 73 games, marred only by the wizardry of Ken Keltner's mitt). Williams enjoyed the daily duels he and DiMaggio would conduct, often at a distance of hundreds of miles. "I think that's what kept him so motivated every day of that summer," Dominic DiMaggio would recall many years later. "He knew everything Joe was doing. Every day, four or five times a day, he'd yell over to me, 'Hey, Dommie! Joe just doubled off Newsom.' 'Hey, Dommie! Joe's 0-for-3 today!' He wanted to know exactly where he was at every moment of the day in comparison to Joe."

Williams received his intelligence from the two men who operated the manual scoreboard at the base of the left-field wall at Fenway Park, a couple of brothers named Walter and Bill Daley. They were privy to everything that was happening all across Major League Baseball via the magic of the Western Union teletype machine, which allowed them to update every inning of every game and allowed Williams a chance to keep informed in what, for 1941, was as close to real time as the human brain could fathom.

"Ted's an incredible storyteller," said Bill (who doubled as the public address announcer at Braves Field across the city when the Sox were out of town). "Sometimes he'll start telling us something in the first inning and then, each time he comes out, he'll add a little, timing it so we get to hear the whole story by the ninth."

Said Walter: "He's president of the Fenway Park Left Fielders' Association. As far as we're concerned he can serve twenty terms."

Fortified with his fix of information, Williams knew where he stood at all times, although after the third of August he would be standing in a lonelier and lonelier place. Williams went 1-for-3, which actually dipped his average to .410, but DiMaggio went 0-for-8 in a doubleheader with St. Louis, a devastating collar that not only finished his latest hitting streak, not only ended an eighty-one-game streak in which DiMaggio had reached base by either a hit or a walk, but also crushed DiMaggio's hopes of ever catching Williams. He was now down to .373, and would never again be as close as thirty points to Ted; a couple of weeks later, in August, DiMaggio sprained his ankle at Briggs Stadium, and he'd spend the rest of the season forgetting about Williams and focusing on getting healthy for the World Series.

There would be no World Series for the Red Sox, who by the first week in August had already fallen seventeen and a half games behind the Yankees, but they were still nearly as much of a drawing card as the Yankees because of one reason and one reason only: the Thumper. The Kid. The Willowy Walloper, the Slugging Stringbean. He made old men gasp: "My, my, my," said Connie Mack, the seventy-eight-year-old owner and manager of the Philadelphia Athletics, who'd been around major league baseball for only fifty-five years. "Doesn't that boy do anything but hit line drives?"

He inspired middle-aged men to do crazy things: A fan in Washington's Griffith Stadium climbed down a twelve-foot wall and emerged brandishing a whiskey bottle in the eighth inning, offering it to Williams. "Can't," Ted said. "I'm working." He stirred valor among the youth: Fourteen-year-old Billy Kane, of South Brewer, Maine, hitchhiked 250 miles just so he could see his hero play in Fenway Park. Unfortunately for young Billy, the Red Sox were off the day he arrived, and he fell asleep in an aggrieved heap in a stadium corridor after ducking under an unoccupied turnstile. The cops found him, and instead of calling a truancy officer, they decided to go a different way: They sent a squad to the Hotel Sheraton and found the inn's most famous resident fast asleep after a long day of skeet shooting. Rousted, Williams went to police headquarters and gave the cops a thrill and a fourteen-year-old boy a greeting he would never forget.

"How'd you like to see tomorrow's game from a box seat?" Ted asked young Billy Kane.

"That'd be great," Billy replied, "but do I really have to sit on a box the whole time?" Ted laughed, got a hit for the kid, and kept his average well north of .400.

He talked hitting incessantly. Unlike DiMaggio, a reluctant star whose reticence was often misinterpreted as arrogance, Williams would fill reporters' notebooks wherever he went that summer, a fresh departure from the ornery bastard he'd been throughout most of 1940. "I'll tell you why I'm hitting .400," he told a group of Philly writers standing around the batting cage at Shibe Park one day. "It's a cinch. I got confidence this year for the first time. When I came up two years ago I thought it would be swell if I could have a pretty fair season. You know, hit around .300 and get a homer now and then. Before I knew it I was hitting .330, but I really didn't think I was that good. I finished that first year at .327, I led the league in runs batted in, and I hit more homers than DiMaggio, but I still didn't feel sure of myself.

"Last year I missed the batting title by six or eight points, and I found myself wondering if I was as good as DiMaggio, Appling, Greenberg, and those other guys. I told myself I was a sap for thinking that way, and I guess it worked. I don't believe there's such a thing as a natural hitter. If that's all there was to it, a guy could lay off all winter and come back in the spring as good as he was the previous midseason. Nobody can do that. Natural hitter, my ass."

He was cocky, and unapologetic about it. He didn't believe in jinxes. Someone asked him about slumps, and he crowed, "I haven't had one this year. I've got more real hits than anybody in the league. If I could run like that Pete Reiser of Brooklyn, I'd be hitting ten, twenty points higher."

Someone asked him if he could hit .400 for seven more weeks.

"Hell yes, I can," he said. "If I don't, who the hell will?"

He was more than talk, of course, more than bluster, more than confidence. Whereas DiMaggio would constantly act as if he were afraid he'd wake up one morning stripped of his powers, where he used coffee and cigarettes as a way of shielding himself from the kryptonite hidden everywhere, Williams didn't only think he was a great hitter, didn't only *know* he was a great hitter, he had proof. He had performance. In what should have been the greatest challenge to his assault on .400, the withering heat of August, he spent the entire month in a staggeringly consistent zone. How much?

From August 1 through August 16, he was 23-for-57. From August 17 through September 1, he was 23-for-55. He started the month hitting .409. He ended it hitting .407. He never finished a workday any higher than .414, but he never finished one any lower than .402, either. And invariably, whenever he seemed on the verge of tumbling south of the magic barrier, that's when he was toughest. On August 7 he woke up at .403, then promptly went 3-for-4 against future Hall of Famer Lefty Gomez ("I prefer taking on the better pitchers"); "Let's just call him 'Ted the King'," Joe DiMaggio's roommate said after that battering. On August 25, Feller kept him hitless ("Most days they'll get the better of you"), and then Ted promptly went seven for his next eleven, hitting his twenty-ninth and thirtieth home runs in the bargain.

His teammates were awed. And they were also concerned. By September 1, DiMaggio's streak had been over for a month and a half, his batting average was fifty points behind Ted's, and with him nursing a bum ankle it was possible that Williams would finish with more home runs *and* more RBIs than him, too. And yet the public—specifically the sportswriters—remained smitten with DiMaggio. Sportswriters selected the Most Valuable Player Award at the end of each season. And one of Ted's Red Sox teammates—speaking anonymously so as not to incur the wrath of those influential scribes—already feared how that vote was going to go.

"How are they going to pick DiMaggio over Williams?" he asked. "Just because DiMaggio is from New York? Just because the Yankees will win the pennant? Yankee pitchers gave their answer when they walked Ted three times in one game last week. You didn't see our pitchers walking DiMaggio, did you? Our pitchers pitch to Joe. Yankee pitchers duck Williams like so much poison. That's one answer. Unless things change later on, it would be a crime to pick DiMaggio over Williams."

Ted himself was, as usual, deferential. "A guy like me," he said September 1, "is lucky enough just to have people talk about me and Joe in the same sentence sometimes. He's the greatest player in the game right now. I'm trying to get there." He wouldn't say it, but he was gaining. That day, he'd clubbed three home runs in a doubleheader sweep of the Senators and barely missed a fourth when, in his last at-bat, a towering shot to right field drifted just foul. Every day now, all of the Boston papers had to run house advertisements pleading with their readers not to call the newspaper offices to find out how Ted had done because they were jamming the switchboard. "We'll give you all you can possibly read . . . and more!" promised the *Boston Post,* and in those first days of September, Williams was giving everyone plenty to read about.

He was walking at an astonishing pace—Cronin had unwittingly assured this earlier in the season when he'd flip-flopped with Ted in the batting order; now, instead of hitting ahead of slugger Jimmy Foxx, he was hitting ahead of Cronin, and was seeing only maybe three or four hittable pitches in the strike zone every day—but he still got his hacks in, too, getting hits in twelve of his first twenty-four at-bats in September, pushing him to .413 by the morning of September 11. That day, in fact, Williams would give a hitting exhibition at a park in East Providence, Rhode Island, that would draw 4,000 people; the night before, only 1,200 had come to watch another presentation by another man who'd been a fair left-handed hitter in his day: Babe Ruth.

The Kid was officially bigger than The Babe now.

And it wasn't only the fans who were amazed at what they saw.

"I've pitched to other .400 hitters, and they've had their share of banjo hits," veteran Yankees pitcher Red Ruffing said. "Not Ted. All of his hits are clean and hard."

"He won't swing at a bad ball," marveled Johnny Murphy, another Yankees pitcher.

"He slugs them inside, outside, high and low," said Marius Russo.

"I'll be the happiest fellow in the world if I hit .400," Williams admitted when the Red Sox made their final tour of New York, the one-year anniversary of his infamous tour of the firehouse. "But I want to be talked about. I want to be remembered when I leave baseball. Who are the players they talk about and remember—Babe Ruth because he hit sixty home runs, Rogers Hornsby because he hit .424, Hack Wilson because he batted in 190 runs, and Joe DiMaggio because he hit in fifty-six straight games.

"Those are the best, top performances in baseball. They're what I'm aiming at."

But as focused as Williams was at the ballpark, as boundless as his ambitions may have been, even he wasn't immune to the humbling powers of a humbling sport. It turned out that .413 would be his high-water mark for the rest of the year. Soon enough, the number began to melt, slightly, almost imperceptibly; there was no great slump, no doubleheader disaster like the one that had kneecapped DiMaggio two years earlier. Just a point here, a point there. Why?

Maybe it was the time demands. The *Life* cover came out. On September 16, an off-day, he'd spent the day in New York on the *We the People* radio program, where he'd explained his success to the nation: "I am not popping off anymore. I am just popping everything out of the ballpark." Ted's girlfriend, Doris Soule, had accompanied him to the appearance, flown back by herself, and gotten a firsthand peek at American fame when her American Airlines plane touched down at Logan Airport at 11:30 that night and she was instantly mobbed by reporters.

"Just say we're good friends," she said uncomfortably.

Part of it might have been the pressure of the chase finally catching up with him. On September 9, he and Cronin had a testy exchange on the field when Ted didn't appear to run with a 100 percent effort after a fly ball. Part of it might have been the law of averages catching up to him: After hitting Bob Feller well for so much of the season, Feller shut him down for a second straight time on September 18, an 0-for-3 that dipped Ted's average to .405. "It's about time I started to get a little even with Ted," Feller said. "After all, he's been wearing me out all season and I've given the matter a lot of study. But I still say he's the best hitter I've ever seen, and I've still got a long way to go to really get even with him."

Still, after hitting his thirty-sixth home run of the season in the Fenway Park finale on September 21, he was sitting at .406. There were six games left, three at Washington (where he'd only hit .318 so far on the season) and three at Philadelphia (where he'd hit .348). Before the question could even be asked, he said, "I intend to play all six games. If you hit .400, it's got to be because you played a whole season."

Ted Williams would make damn sure that no one could ever accuse him of backing into a batting record.

———————•———————

Charles Lindbergh sensed that there was momentum to his cause now. He didn't much care that in many of the cities where the America First Committee held its rallies, it was denied use of the best arenas, stadiums, or convention halls. This, he said, was just further proof of the Roosevelt administration's single-minded quest to drown out any voice urging the United States to steer clear of a war it could not possibly win. If anything, those snubs made Lindbergh more determined than ever to narrow the scope of his speeches, to kick up the rhetoric and make his message as clear and precise as possible. And the people who came to hear him invariably ate up every word.

In Oklahoma City on August 29, the AFC had been exiled to Sandlot Park, a baseball diamond located outside the city limits. Eight thousand people came anyway, and Lindbergh whipped them into a frenzy. "It seems to me," he said, "that the quickest way for Germany to lose a war would be to attack America and that the quickest way for America to lose a war would be to attack Germany. England may turn against us, as she has turned against France and Finland. Reasons are always found to justify whatever action a nation takes in time of war."

These words infuriated Churchill, they incensed Roosevelt, they enraged most members of Congress, regardless of party affiliation, who understood that whether or not you supported joining the war, there was a clearly determined boundary between who the good guys were and who the bad guys were, at least when it came to distinguishing England and Germany. But Lindbergh couldn't hear them. All he heard were the cheers. All he heard were the shouts of "Down with Roosevelt" and all he could see were the placards calling the president a warmonger. And so he made plans for what would surely be his finest hour, September 11, in Des Moines.

Earlier that evening, Roosevelt would address the nation, telling of his orders to the navy to shoot first if Axis raiders entered American defense zones in the Atlantic, saying, "We can no longer stand by as the Nazis imperil the sea."

"No matter what it costs," Roosevelt vowed, "we will keep open the line of legitimate commerce in these defense waters. There will be no shooting war unless Germany continues to seek it. Let this warning be clear: From now on, if German or Italian vessels of war enter the waters, the protection of which is necessary for American defense, they do so at their own peril. Upon our naval and air patrol—now operating in large number over a vast expanse of the Atlantic Ocean—falls the duty of maintaining American policy of freedom of the seas—now.

"Hitler already is seeking to establish footholds and bridgeheads in the New World through conspiracy after conspiracy. The Nazi danger to our Western world has long ceased to be a mere possibility. . . . You seek to throw our children and our children's children into your forms of terrorism and slavery. You have now attacked our safety. You shall go no further."

Across the country, men and women were instantly galvanized. Morning-after polls revealed that even those who'd clung stubbornly to the notion of avoiding war at all costs had shifted their opinions. One survey said that some 92 percent of all Americans supported the president's action. It was a stunning victory for Roosevelt (still wearing a black armband to mourn his recently deceased mother), whose voice had never sounded fuller, stronger, more defiant. Even in Des Moines, where 7,500 people had gathered to listen to Lindbergh speak, the crowd had been overwhelmingly supportive of Roosevelt's message, breaking into applause on eleven different occasions. Lindbergh either didn't hear this, didn't recognize it, or he didn't care. Because when it was his turn to speak, he didn't waver a word from the prepared text in front of him.

"The three most important groups which have been pressing this country toward war," Lindbergh said, "are the British, the Jewish, and the Roosevelt administration."

There was scattered applause, and a few boos, but the room remained mostly quiet. From the start, this was a different kind of Lindbergh speech: harder, angrier, more pointed. England was his first target.

"Her position is desperate," Lindbergh asserted. "Her population is not large enough and her armies are not strong enough to invade the continent of Europe and win the war she declared against Germany. Her geographical position is such that she cannot win the war by aviation alone, regardless of how many planes we send her. Even if America entered the war, it is improbable that the Allied armies could invade Europe and overcome the Axis powers. If it were not for her hope that she can make the United States responsible for the war financially, as well as militarily, I believe that England would have negotiated a peace in Europe many months ago and be better off for doing so."

The room grew more still. Next on his hit list were the Jews.

"The persecution they suffered in Germany would be sufficient to make bitter enemies of any race. No person with a sense of the dignity of mankind can condone the persecution of the Jewish race in Germany. However, instead of agitating for war, the Jewish groups in this country should be opposing it in every possible way, for they will be among the first to feel its consequences."

Now there was complete silence. Meaning that everyone in attendance—and everyone else listening on the radio—could hear with crystal clarity what came next.

"Their greatest danger to this country," Lindbergh said of the Jews, "lies in their large ownership and influence in our motion pictures, our press, our radio and our government."

There were a few audible gasps in the audience. And then this:

"I am not attacking either the Jewish or the British people," Lindbergh said. "Both races, I admire. But I am saying that the leaders of both the British and the Jewish races, for reasons which are as understandable from their viewpoint as they are inadvisable from ours, for reasons which are not American, wish to involve us in the war. We cannot blame them for looking out for what they believe to be their own interests, but we also must look out for ours. We cannot allow the natural passions and prejudices of other peoples to lead our country to destruction."

Over the next sixty-five years, Lindbergh admirers have attempted to reinterpret what he intended to say, have insisted that he was caught up in the moment and misrepresented his message. No one can know for sure what truly lurked in Lindbergh's soul. But these words leave little to the imagination: He considers "the Jewish people" apart from the rest of America, "their own interests" differing from "ours." They are "other peoples."

The words were chilling, and their impact was immediate. Dorothy Thompson, the widely read *New York Post* columnist who was a staunch and unabashed Roosevelt supporter, seethed, "In effect, Lindbergh is saying: 'We don't really want to do anything against you fellows, and we won't if you don't oppose us. But if you do—well, remember what has happened to you elsewhere. The plain word for that is 'blackmail.' "

"You have seen the outpourings of Berlin the last few days," White House press secretary Stephen Early said. "You saw Lindbergh's statement last night. I think there is a striking similarity between the two." The Committee to Defend America was even more pointed in releasing a scathing indictment: "But he should know that this persecution was brought about in Germany by exactly the kind of thing he said at Des Moines."

Mrs. David de Sola Pool, national president of Hadassah, the Women's Zionist Organization of America, called upon all members to "expose what lies beneath this effort to besmirch a loyal group of American citizens. Coming at a time when we must close our ranks and present a united front against the aggressors who would divide and bedevil us, the speech of Mr. Lindbergh is a warning to all who remember the anti-Jewish campaigns of the Nazis and the use to which they were put."

And Kenneth Leslie, editor of *Protestant Digest*, seeking to prove that this wasn't merely a Jewish concern, wrote: "Lindbergh revealed the true nature of the America First Committee, through his open appeal to anti-Semitism as a political principle and finally accomplished the transformation of that committee into the National Socialistic Party of America. The danger here is even greater because anti-Semitism in pre-Nazi Germany was practically non-existent, while in America it has been assiduously cultivated in preparation for this Des Moines zero hour."

A few days later, in the midst of a heated policy debate, Rep. Luther Patrick of Alabama waved a copy of *Mein Kampf* and said, "It sounds just like Charles A. Lindbergh. Now Lindbergh even tracks him so closely that he says we are being pulled into the war by the seat of the pants by President Roosevelt and the Jews. Lindbergh has turned sour on the United States. Any barber is his equal and any justice of the peace his superior in the matter of international relations."

It took thirteen days, but American First finally answered on behalf of its most notable member. "Colonel Lindbergh and his fellow members are not anti-Semitic," the statement read. "We deplore the injection of the race issue into the discussion of war or peace. It is the interventionists who have done this. America First has invited men and women of every race, religion and national origin to join this committee, provided only that they are patriotic citizens who put the interests of their country ahead of any other nation. We repeat that invitation."

By now, though, few were listening. They'd already heard more than enough.

———————●———————

Five more hits.

That was the magic number, Ted Williams was told. Five hits in those last six games ought to get him home as a .400 hitter, assuming the men who would be pitching for the Senators and the Athletics continued to sprinkle in as many walks as everyone else had been issuing. Ted was averaging about three official at-bats per game thanks to all those bases on balls. So, if he went 5-for-18, he'd be sitting at exactly .40024. And that would count as a .400 hitter by anybody's standard.

"I'd like a little more breathing room than that," he said.

Actually, in that final week of the 1941 season, Ted Williams had more than enough time to take as many deep breaths as he wanted. He'd start with a day off in Washington. Then three games in two days there. Then there'd be two more off-days on Thursday and Friday in Philadelphia, because Connie Mack, the owner of the cash-strapped A's, figured it would make sound business sense to move Friday's scheduled game to Sunday, building a doubleheader that, coupled with interest in Williams's march, might give the A's a good chance to squeeze a good gate out of the dying season.

Williams was unfazed. "Just means extra batting practice for me," he said.

"That's the reason we plan to go to Philadelphia right after the double-header in Washington Wednesday," Joe Cronin said. "We all want to see Ted stay right up there and it ought to help him get in some batting practice on the off-days at Shibe Park Thursday and Friday. To lay off three days this week—today, Thursday, and Friday—might mean Ted wouldn't be meet-ing the ball squarely Saturday and Sunday against the A's. So that's why we're planning to have Williams out there hitting those idle afternoons."

Good thing, too. In the first game, Ted went precisely according to plan—1-for-3—even if the hit was a scratch double off Sid Hudson, a gift from the official scorer after Doc Cramer couldn't hold on to the ball after a short run. He was at .405, but that was fine, he was right on pace, right where he needed to be. But the pace stalled terribly on Wednesday. The Sox swept a doubleheader from the dreadful Senators, who threw a couple of knuckleballers at them, one right-handed, one left-handed. Dutch Leonard, who'd served up the pitch on which DiMaggio had tied George Sisler's hitting-streak record earlier in the summer, stifled Williams in the first game, while a kid southpaw named Dick Mulligan—who would pitch in exactly twenty-five games in his major league career, winning three—nearly did the same in the nightcap. Bill Grieve, the first-base umpire, gave Williams a boost in the fourth inning of the second game, extending his arms and barking "Safe!" after Williams bounced a slow roller toward sec-ond baseman Jimmy Bloodworth. It was only Ted's fifth infield single of the season, and it came by an eyelash, and it was his only trip in seven at-bats, and that alone kept his average propped up at .401. Cronin, doing his best to imitate Tommy Henrich's selfless play during one of the crisis points of DiMaggio's streak, had laid down a sacrifice bunt in the ninth in-ning of the opener, with Boston up five runs, in the hope of buying Ted an extra at-bat, but Williams wound up drawing a walk.

Now, Williams was officially staring at the abyss, his average as low as it had been since the middle of July, and he would have almost seventy-two hours to think about the task at hand.

"It was the first and only time that year that .400 seemed to be weighing on his mind," Dominic DiMaggio would recall many years later. "Who could blame him? This is something he'd wanted to do his whole life, and six months of effort had gone into giving him a chance, and if he lost out in the final few days he knew he'd be kicking himself for a long, long time."

Ted spent the off-days hitting, and thinking, and hitting, and worrying, and hitting, and visualizing, and hitting. Friday was a gorgeous, sunny day, perfect for baseball, perfect for the game that should have been played that day if not for Mack's creative accounting.

The amateur mathematicians were back at work again, needing to rejigger their figures. Now, they determined, Ted would need to go 5-for-12 across the three games. Even 4-for-12 wouldn't get it done, leaving him at .3991. Stories in the morning newspapers were saying that Mack had already told his pitchers that they should come after Williams, and not walk him on purpose. Williams appreciated that. He started feeling better about his swing, too, especially after blasting one over the wall, out onto Twentieth Street, even though the batting cage was set up fifty feet in back of home plate.

"Coming to Shibe Park at this time of the year is another headache," Williams said. "During the summer, Shibe is a happy hunting ground for all the hitters, but in the fall the shadows are bad and you don't get a good look at the ball. I'm not alibi-ing, I want to hit over .400, but I'm going to play in all three games even if I don't get a ball out of the infield. A batting record's no good unless it's made in all the games of the season. I'll play even if it means finishing at .360. All's I need is five hits the next two days. Only five. I can get 'em."

Williams's unwillingness to even consider sitting out and sitting on .401 impressed the hell out of his manager. "You've got to admire the Kid for being so courageous about it," he said. "But I'll tell you one thing: I may yank him in that second game Sunday if he's got his hits. Why? Because it's the toughest, roughest ballpark in the world to hit in late in the day at this time of year. Shibe Park with its high stands all around the relatively small playing field have shadows that make it tough for a batter in late September. Plus, we go on the new time Sunday, and with the first game starting at 1:30 it'll be pretty dark when that second game gets under way. I feel I have obligations and I may decide to take him out of the second game, even if he doesn't like it."

By the close of business on Saturday, though, it looked like Williams might need every available at-bat Cronin could find for him. Facing another knuckleballer, Roger Wolff, Ted drew a full-count walk in the second inning and then doubled sharply in the fourth, nudging the average to .402, giving a quiet thrill to the tiny crowd of a thousand or so fans. But in the fifth, he flied out lazily to right field, and in the eighth he popped up to first, and that left his average right on the precipice, at .4004, and he figured that would be it for the day. But the Sox mounted a rally in the top of the ninth, and with two outs Williams got one last surprise at-bat. Some surprise. He whiffed on a low-breaking knuckler, and suddenly he had a genuine dilemma on his hands.

Technically, his average stood at .39955. Officially, that would be rounded up, and for the rest of time, had Williams opted to sit out the doubleheader on Sunday, the record book would reflect that he hit precisely .400 for 1941. Because of this, Cronin felt an obligation to offer his star one last chance to preserve his place in the historical firmament. But before he could even broach the subject, Williams waved it off.

"I'm playing," he said. "And that's that."

There was little doubt that .400 was the prime thing on Williams's mind as he left the ballpark. As much as everyone from Joe Cronin to Hugh Duffy had told him to relax, to not worry about .400, to keep doing what he was doing, it was impossible *not* to think about it. It was impossible *not* to think of balls that had landed just foul during the past six months, of bad-hop grounders called errors, of screaming line drives hit right at somebody's mitt. For Joe Cronin, it was torturous to think of those 12 to 15 sacrifice flies that, in other years, would not have qualified as official times at-bat; if that rule had applied this year, Williams would be sitting at .411, minimum. If.

Still, Williams's roommate that summer, pitcher Charlie Wagner, always remembered that, as completely as .400 surely occupied Ted's thoughts, it never occurred to him that he wouldn't get there.

"It wasn't a nervous confidence," he said. "We didn't talk about it because there was no discussion on hitting between us, ever. All Ted wanted to know was who was pitching. In those days, teams didn't list the pitchers for the next day because everyone was afraid of the gamblers' influence. So Ted always had to wait until he got to the ballpark to see who was pitching."

Ted went for a long walk that night, but was in bed early, up early enough to wolf down a big breakfast, and to the park early enough to take a couple of extra swings in the batting cage. He started tinkering with his right foot, pointing it more toward third base. The sky was cloudy, the weather gloomy, with more than a trace of rain in the forecast, and Williams hoped the storms would hold off long enough for him to take an honest shot at his life's ambition. Cronin, meanwhile, told his team that he'd start handing out fines if he heard anyone offering Ted advice. "I really don't see any batter anywhere who can qualify as a coach for Ted's hitting," he told them.

Ten thousand people showed up at old Shibe Park, a hefty enough number to bring a smile to Connie Mack's face. Williams was impatient. He started pacing in the dugout, yelling encouragement at his teammates even before the first pitch, driving everyone crazy. "He was always pumped up on adrenaline," Bobby Doerr recalled. "But that day, he was sky high from the moment he walked into the dugout."

The Athletics were planning to honor Lefty Grove, who'd won the first 195 games of his career as an A, between games, and Williams found himself wishing he were facing a veteran like Grove today, someone he was familiar with. Instead, he'd get a couple of kids—Dick Fowler, a rookie just up from Toronto, and Fred Caligiuri, freshly recalled from Wilmington. Williams was hitting fourth, and when the Red Sox were retired in order in the first, he had to wait an extra fifteen minutes to get his first chance. When he did, he had two messages waiting for him.

The first came from Bill McGowan, the home plate umpire. Just before Ted stepped into the batter's box, McGowan came from behind him and bent over to clean off home plate. Without looking up, McGowan told Williams, "To hit .400, a batter has got to be loose. He's got to be *loose.*"

Just as McGowan returned to his post, Frankie Hayes, the Athletics' catcher, looked up at Ted through his mask.

"Mr. Mack told us if we let up on you, he'll run us all out of baseball," Hayes said. "I wish you all the luck in the world, but we're not giving you a damn thing."

Fowler threw two balls, then came in with a fastball and Williams ripped it cleanly, right through the hole between first baseman Bob Johnson and second baseman Crash Davis. The crowd roared its approval, and so did the Sox dugout. He was at .4008. He was legit. And he wasn't finished. In the fifth, Fowler came with another fastball, and this time the only hole in play was the one Williams nearly bored through the sky: The blast landed on Twentieth Street, some 440 feet away. Now he was at .4022. An inning later, this time facing lefty Porter Vaughan, he smoked a hard ground ball that found the same hole the first one did; he was at .4035. Then, in the seventh, he cracked a line drive right over Johnson's head: .4048! Even when he reached on an error his final time up, shaving the average to .4039, he'd all but clinched his place not only in the record books, but in one of the great baseball fables of all time.

"It wasn't in him to ever take the easy way out," Doerr said. "Doing it that way was just pure Ted."

Cronin didn't even bother asking Ted if he wanted to take the second game off. Why would he? He smashed a single his first time up, once again finding that comfortable hole between second and first (.4052) and then provided the coup de grace in the fourth, bludgeoning a 2-and-1 fastball from the overmatched Caligiuri with such force that after it cleared the right-centerfield fence, the ball plunked into the loudspeaker horns perched high on the wall, punched a hole in one of them, then fell back onto the field. For the rest of his life, Williams would say, "That was the hardest-hit ball of my career." Dominic DiMaggio would counter: "It might have been the hardest-hit ball of *anyone's* career."

His last, anticlimactic at-bat of the season was a lazy fly ball in the seventh, and that was it, his final average resting forever at .4057, rounded up forever to .406, and if you count all those sac flies that weren't . . . well, he could have hit as high as .419.

But .406 would do just fine.

"If there's ever been a ballplayer who deserved to hit .400, it's Ted," Cronin said. "He's given up plenty of chances to bunt and protect his average in recent weeks. He wouldn't think of getting out of the lineup to keep his average intact. I tell you, I never came closer to bawling right out loud on a baseball diamond than when Ted got that third hit. I really filled right up. I was so happy that the Kid had done the trick without asking or being given any favors. I guess I was no different from the whole rest of the club."

McGowan, granted a front-row seat to the whole afternoon, was ebullient in describing what he'd just seen. "Don't let anyone tell you those kid pitchers weren't bearing down on Ted. That single Ted hit in the seventh inning against Vaughan was off as beautiful a curveball as I've seen. The count was 3-and-2 at the time, and every one of Vaughan's pitches to Ted was a curve. Six straight curves, and I called two of them strikes. He made the grade the hard way."

Oddly, after a season and a summer when he'd barely been able to keep his gums from flapping, Williams himself was strangely subdued afterward. "There's no doubt that this even surpasses the All-Star homer as my biggest thrill," the Kid said. "I never wanted to do anything harder in my life."

Someone asked, "What about the MVP, Ted?"

"Gee," he said with a wide grin, "do you think there's any chance? Even if I don't, I'll be satisfied with that thrill out there today. I wasn't saying much about it, but I never wanted anything more in my life."

11

"WE CAN'T GO AROUND WITH SAD FACES."

SPORTS, SOLDIERS, SOLIDARITY, AND A DATE
WHICH WILL LIVE IN INFAMY

Bob Feller is sworn into the Navy by Lieutenant Commander Gene Tunney (R), as Chicago recruiting officer Lieutenant David N. Goldenson looks on (December 9).

The sporting diversions of summer dissolved too quickly, disappearing into the ether just as autumn arrived, leaving an anxious nation mostly alone to confront the ever-darkening specter. Whirlaway maintained a grueling pace throughout the rest of the racing season, Warren Wright and Ben Jones choosing to enter him in some twenty races in 1941, and his summer was capped by an August victory in the Travers Stakes at Saratoga, the unofficial "fourth leg" of the Triple Crown. And while that was historic—through 2006, he remains the only horse ever to win the Kentucky Derby, Preakness, Belmont Stakes, and Travers in the same year—by then Whirlaway had become almost a victim of his own successes, his own high standards, and his triumph was greeted by a vast national yawn. Billy Conn kept himself busy filming a forgettable piece of cinematic gold called *The Pittsburgh Kid* and enjoying life with his beautiful young bride, taking his first extended sabbatical from the rigors of ring life.

Joe Louis enjoyed no such vacation and rapidly reaffirmed his place as America's most prominent, and most indomitable, sporting hero. On September 29 he returned to the Polo Grounds for the first time since conquering Conn and hammered Lou Nova, the number-one contender, providing 56,549 fans with an old-school Louis performance, the champion finally flooring Nova for good one second before the end of the sixth round. There were some—including President Roosevelt, who'd specifically rearranged his schedule so he could hear the fight on the radio—who figured Nova could finish what Conn (now juking out of the way of some brutal reviews for *The Pittsburgh Kid*) had started. They were sadly mistaken.

"I forgot to duck," Nova explained.

By then, Joe DiMaggio had returned from his injured foot in grand style, finishing the season with a .357 average and thirty homers, his 125 RBIs five more than Ted Williams's, depriving the Kid of winning the Triple Crown (though he would win two others before his career was through). DiMaggio's teammates never forgot how meaningful DiMaggio's Streak had been to their cause, and had started to bristle in August when, with Williams chasing .400, much of the national sentiment seemed to shift away from Joe as the American League's Most Valuable Player. They wanted to show DiMaggio how indispensable they thought he was. So on August 29, after a terrible train ride from St. Louis to Washington, one sweltering sauna to another, DiMaggio made plans with his roommate, Lefty Gomez, to get a big meal at the Hotel Shoreham's restaurant and relax, maybe try to find someplace in the District where it was less than 99 degrees. That night Gomez was taking an especially long time to get ready, which had Joe antsy.

"Let's go, Lefty," he nagged. "All the steaks will be gone."

But Gomez wouldn't be budged. On the way to the elevator, he told DiMaggio, "Hey, come with me, I just remembered I need to stop by [reserve outfielder George] Selkirk's room."

"I'll get us a table and order," Joe said. "I'll meet you downstairs."

"No, no, stay with me," Gomez insisted. "It'll only take a minute."

DiMaggio grunted. "Okay," he grumbled, "but hustle it up."

Gomez knocked on the door of room 609-D. Selkirk answered, and waved Joe in. And when he entered the room, he was greeted by the sight of forty men—players, coaches, writers—with raised champagne glasses. There was a toast, then three cheers, then singing, and finally Gomez presented his roommate with a gift-wrapped package. DiMaggio opened it, and gasped: It was a sterling silver humidor from Tiffany's. On the top was a statuette of DiMaggio, swinging Betsy Ann. On one side was the number 56, for The Streak; on the other, 91, for the number of hits he'd collected during The Streak. The inscription is what finally got DiMaggio.

PRESENTED TO JOE DIMAGGIO BY HIS FELLOW PLAYERS ON THE
NEW YORK YANKEES TO EXPRESS THEIR ADMIRATION FOR HIS
CONSECUTIVE-GAME HITTING RECORD IN 1941.

Below that were the engraved autographs of all his teammates. DiMaggio would keep the humidor in his study until the day he died.

"The single greatest gift," he would say, "that I ever received."

DiMaggio would help write the perfect final chapter to a storybook season little more than six weeks later when the Yankees crushed the Brooklyn Dodgers in five games in one of the most hotly anticipated World Series ever. DiMaggio wasn't a dominant offensive force in the Series, collecting only five singles and driving in but a single run, but he did find himself squarely in the middle of one of the most infamous, and improbable, sequences in the history of the Fall Classic.

On October 5, a swelteringly unseasonable 90-degree day in Brooklyn, the Dodgers were holding a 4-3 lead with two outs and nobody on in the top of the ninth, on the verge of tying the Series at two games apiece. Hugh Casey, a curveballing specialist known to occasionally mix a spitball or two into his repertoire, threw a sharp-breaking full-count pitch to Yankees outfielder Tommy Henrich, and Henrich took a weak swing chasing it. The game was over.

Only it wasn't. Though the 33,813 people inside Ebbets Field had already begun celebrating, though a brigade of cops had already stormed the field anticipating the need to keep peace, few of them noticed that the baseball had skipped past Dodgers catcher Mickey Owen—who'd committed only three errors all year, who'd allowed only two passed balls in 128 games, and who was now lumbering toward the backstop to retrieve the ball. Henrich was on first base, granted one of the grandest reprieves in sporting history.

DiMaggio, up next, promptly lined a clean single, extending the rally, reducing Ebbets Field to a somber tomb of inevitability. Charlie Keller followed with a double to right field that plopped against the large screen set atop a nineteen-foot wall, scoring Henrich with the tying run and DiMaggio with the go-ahead run—the only run DiMaggio would score all series, in fact. Before the inning was over, the Yankees would add two more runs, win the game 7-4, and the next day they would close out the Series with a 3-1 victory that caused hearts to shatter all over the Borough of Churches, and so moved a young sports columnist writing for the *Philadelphia Record* that he could barely contain his emotions from spilling onto his typewriter.

"It could only happen in Brooklyn," Red Smith surmised. "Nowhere else in this broad, untidy universe, not in Bedlam nor in Babel or in the remotest psychopathic ward . . . only in the ancestral home of the Dodgers . . . could a man win a World Series game by striking out."

"What happened in Brooklyn," Smith concluded, "should have happened in Berlin."

———————●———————

Professional football took its time establishing a bridgehead in New York City. The National Football League, founded in 1920, had Midwestern roots, and ancient ties to a small-town America where cities such as Green Bay, Wisconsin; Pottsville, Pennsylvania; and Muncie, Indiana could play host to "major league" teams. Five years later, with the league desperately wanting to crack into the nation's one true media market, the league contacted Timothy Mara, son of a New York City policeman, owner of one of the city's most colorful personalities and operator of one of its most successful legal bookmaking operations, and asked if he'd like to buy into the league for five hundred dollars. It was an offer Mara couldn't possibly refuse. "In New York," he told his nine-year-old son Wellington, "an empty store with two chairs in it is worth that much."

It wasn't until December 6 of that year that Tim Mara started to believe he hadn't made a terrible mistake. Already he was drowning in red ink, the team having lost $45,000. Mara was desperate to find a buyer to rescue him from his folly. But a fateful break in the schedule changed Mara's mind, and probably changed the course of pro football forever. Red Grange, the sensational college football star from the University of Illinois, had just signed with the Chicago Bears. Just ten days earlier, on Thanksgiving Day, he'd made his debut against the Chicago Cardinals, drawing 36,000 people to Wrigley Field, and in those haphazard early days of the NFL the Bears managed to squeeze two other games in the next week, drawing huge crowds in Columbus and St. Louis. New York, then as now a big-ticket town, wanted to get in on the fun, and it just so happened the Bears were scheduled to play in the Polo Grounds on December 6. All 65,000 tickets sold in a flash. On game day, 10,000 more people managed to con their way into the stadium, and while the Bears soundly thumped his team 19-7—highlighted by a thirty-five-yard interception return for a touchdown by Grange—Tim Mara decided that day that pro football really might work in New York.

Now, sixteen years and one day later, the Giants were one of the league's marquee franchises, with four championships to their credit, with a modest but growing base of season-ticket holders, with a core of fan-favorite players who inspired rabid devotion among the faithful. One such icon was Alphonse "Tuffy" Leemans, a single-wing tailback who, as a first-year player in 1936, had led the NFL in rushing and become an immediate star in New York, moving in the same circles as another rookie from the sporting class of '36, Joe DiMaggio.

Leemans's reputation as a workhorse endeared him to the fans, even if it limited his effectiveness in ensuing years. By the end of 1941, with the Giants having already won eight of their first ten games to clinch first place in the Eastern Division, the team decided to honor Leemans during its final regular-season game, against the crosstown rival Brooklyn Dodgers. And so on a cloudy, 32-degree afternoon, 55,051 people flooded the Polo Grounds to salute Tuffy, and just before the two o'clock kickoff he received a silver tray, a silver trophy, a gold wristwatch, and $1,500 in U.S. Defense bonds.

Soon enough, the crowd settled into their seats and prepared to watch the Giants and the Dodgers, who enjoyed just as heated a rivalry with each other as their baseball namesakes did. The Dodgers had already handed the Giants one of their two losses earlier in the year, and they started this game quickly, too, marching down the field rapidly, setting themselves up first-and-goal at the Giants' four-yard-line. The crowd was lost in the game, lost in the excitement, Giants fans shouting for a goal-line stand, Dodgers fans yelling for a quick touchdown. The Dodgers approached the line of scrimmage. Center Earl Svendsen snapped the ball to quarterback Rhoten Shetley.

Just then, a burst of feedback pierced the din as a primitive loudspeaker system clicked on.

"Attention please!"

Play halted. The crowd buzz quieted.

"Here is an urgent message! Will Colonel William J. Donovan call Operator Nineteen in Washington, D.C., immediately!"

It seemed an odd announcement in the middle of a football game. So did the one that followed a little bit later, summoning Wendell Willkie, the leading Republican who'd run unsuccessfully against Franklin Roosevelt thirteen months earlier. Most of the crowd turned back to the game, watched the Dodgers take a 7-0 lead, and wondered who Colonel William J. Donovan was. Those who knew the answer to that question—he was a millionaire Wall Street lawyer who'd served in France during the Great War as part of New York's 69th Regiment, the "Fighting Irish," who'd been known as "Wild Bill" ever since serving under Black Jack Pershing in Mexico before that, and who had recently been named chief of a burgeoning intelligence operation called the Office of Strategic Services—might have had an inkling that something was up. Donovan himself found out soon enough. When he contacted Operator Nineteen, he was patched through to James Roosevelt, the president's son.

"The Japanese bombed Pearl Harbor this morning," James said.

Across the nation, as those same words were repeated a million times in the next few hours, neighbor to neighbor, brother to brother, wife to husband, announcer to listener, the shock that might have accompanied that piece of news was muffled ever so slightly as almost everyone had the same question: *What's Pearl Harbor?*

Wild Bill Donovan knew, though, and he knew what it meant.

"Good God," he gasped on the phone.

"The president needs you in Washington, Bill," James Roosevelt said. "Could you come immediately?"

Of course he could. There might not have been two men in the United States more diametrically opposed politically than Franklin Roosevelt and William J. Donovan, who'd been classmates at Columbia Law School. Donovan was a Republican, and an outspoken critic of the New Deal, but in those simpler times that simply made a man a worthy adversary, not a pariah. Shortly before midnight he would be ushered into the Oval Office, where Roosevelt was waiting for him. "They caught our ships like lame ducks! Lame ducks, Bill," Roosevelt raged. "It's a good thing you got me started on this."

Roosevelt was referring to rudimentary intelligence operations that Donovan had suggested and pushed forward in his new role with the OSS, the model and forerunner to the Central Intelligence Agency. By then Roosevelt had assembled a full accounting of just how horrific the attack had been. The entire U.S. Pacific Fleet lay in ruins. Eighteen ships had been sunk or rendered unusable. One hundred eighty-eight planes were destroyed, and another 159 were badly damaged as they'd sat helplessly, bunched together like cordwood to fend off possible sabotage.

And 2,403 Americans had been killed.

Roosevelt had already spoken with Winston Churchill, who had called from Chequers, his country residence, when he heard the news on the radio. Less than four months earlier, Roosevelt and Churchill had secretly met aboard warships in a secure anchorage at Argentia, Newfoundland, officially to establish a vision for a postwar Europe, really to formalize the unwritten alliance between the United States and the United Kingdom. Roosevelt had traveled to the meeting on the heavy cruiser USS *Augusta,* escorted by three battleships, while Churchill traversed the Atlantic on the battleship HMS *Prince of Wales.* The eight-point agreement, the Atlantic Charter, signed on August 14, had all but clinched, in many American minds, the inevitability of U.S. participation in a shooting war. It had also strengthened the friendship between two old political survivors.

"It's quite true," Roosevelt said grimly. "They have attacked us at Pearl Harbor. We are all in the same boat now."

Churchill, while offering sympathies, understood that this was probably the most fortunate thing that had happened to England in three years.

"This actually simplifies things," he said. "God be with you."

Back at the Polo Grounds, the news began to filter through the stands, ever so gradually. Some fans had brought a relatively new invention with them to the stadium, a portable radio, and they were charged with distributing and disseminating whatever bulletins came inching through their tiny speakers. On the Giants sideline, a priest named Father Benedict Dudley, the team chaplain, walked over to twenty-five-year-old Wellington Mara and told him the news.

"What does this mean, Father?" Wellington asked, though he already suspected he knew the answer.

"I think it means war, Well," Father Dudley said. "God help us all."

For the first time, sports would have to truly confront its place in the larger picture. No longer could it serve as an escape, because now there was no fleeing someone else's war. Soon enough, it would be our war, too. It would take a while to get used to that notion, and nowhere was this better exemplified than in the opposite halftime locker rooms at the Polo Grounds that day, located up a steep set of wooden stairs behind what served as center field during the baseball season.

"At halftime, our coach, Steve Owen, told us about Pearl Harbor," Jim Poole, a Giants end, would recall for sports columnist Dave Anderson fifty years later. "He gave us such a bad account of all the bad things that happened there, it was like we didn't want to go back out on the field."

In the other dressing room, Dodgers traveling secretary Frank Scott alerted Brooklyn coach Jock Sutherland of the grim news. "Don't mention it to the players, Scotty," Sutherland said. "They'll get upset. We've got another half to play."

But this kind of news didn't keep for long. Most of the Dodgers had already heard sketchy reports of what happened, even if nobody was discussing it openly. They quietly returned to the field and methodically did what they had to do, winning the game 21-7, ending their season 7-4, sending the Giants off to the NFL Championship Game in two weeks on a sour note that hardly anyone on the Giants seemed to notice.

"Things," Wellington Mara would say, "were already pretty sour."

Whatever doubt may have lingered as to the gravity of the day's events vanished midway through the fourth quarter, when again the Polo Grounds' public address system clicked on and another announcement came rushing out of the sky: "Attention, please! All navy men in the audience are ordered to report to their posts immediately. All army men are to report to their posts tomorrow morning. This is important!"

Those who didn't have posts to rush to went home, and those who didn't have radios in their homes sought out neighbors who did, and throughout the rest of that terrible Sunday came a fuller and richer and bloodier picture of what had happened, and what was to come. Roosevelt would address the nation the next day. Emperor Hirohito of Japan didn't wait that long to inform the world of the inevitable: that a state of war now existed between the United States, the United Kingdom, and the Empire of Japan.

"It has been truly unavoidable and far from our wishes that our Empire has now been brought to crossed swords with America and Britain," he said. "Patiently we have waited and long have endured in the hope that our government might retrieve the situation in peace, but our adversaries, showing not the least spirit of conciliation, have unduly delayed a settlement and in the meantime they have intensified the economic and political pressure to compel our Empire to submit."

U.S. Secretary of State Cordell Hull rose quickly to dismiss Hirohito's justifications.

"This government has stood for all the principles that underlie fair dealing, peace, law and order, and justice between nations and has steadfastly striven to promote and maintain that state of relationship between itself and all other nations, he said. "It is apparent to the whole world that Japan in its recent professions of a desire for peace has been infamously false and fraudulent."

That world had been a teetering tinderbox for three years already, but it now understood the sad reality of what was dawning. The *New York Times*, unwittingly or not, lent credence to these suspicions the morning after Pearl Harbor when it referred to the last great conflict into which the United States had entered. For twenty-three years it had been known as the Great War. Now, in the morning editions of December 8, 1941, it was given a new name: World War I.

The distinguishing Roman numeral hadn't been necessary before.

It was now.

———————●———————

The day after the first news flashes crackled across the country, delivering news of the impossibly horrific events at Pearl Harbor, things moved very quickly.

"Yesterday, December 7, 1941—a date which will live in infamy—the United States of America was suddenly and deliberately attacked by naval and air forces of the Empire of Japan," Roosevelt said, in asking Congress for a declaration of war. "The United States was at peace with that nation, and, at the solicitation of Japan, was still in conversation with its government and its Emperor looking toward the maintenance of peace in the Pacific." In the burgeoning age of mass communication, that one paragraph would be broadcast and rebroadcast more than any other ever uttered by any man.

Roosevelt's six-and-a-half-minute speech ended as it had to end, concluding at last his yearlong pledge to spare the nation the horrors of a new war. He believed he'd done all he could.

"No matter how long it may take us to overcome this premeditated invasion, the American people, in their righteous might, will win through to absolute victory. I believe that I interpret the will of the Congress and of the people when I assert that we will not only defend ourselves to the uttermost but will make it very certain that this form of treachery shall never again endanger us.

"Hostilities exist. There is no blinking at the fact that our people, our territory and our interests are in grave danger. With confidence in our armed forces, with the unbounding determination of our people, we will gain the inevitable triumph. So help us God.

"I ask that the Congress declare that since the unprovoked and dastardly attack by Japan on December 7, 1941, a state of war has existed between the United States and the Japanese Empire."

It had taken Congress four days to reach agreement on declaring war in 1917; it took precisely thirty-three minutes this time. The vote was 82-0 in the Senate, 338-1 in the House, with the lone dissenting vote coming from Jeannette Rankin, a Republican from Montana who'd also voted against the war in 1917 (although that time, 48 other congressmen stood with her). Of Rankin, John F. Kennedy would one day say, "Few members of Congress have ever stood more alone while being true to a higher honor and loyalty," but on the afternoon of December 8, 1941, she was heckled by her fellow lawmakers so fiercely that she sought exile in a telephone booth off the main Capitol corridor until everyone left the building. Three days later, when both houses voted by acclamation to declare war on Germany and Italy, too, Rankin backed off ever so slightly, stating "Present" when her name was called, abstaining rather than voting no.

The voting done, Garrett Whiteside, clerk of the Senate Committee on Enrolled Bills, delivered the official declaration to the White House for the president's signature. Twenty-four years earlier, working in the office of the House bill clerk, Whiteside had been sitting behind a desk when the chairman of the Foreign Affairs Committee had wandered into the room, asking if he could use a typewriter. Instead, Whiteside had taken the dictation for the formal U.S. declaration of the last Great War.

Now, just past four o'clock, he handed another one to the President of the United States. At precisely 4:10 P.M., Franklin Delano Roosevelt signed his name to the bottom of the resolution. The United States, officially, was at war.

———————●———————

Everywhere, American life on December 8 and beyond was markedly different than it had been up to the predawn hours of December 7. Recruiting stations in all forty-eight states were jammed with men eager to volunteer for the cause. The president ordered the Capitol dome to be dimmed, and it would stay that way for much of the next four years. In New York City, the lights of Broadway continued to blaze, but one unfortunate and ill-timed production never did get the opportunity to see its name immortalized in the Great White Way's neon bulbs. Jose Ferrer's production of *The Admiral Had a Wife* was supposed to have its last out-of-town preview in Wilmington, Delaware, on December 8 before holding a grand premiere in New York on the tenth. The play was a comedic farce starring Uta Hagen, Richard Hale, and an unknown burlesque skit player named Red Buttons, and the premise was simple enough: The wives of a certain gaggle of admirals were really running the navy. It was the setting that was troublesome: Pearl Harbor. The show never made it to Wilmington, much less New York, and was never performed publicly again.

The name of the war's first casualty was announced, Robert Niedzwiecki, twenty-two, of Grand Rapids, Michigan. The War Department sent his father, Peter, the grim news in a brief note: "Your son, Robert, died at 10 a.m. December 7. Battle casualty, result of machine gun and shrapnel wounds."

Charles Lindbergh, conspicuously silent for two days, surfaced on December 9, three days before the America First Committee would officially announce it was ceasing operations for the foreseeable future. "We have been stepping closer to war for many months," he said. "Now it has come and we must meet it as united Americans regardless of our attitude in the past toward the policy our government has followed. Whether or not that policy has been wise, our country has been attacked by force of arms and by force of arms we must retaliate. Our own defenses and our own military position have already been neglected too long. We must now turn every effort to building the greatest and most efficient Army, Navy and Air Force in the world. When American soldiers go to war it must be with the best equipment that modern skill can design and that modern industry can build."

Roosevelt, suddenly recast as a war president, would become a regular radio presence in the early hours of the conflict, when each day the news seemed to grow darker and bleaker: Japanese submarines were spotted off the coast of San Francisco. A panic seized Manhattan when false reports of an air raid spread. The Japanese army, gaining momentum after its unconditional triumph at Pearl Harbor, blazed through the South Pacific: Wake

Island, Hong Kong, the Philippines. Things were not looking good, and Roosevelt saw no reason to soften the truth.

"So far all the news has been bad," he admitted on December 9. "Our enemies have performed a brilliant feat of deception, perfectly timed and executed with great skill. We are now fighting to maintain our rights to live among our world neighbors in freedom and common decency, without fear of assault. On the road ahead lies hard work—grueling work—day and night, every hour and every minute. It is collaboration so well calculated that all the continents of the world, and all the oceans, are now considered by the Axis strategists as one gigantic battlefield. Germany and Japan are conducting their military operations in accordance with the joint plan."

The entire country was in a state of flux, and nowhere was the uncertainty more pronounced than in sports, which wanted to do its best to remain relevant without being inappropriately intrusive. Back in the First World War, baseball had come within hours of shutting its doors when Congress issued a "work-or-fight" order, declaring that all men of draftable age either join the army or a military-related industry by July 1, 1918. Baseball, initially, wasn't on the list of exempt industries, but at the last moment it was granted a reprieve. The season was shortened to 126 games, the World Series began the first week in September, and the war was over two months later.

This new war had already wreaked havoc on sports across Europe and Asia. The 1940 Summer Olympics, originally awarded to Tokyo, were removed from Japan after the start of the Sino-Japanese War in 1937. Moved to Helsinki, Finland, they, too, were ultimately canceled as the war's blood began to spread ever deeper into European soil. The Winter Olympics scheduled for that year had an even more hectic itinerary. Originally set for Sapporo, Japan, they were stripped from the Japanese at the same time the Summer Games were and moved to St. Moritz, Switzerland. But a dispute between local organizers and the International Olympic Committee forced a switch again, this time to Garmisch-Partenkirchen, Germany, site of the 1936 Winter Games. The war's onset made that site even more unfeasible than the others, and the Games were canceled altogether. All international golf and tennis tournaments were suspended for the duration, as was the Tour de France bicycle race, as was the World Cup soccer tournament. Only England had tried to maintain a semblance of sporting normalcy, conducting Triple Crown races as planned and keeping as regular a soccer schedule as it could, considering so many footballers were now otherwise engaged.

"This is my third war, and I think the game will go safely through this one as it did through the Spanish-American and the last World War," Washington Senators owner Clark Griffith said. "They encouraged us to keep the game going in the last one. We played on in 1917 and while we lost twenty-eight games when the season was shortened, we played the World Series that year and came back strong."

Said Connie Mack, who would soon celebrate his seventy-ninth birthday: "We can't go around with sad faces. We must be cheerful. Sports do a great deal to keep morale. During the last war the 1918 season was curtailed, but later we thought that was a mistake."

So baseball bided its time, deciding to wait for a directive from the president who, for the time being, was otherwise occupied. The winter meetings went on as scheduled in Chicago, where it was announced that $100,000 worth of receipts from the 1942 All-Star Game, assuming it was played, would be set aside to purchase sports equipment for the armed forces. The only transaction of note was Mel Ott, the Giants' slugging outfielder, replacing Bill Terry as manager of the team, something that in other years, under other circumstances, would have delighted Brooklyn Dodgers fans to no end. It was Terry who, when asked several seasons earlier how he viewed the Dodgers' chances of challenging the Giants in the National League, had replied, "Are the Dodgers still in the National League?" That had filled Brooklyn fans with blind fury for years, and they'd lusted for vengeance. Now, Terry's demise merited merely a quiet paragraph in the morning papers, a photograph in the afternoon dailies.

On December 13, the first cold blast of reality hit sports, when Gov. Culbert L. Olsen of California telegraphed authorities in Pasadena, forwarding a request of the army that the Tournament of Roses and the January 1 Rose Bowl between Oregon State and Duke be canceled "for reasons of national defense and civilian protection." He said that would likely mean cancellation of East-West All-Star Game in San Francisco, too.

Gen. John L. DeWitt of the Western Defense Command explained, "The congestion of the state highways over a large area, incident to this tournament and football game, and its serious obstruction to their use in defense work, the concentration there of a large police force now needed for defensive services, the unusually large gathering of people, known to the enemy, exposing them to the dangers now threatening, require that plans for the tournament and football game be abandoned."

That was just the first sporting blow to California, which most of the nation understood was the state most vulnerable to enemy attack. Within days the NFL's Pro Bowl, scheduled for Los Angeles, was also canceled. Most disappointing of all, however, came the announcement on December 15 that the Santa Anita Handicap, one of the showcase events of the Thoroughbred racing calendar, would be canceled, and that the entire Santa Anita meet was also likely to be wiped out. This was a devastating blow, because Santa Anita officials had already received a commitment from Warren Wright that Whirlaway intended to race in the Handicap, and to spend the winter months training at the track. Knowing this, they had arranged for the richest meet in racing history, with purses totaling well over a million dollars. The Handicap, which had been scheduled for March 7, 1942, had already drawn not only a record amount of entries, but interest: Every seat for Handicap day had already been sold.

There was talk that the army might relent after a few weeks' time and loosen its restrictions. The Rose Bowl couldn't wait; Oregon State agreed to accept Duke's offer to play the game at fifty-thousand-seat Duke Stadium in Durham, North Carolina. But Warren Wright decided to keep his prized colt in California and wait to see how events unfolded. On December 8, Whirlaway had been named "Horse of the Year" in a closer-than-expected vote over Alsab, the year's best two-year-old, and Wright and Ben Jones both figured Whirlaway would be even better in 1942.

"Plus," Ben Jones would admit later, "we wanted that money record. That wasn't something you could talk about in December of 1941, though."

Ben Jones, Warren Wright, and Whirlaway would sit tight and wait to see what would happen with the world. Same as the world would.

———————●———————

Hank Greenberg had made the most of his seven months in the army. He'd settled easily into the anonymous life of a G.I., and while the pay wasn't near as good as he was used to, he didn't miss the daily glare and the constant interrogations he dealt with in his other world, as the highest-paid baseball player in the country. His commanders said he was "a good joe" and "a regular guy," and the other soldiers at Fort Custer commented on how "down-to-earth" and "normal" he was. He'd actually made a rapid ascent through the enlisted ranks, earning three different promotions—to private first class, to corporal, and finally to sergeant—which meant his monthly take-home pay had almost tripled, to sixty dollars a month.

Still, when the army announced it would start granting early discharges for draftees older than twenty-eight, Greenberg had inquired. He'd be thirty-one in January, and was at least eight or nine years older than just about every other draftee in his regiment. The army agreed. The paperwork was done, but, the army being the army, it took a while to process. Finally, Greenberg was given a discharge date.

December 5, 1941.

"Baseball season is a long way off," he said three days before that. "When I get out of the army, I'm going home to New York for a while and I'll do some planning there."

Freshly discharged, Greenberg got a quick reminder of all that he'd been missing for the past 180 days. For the benefit of photographers, he carried his army equipment to the warehouse three different times to accommodate everyone, he made his bed twice, and repeatedly went through the motions of picking up his final pay stub from the army—ten dollars in back wages. He hustled home to Detroit, checked back into the Leland Hotel, and planned to enjoy a night on the town with friends. He chatted about the possibility of the Tigers trading Rudy York, which might allow him to return to first base, his preferred position. The next day he had a wisdom tooth extracted and revealed that he would be "on-call" for the next ten years as a member of the army reserve.

"I'm ready to go back if I'm needed," he said. "I hope I'm not needed. For the next few days I hope to forget about baseball, the army, and everything else and concentrate on re-acclimating myself to civilian life. It's good to be around again. I feel fine and I'm in pretty good shape from playing handball. I expect to play a lot more handball and squash between now and when I leave for training camp next February. I don't expect to be there early."

On his way back to his parents' house in the Bronx, Greenberg stopped in Philadelphia to visit some old friends. It was there that he first heard the bulletins about Pearl Harbor. And it was there that he first understood that his furlough was going to be a brief one. It wasn't 100-percent guaranteed that Greenberg would be recalled, at least not immediately, not with the glut of fresh volunteers who would soon be signing up for the action. But he never even thought twice about it.

"I'm going back in," Greenberg said on December 9. "We are in trouble and there's only one thing to do, return to the service. I have not been called back. I am going back of my own accord. It isn't anything particularly credible to me. That's what we are all going to do, isn't it? There are a million men or so in the service ready to defend the country. It's our job."

A long layoff could hurt your baseball career, he was reminded.

"Baseball," he said, "is out the window as far as I'm concerned. I don't know if I'll ever return to baseball. If I do, all right. If not . . . well, that's all right, too."

That same day, Bob Feller walked down State Street in Chicago, ducked unnoticed into the Palmer House Hotel, and was quickly surrounded by a gathering of baseball writers in town to cover the winter meetings. Though he'd already won 107 games, struck out 1,233 major league hitters, and earned well over $100,000 as a member of the Cleveland Indians, Feller had only recently turned twenty-three years old, having entered the world exactly eight days before the Armistice ending World War I was signed in 1918. Along with Joe DiMaggio and Ted Williams, he was part of a generation of extraordinary talents who'd joined baseball within the last half decade, all of them well under thirty, which made all of them likely candidates to be spending the foreseeable future out of home whites and inside dress greens.

Feller decided to lead that parade. That morning, he'd applied to the Great Lakes Naval Training Station in Great Lakes, Illinois, for enlistment in the U.S. Naval Reserve as a chief boatswain's mate, the rating given navy physical training instructors. Lt. Comdr. Gene Tunney, formerly the heavyweight champion of the world, accepted Feller's application personally. He didn't expect there to be any complications.

"I want to go where I can do the most good," Feller said. "Count me out for the coming season—maybe a lot longer. Tell the rest of the guys good luck and watch that first one. This is a big game we're in now, and I've got to do my share."

"How about reveille, Bob?" a reporter from the *Cleveland Press* asked. "Think you'll make it on time?"

"I had to get up early when I was a kid to milk the cows and get to school," said Feller, who grew up on a farm in Van Meter, Iowa. "I guess I'll get up without much trouble."

"You should be okay pitching," the reporter said, before giving a little insight into the kind of fervor that had already swept across most of the nation. "Even if the grenade doesn't explode, you should do all right just beaning one of those filthy Japs."

Feller said that he and his Indians teammate Soup Campbell had often discussed what branch of the service they wanted to pursue, and Feller said, "Whatever it was, I wanted to make sure it wasn't too soft. I want to do what the fans think I should be in there doing. If they want me pitching grenades, that's my dish. If it's flying a combat plane or in the air service elsewhere, or in the navy, I'd prefer to be there. When I'm in uniform, I want to 'keep pitching,' as it were."

Feller had reason to talk this way because throughout the second half of the 1941 season, for the first time in his life, Indians fans had started to treat him with something other than reverential devotion. His story, told and retold a thousand times the past few years, had been an irresistibly American fable: At twelve he'd been a child prodigy, Mozart with a mitt, playing in men's amateur leagues. At fourteen he played in a fast semipro league. His first game as an Indian, as a seventeen-year-old in 1936, he'd faced nine St. Louis Cardinals in an exhibition game and struck out eight of them. Later, in his first real start, he'd fanned fifteen St. Louis Browns. To Indians fans who hadn't had much to cheer for since the 1920 championship team, he was looked upon as a messiah and treated like a savior.

That had started to turn in 1940, when Feller, along with several other prominent teammates, had engineered a mutiny that cost manager Ossie Vitt his job, even though the Indians finished in second place, just one game behind the Tigers. Early in '41, he'd come across as something of a spoiled, petulant child when he'd railed at opposing teams who tried to steal signals against the Indians, hinting he'd start planting baseballs in their ears if they didn't stop. But the thing that really alienated Feller with his normally adoring public was his position on the draft. He had a relatively low number, and it wasn't likely he'd be called during the season anyway. Still, on June 6, with the Indians sitting atop the American League standings, the team hinted that if Feller was called up in August, they'd likely ask for a postponement that would allow him to finish the season.

"I wouldn't think it would be too much out of line to ask deferment for thirty days or so if it's near the end of the season," Roger Peckinpaugh, the Indians' new manager, said. Both Feller and C. C. Slapnicka, the Cleveland vice president who'd signed and nurtured Feller, anticipated how that might sound to a ticket-buying public bidding farewell to army-bound sons, brothers, and neighbors every day, and tried to muffle the controversy. Feller himself indicated he'd never seek a deferment, saying, "Everybody has to do his duty, and if they call me I'll do the best I can," while Slapnicka added, "Bobby's really tickled to death at the chance to serve. If we were in the war, he would not have to be drafted because he would enlist."

Then, a few weeks later, Feller was asked if he'd maybe be able to pitch for the Indians on weekends if he were drafted. Feller, laughing at the absurdity of the notion, said, "Gee, maybe I'll look into that," but his sarcasm didn't quite translate in the newspapers. There was another backlash. Somewhere, Hank Greenberg was either shaking his head in sympathy or muttering to himself: *Better you than me, kid.* Feller tried to spin his words like one of his curveballs: "Honestly, I haven't given any thought to that possibility. How about transportation? I don't see how I could arrange that unless Cleveland moved its ballpark to wherever I happened to be."

By now, though, his reputation had taken too much of a hit. It wasn't helped at all when it was revealed that Feller's mother had appealed to his local draft board that Feller was not only the sole provider for his family, but also was needed desperately at home since his father, Bill, was gravely ill. This was a standard plea available to and utilized by every draft-age kid in the country if the situation warranted. But those kids weren't Bob Feller. And so they didn't have to answer to "rocking-chair patriots," as one Cleveland sportswriter called them, who even now, after Feller became the first major leaguer after Pearl Harbor to voluntarily raise his right arm and take the naval oath, questioned everything about the sincerity of that tactic, criticized him for not seeking more hazardous duty. Some even had the gall to wonder if his father was really as sick as he was said to be.

Things hadn't changed a bit since Hank Greenberg had all but fled to the army seven months earlier. This was typical of the letters that flooded the Cleveland newspapers in the days and weeks after Pearl Harbor, after Feller went off to begin basic training, leaving behind a baseball career in which he'd seemed a shoo-in to become the third person in history to win four hundred games. It was signed "J. Miller, ex-first sergeant, AEF":

"Bobby Feller soured himself on the public when he said he wouldn't seek deferment—but let his mother and yourselves in the newspaper field go to bat for him. Anyone would be silly to think he didn't know what his mother was writing to the draft board seeking exemption on account of having dependants.

"It seems funny that his father developed a sickness after he became eligible for the draft. After he built them a $25,000 house on the farm then they couldn't keep it up if he didn't stay and play ball for a big salary and let some poor boy who helped at home go.

"He is a poor example for an American boy to follow, in that he shirked his duty to his country in time of war and stood in the background while others endeavored in various ways to have a deferment.

"Greenberg accepted his draft call in a spirit that had no question and sacrificed his career, but Bobby Feller tried to hide behind his mother's apron strings and the sportswriters' hints for deferment."

Sixty-four years later, Bob Feller, age eighty-seven, sighed when reminded of the things some people were saying about him in December 1941.

"It was a terrible time," he said. "I don't think people can be held accountable for what they say in a time like that. I don't know why they would say a thing like that. Here's what I do know: I went to the service knowingly, I went willingly, and if I was sacrificing something, that was fine, because a lot of other fellows were, too."

He paused.

"We had a war to win," Bob Feller said. "In the end, that was more important than any damned ball game."

Epilogue

A general view of the crowd in Times Square as the year 1941 melted into 1942. This scene, captured at the stroke of midnight, was photographed from the Marquee of the Hotel Astor.

If you didn't know any better, you would have sworn the past twenty-four days had been nothing more than a bad nightmare, a bloody hallucination. The people had been piling into the cordoned-off streets for hours and not one of them had come empty-handed; they carried pots and pans and whistles and buzzers, they lugged trumpets and drums and cowbells. In their jackets they carried snifters and flasks, they brought pocketfuls of cigars and cigarettes. They had all been walking on eggshells for three and a half weeks, unable to sleep, unable to work, unable to think of much of anything besides the fact that the world was going to hell faster than any of them could keep up. They'd celebrated Christmas and Hanukkah with restraint, mostly choosing to observe the spiritual side of the holiday season. They'd kept their radios tuned constantly to news reports, they'd emptied newsstands of papers and magazines, they talked to each other constantly, swapping rumors and worries, and to be honest, most of them were working on their very last nerve.

So for one night, at least, they'd decided to say: The hell with it.

For one night, the last night of a troubled year and the first morning of a new one that simply *had* to be a damned sight better, they did what came naturally. They came to Times Square, again, in even larger numbers than they had the year before, in even louder voice, in even greater spirits. By nine o'clock, the cops estimated that 200,000 of them were already milling about. By eleven o'clock that number was closer to half a million, and this time the revelers weren't containing themselves merely to Times Square proper. The fringes of the main celebration were also teeming with people, maybe a half million of them, maybe more.

"I hope the Japs and the Jerrys don't know about this," one cop said, marveling at the piles of humanity that continued to flow through the city about a half hour before midnight this New Year's Eve, before 1941 would melt into 1942. "If they did, they could win the war in about fifteen minutes, because I think everyone in the country is in New York City tonight."

"If Axis ears didn't hear last night's revelry in Times Square," the *New York Times* would proclaim in its first editions of the New Year, "it wasn't that New Yorkers didn't try."

The war was still foremost on people's minds, and it was a prominent co-host to the festivities. Fire trucks were stationed beside the Times Tower in Father Duffy Square. Police emergency trucks, ambulances, radio patrol cars, and mobile broadcasting units lined the streets, poised to provide relief at the first sign of worry. Signs and loudspeakers were fastened to light posts to give air raid warnings if they became necessary. A sign on the west end of the Square warned: IN CASE OF ALARM, LEAVE TIMES SQUARE. WALK WEST. DO NOT RUN. At the entrance to one of the city's most popular theaters was another attempt at reassurance: THE NEW YORK PARAMOUNT IS THOROUGHLY PREPARED FOR ANY EMERGENCY. OUR WELL-TRAINED STAFF OF 160 HAS BEEN DRILLED TO MAINTAIN THE SAFETY OF ITS PATRONS AT ALL TIMES. All of this gave a different tone to this evening compared to past New Year's Eves. But not one Broadway bulb was dimmed. Not one ordinance was passed suggesting that the people keep the noise down, even though Mayor Fiorello LaGuardia had pondered issuing a formal warning, urging people to stay home this night and not gather en masse, creating an inviting target.

"You can't hold people prisoner in their houses," the Little Flower had finally reasoned. "If you do, you're no better than the people we're fighting against."

When the theaters let out—after the people had seen sold-out performances by Eddie Cantor in *Banjo Eyes* at the Hollywood Theater, or Helen Hayes in *Candle in the Wind* at the Shubert, or Boris Karloff in *Arsenic and Old Lace* at the Fulton, or *The Corn Is Green* with Ethel Barrymore at the Royale, or *Clash by Night* with Tallulah Bankhead and Lee J. Cobb at the Belasco—the crowds grew so dense on the sidewalks that they could move only inches at a time. To blow their horns, revelers had to throw their heads backward and aim them skyward. Bells had to be held above their heads and shoulders. Yet nobody minded. Nobody complained. Nobody bickered. Even New York, with its famously quick temper, seemed to realize something: For now, and for the foreseeable future, we were all teammates. Praise the Lord and pass the bottle.

A few minutes before midnight, just before Thomas Ward would fulfill his annual duty for the twenty-eighth straight time and start lowering the three-hundred-pound New Year's ball, the loudspeakers dominating the Square sprang to life, not with an air-raid warning, but "The Star-Spangled Banner" instead. At the apex of the triangle defining the north end of Times Square stood singer Lucy Monroe, surrounded by policemen and firemen, flanking a large, hand-painted sign that read REMEMBER PEARL HARBOR. Standing sentry beside the young singer was the eight-foot bronze statue of Father Patrick Duffy, who'd been a military chaplain and was frozen forever in this monument in military garb, a helmet at his feet, a Bible in his hand, poised in front of a seventeen-foot Celtic cross.

There was a momentary hush when Monroe started, and then the crowd joined in and Times Square echoed with the sound of the National Anthem as it poured from a million throats. The radio networks picked it up, broadcasting it across the nation. When it was over, at 11:59, Ward finagled a few levers, pushed a couple of buttons, and the sacred ball began its sacred descent, and the din grew thick, and the horn-and-bell chorus swelled, shrill cheering and hoarse shouting spilling through the streets. Torn paper fluttered from hotel windows in the Square, turning and twisting in the brilliant paths of movie searchlight beams. Colored serpentines twisted and writhed in the wind eddy.

And then it was here: midnight, 1942, a new year, a fresh start, and soldiers and sailors and Coast Guarders and servicemen of all colors and all nations were suddenly and swiftly hoisted onto the crowd's shoulders. On Forty-third Street, a cluster of men wearing gray Australian fliers' uniforms were chatting quietly among themselves when, without warning, they were grabbed and lifted into the air like football heroes who'd just scored the winning touchdown. On down the block, two U.S. soldiers, three British sailors, and a 44th Division sergeant were given the same treatment.

Longtime New Yorkers couldn't remember a more boisterous celebration, even in peacetime, certainly not compared to the last wartime New Year's Eve. That had been December 31, 1917, eight months after the United States had entered World War I. That time there were more cops than celebrants, the streets were glazed over with ice, and Times Square had been blacked out because of a coal shortage and it was necessary to conserve power. That evening, twelve people died in the extreme 2-degree cold; there was little chance of that happening now, on a 42-degree night. Perhaps the grandest difference was visible at the esteemed Waldorf-Astoria, which on this night was packed with four thousand guests enjoying a lavish four-course meal for fifteen bucks a head. In 1917 it could serve only vegetable plates.

The State Liquor Authority announced that some 2,091 New York bars had bought special all-night licenses in anticipation of the masses not wanting to let go of the night until they absolutely had to. Only a funny thing happened. The post-midnight clamor lasted thirty-seven minutes, but as soon as the racket died down, it seemed as if the people vanished like magic. The Square was actually reopened for traffic by one o'clock. Quiet revisited the streets. Reality returned.

Soon there would be more awful news to digest from Manila, on the verge of falling at last to the Japanese. There would be Adolf Hitler's cheery New Year's greeting to the Germans—"He who fights for the life of his people, for his daily bread and his future will have victory, but he who is animated by Judaic hate and seeks in this war to annihilate all peoples will be destroyed." There would be room in the newspapers for brief snippets of comic relief—in Rochester, New York, a native-born American named Norman W. Fuehrer told Country Judge William C. Kohlmetz that he had tired of his friends greeting him as "Der Fuehrer," and his application to change his name to Scheer was approved, effective February 4—but these ever-too-fleeting moments would be replaced by more hard news, more depressing quotations, such as this one from Japanese prime minister Hideki Tojo: "The war has only just begun. Although the Japanese forces are fighting with the greatest energy, the war will be long in duration. As Britain and the United States have now started desperate counter-action to maintain the old order, there is no alternative for Japan but to continue the war to the end to achieve the great ideals for which she has been striving."

The waiting was over at last. The warring had just begun.

———————●———————

Sports would survive the war, even if it became a diminished product for the duration, certainly nowhere near the sublime levels it so often reached throughout 1941.

Baseball, the quintessential American game, set the example almost immediately. On January 14, 1942, Commissioner Kenesaw Mountain Landis had written a letter to President Roosevelt, seeking counsel on what should be done with the nation's pastime now that so many of its fans had marched off to war, soon to be joined by a great number of its players. "Baseball is about to adopt schedules, sign players, make vast commitments, go to training camps," Landis wrote. "What do you want us to do? We await your order."

Roosevelt responded the very next day, and his suggestion confirmed what had long been suspected but never verbalized, the fact that sport had become an integral part of the national fabric, essential not only to leisure but also to the quality of life itself.

"I honestly feel it would be best for the country to keep baseball going," the president wrote in what became instantly known as the "Green Light Letter." "There will be fewer people unemployed and everybody will work longer hours and harder than ever before. And that means that they ought to have a chance for recreation and for taking their minds off their work even more than before.

"Baseball provides a recreation which does not last [for more than] two hours or two hours and a half, and which can be got for very little cost. And, incidentally, I hope that night games can be extended because it gives an opportunity to the day shift to see a game occasionally.

"As to the players themselves, I know you agree with me that individual players who are of active military or naval age should go, without question, into the services. Even if the actual quality of the teams is lowered by the greater use of older players, this will not dampen the popularity of sport.

"Here is another way of looking at it—if three hundred teams use five thousand or six thousand players, these players are a definite recreational asset to at least twenty million of their fellow citizens—and that, in my judgment, is thoroughly worthwhile."

The brand of baseball played across the next four seasons would hardly be memorable, as more and more able-bodied players departed for the service, replaced by the aged and the infirm. Even the St. Louis Browns, the worst team in baseball history, managed to win the 1944 American League pennant, and a year later the Browns had a one-armed outfielder named Pete Gray who managed to play in seventy-seven games. But Roosevelt was right. People still came to the games. They still rooted for the players, even if they didn't possess household names. They still cared about sports, even if it wasn't with the fervor they showed in 1941, but that wasn't unusual. Sports had never meant more to people than it did in 1941. And in many ways, it would never mean quite the same to them ever again. How could it?

Baseball not only endured, it prospered in later years, and so did the men chiefly responsible for allowing it to reach the iconic status it attained in 1941.

Joe DiMaggio and Ted Williams both played through the 1942 season before entering the service. DiMaggio's military career was largely ceremonial, while Williams, not surprisingly, became a hero, serving two different tours in two different wars, once having to crash-land his plane while flying a mission over Korea in 1951. On November 11, 1941, DiMaggio was named the American League's Most Valuable Player for 1941 in one of the closest votes ever, DiMaggio receiving 291 points to Williams's 254, fifteen first-place votes to Williams's eight. Though the Boston writers howled in protest, even Williams himself admitted that he believed DiMaggio deserved the award based on how his Streak had helped propel the Yankees to the pennant, while his own batting heroics could draw the Red Sox within no closer than seventeen games of first place.

Williams did win the MVP Award twice; incredibly, he didn't win in either 1942 or 1947, when he won the Triple Crown. In 1942, his staggering numbers—.356 average, 36 homers, 137 RBIs—somehow lost out to Yankee second baseman Joe Gordon's .322, 18, and 102. It was also in that summer that he resumed a war with sportswriters that would last his entire career and probably sabotage him in 1947, when again his stats—.343, 32, and 114—overwhelmed the figures of the MVP winner—.315, 20, and 97. That time, even Joe DiMaggio had to admit, the trophy probably should have gone to Terrible Ted.

The three seasons DiMaggio lost to the war robbed him of his prime years, and when he returned to the Yankees, he was never quite the same player he'd been in his first six seasons. He still finished one of the game's legendary careers with a .325 lifetime average, though the most incredible of all his achievements may have been the fact that despite hitting 361 lifetime home runs, he struck out only 369 times. His would be one of the truly extraordinary American lives, his later years including a brief marriage to Marilyn Monroe and a comfortable retirement as a commercial pitchman who, each time he was introduced in a baseball stadium, received the title of "Greatest Living Ballplayer." He died March 8, 1999, in Hollywood, Florida.

Williams played nine years longer than DiMaggio and wound up with 521 lifetime homers to go along with a .344 career average, fulfilling his life's ambition; whenever he walked down any street in any city in America, people really did say, "There goes the best damned hitter who ever lived," and they weren't kidding. He never sulked about the time he lost to the wars, and let other people speculate that if he'd simply maintained his average home run output during the nearly five full years he sacrificed to service, he would have wound up with at least 681 home runs, if not more. Since 1941, only four men have ever made a legitimate run at .400: Tony Gwynn of the San Diego Padres, who reached .394 before a player's strike cut off the final month and a half of the 1994 season; George Brett, who hit .390 for the Kansas City Royals in 1980 and was still at .400 in mid-September before fading; Rod Carew of the Minnesota Twins, who flirted with .400 all across the summer of 1977 before settling at .388. And Theodore Samuel Williams, who hit .388 in 1957, the summer he turned thirty-nine years old. Had he just sprinkled five more hits among the 420 at-bats he accumulated that season, Teddy Ballgame would have reached the hitter's pinnacle of .400. Again.

———————●———————

Joe Louis was one of the five most famous men in America, which meant that when he joined the army in 1942, he became one of the nation's most famous soldiers, even if his wartime exploits never matched those of the other names on that list, the Pattons, the Eisenhowers, the Bradleys, the MacArthurs. Mostly he spent his service time engaged in two pastimes: fighting dozens and dozens of exhibitions designed to build the morale of thousands of foot soldiers, and playing countless rounds of golf, mostly designed to boost the ego of high-ranking officers. It was during one of these latter pursuits that Louis found himself in Fort Bragg and met an old friend who was stationed there: Ed "Porky" Oliver, the man who'd twice been plucked out of golf tournaments in 1941 and ordered to his local draft board back in Delaware. Louis knew of a wonderful nine-hole course at nearby Camp Shanks and asked his pal Porky to come up to play a round sometime; Oliver laughed, saying that the idea probably wouldn't sit well with Gen. George C. Marshall, who happened to be chief of staff of the army, and happened to be residing that very moment at Fort Bragg.

"Hell, don't worry about that," Louis said. "I know the guy. I'll fix that."

He was Joe Louis. He fixed it. And so one day shortly thereafter, Oliver found himself in a jeep, speeding, trying to outrace the setting sun so he could meet Louis on the first tee. By the time he arrived, Louis determined that they would have time to play only eight holes. Which, by Louis's calculation, meant that Oliver would have to spot him only two holes for their friendly side wager. Oliver knew Louis was better than that, knew he was being hustled, but he also knew he had little choice but to agree. Louis was a sergeant. He outranked him.

Louis easily won the match, and soon Oliver had to even up.

"A player like you, and you want two shots in an eight-hole match?" Oliver muttered. "There oughta be an investigation."

Louis thought about this for a second and figured out a compromise.

"Tell you what, Porky," the champ said. "Now we can box four rounds. And I'll spot you the first three. How's that sound?"

Oliver figured he'd quit while he was ahead.

Golf had become Louis's passion, mostly because he'd come to realize that his greatest boxing challenges were all in his past, that the war would wipe out what remained of his prime. After he'd thumped Lou Nova in late September 1941, it was clear that there was only one fight that America wanted to see, and that was a rematch with Billy Conn. Conn, recovering from both Louis's assault on his chin and the movie critics' battering of *The Pittsburgh Kid,* won three times in the winter of '42, against Henry Cooper, J. D. Turner, and Tony Zale. Louis, looking as sharp as ever, pounded Buddy Baer in a rematch on January 9, knocking Baer down three times before the fight was stopped at 2:56 of the first round, and also dispatched Abe Simon, who was twice saved by the bell, in the second and fifth rounds, before finally succumbing in the sixth. Both Louis and Conn were headed to the army, but the public couldn't be denied their desire to watch one last million-dollar fight before commercial prizefighting closed up shop for the duration. A date was tentatively scheduled for June.

Then, in May, Private Conn was granted a three-day leave so he could attend the christening of his firstborn son, Timothy. Art Rooney, gadfly owner of the Pittsburgh Steelers, was the godfather; more important, he was an old friend of Greenfield Jimmy Smith, and he coaxed his pal to patch things up with his son-in-law since there was a war going on and, hell, who knew what that could mean. So Greenfield Jimmy went to the baptism, and he hosted the reception afterward, and he had a few drinks, and then a few more, and then he suggested to Billy (probably in a tone that Billy felt was something less than respectful) that it was about time he started going to Mass with his wife and his young son, and then he mentioned that, by the way, he could kick the shit out of his son-in-law without breaking a sweat, and . . .

Well, Billy Conn had been nine minutes away from being the heavyweight champion of the world not so long ago, and he'd heard quite enough. He rushed at his father-in-law, and he swung, and the old man ducked just in time, and the force of Billy's fist smashed into the top of Greenfield Jimmy Smith's hard skull, and Billy had been around long enough to know a broken hand when he saw one. The fight was off. Soon enough, *all* fighting-for-profit was off, replaced by fund-raising exhibitions of which Joe Louis was usually the biggest draw.

The war wasn't kind to either man. Conn came back heavier, Louis thicker, and when they finally had their rematch, on June 19, 1946, at Yankee Stadium, it was a disappointment; 45,266 witnesses and the first-ever live television boxing audience watched them stumble around each other before Louis finally dropped Conn in the eighth round. The one memorable thing drawn from the fight came during training, when Louis uttered the single most famous quote of his life, in describing why he believed he'd beat Conn again.

"He can run," Louis said, "but he can't hide."

Many years later, on another stop along their endless banquet tour, Louis sidled up to Conn, smiled, and asked, "Hey, Billy, is your father-in-law still kicking the shit out of you?"

Joe Louis held the title for three more years, retiring after twice defeating Jersey Joe Walcott in bruising bouts in 1949. His later years were marred by a sad, ongoing battle with the Internal Revenue Service and by personal bankruptcy, which prompted two ill-fated comebacks. He lost a tough fifteen-round decision to Ezzard Charles on September 27, 1950, and was sent out of boxing for good by Rocky Marciano, who pummeled him into retirement with an eight-round butchering on October 26, 1951. Still, the quiet dignity that his handlers hammered into him so many years before never vanished, inspiring the sports columnist Jimmy Cannon to summarize Louis's life thusly: "He's a credit to his race. The human race." Louis died on April 12, 1981.

Billy Conn had a much happier go of life after boxing. Though he made a brief comeback after announcing his retirement following the second Louis fight, he never again wore a championship belt and never much fretted about that. After spurning Hollywood, he and Mary Louise settled in Pittsburgh and were happily married for just under fifty-two years. Three years before he died of pneumonia on May 29, 1993, a seventy-two-year-old Conn came across a robber in a convenience store on Beechwood Boulevard in downtown Pittsburgh. Conn did exactly what his instincts had always told him to do. He floored the bum.

"I interrupted him," Conn explained afterward. "I guess he won't be robbing too many more stores. I hit him with a left. You've got to go with your favorite punch. These kinds of things, they happen once in a while."

———————●———————

History hasn't treated Whirlaway as kindly as it's taken care of the other sportsmen with whom he shared the nation's headlines during the defining year of his life. That is something that would have been impossible to believe in 1941, and would have seemed even less likely in 1942, when Whirlaway became the single-most-popular athlete in the United States. It was going to be hard to top 1941. Warren Wright and Ben Jones had raced Whirlaway twenty times, an extraordinary schedule even in an era when championship horses weren't retired to stud farms fifteen minutes after winning the Derby. And the horse's workload would only get more grueling as his popularity grew.

In an effort to convince Washington that racing, like baseball, provided an essential boost to national morale, racetrack operators pledged to set aside one day during each meet in 1942 when the entire day's receipts would go toward war relief. And there was no greater drawing card in the sport than the four-year-old Whirlaway. Wright and Jones, believing their colt now had a higher purpose (and also with their eyes still fixed on Seabiscuit's record), bought into this patriotic fervor completely, and they would race Whirlaway an unbelievable *twenty-two* times during 1942; by contrast, Secretariat, who would win the Triple Crown in 1973 in just as crowd-pleasing a fashion as Whirlaway had, raced only twenty-one times *in his entire career.*

Whirlaway would race in Brooklyn, in Boston, in Trenton; he would draw massive crowds in Rhode Island and New Orleans and in Illinois; he would raise hundreds of thousands of dollars for the war effort, and on July 15, in front of thirty-three thousand screaming, chanting fans, he would capture the Massachusetts Handicap at Suffolk Downs to push his career earnings to $454,336, blazing past Seabiscuit into the all-time lead. He became racing's first half-million-dollar horse a few weeks later, and might well have kept racing throughout the duration of the war if not for the fact that he pulled up lame on June 26, 1943, finishing fifth in the Equipoise Mile at Chicago's Washington Park. The heavy workload had finally caught up to Whirlaway, and he would never race again, sent off to an easy retirement first in the lazy bluegrass of his Kentucky home, later in the fields of France, after Wright's estate sold Whirlaway on September 20, 1952, to Marcel Boussac, one of Europe's most celebrated breeders and owners. It would be an unhappy final few months for the championship colt, who was clearly upset at being moved from his home, and he would survive only until April 8, 1953. Whirlaway was buried in a grave in Normandy, not far from the American cemetery there, a fitting final resting place for a horse who'd raised so much money and worked so tirelessly for the war effort.

Still, Whirlaway isn't always remembered as reverently as Secretariat is, or Affirmed, or Seattle Slew. Part of that may be the fickle nature of fame. Part might be because the same troika who guided Whirlaway reunited seven years later in leading another Calumet Farms prodigy, Citation, to the Triple Crown. Eddie Arcaro, much as he adored Whirlaway, always gave Citation the edge, and the fact that after Citation there was a twenty-five-year drought before the next Triple Crown winner has added a mystique to Citation that Whirlaway simply can't match. Still, for a horse that Ben Jones often admitted "nearly killed me teaching him how to run straight," he ran straight enough to be among the most consistent performers in his sport's history. In sixty lifetime starts he won an astonishing thirty-two times, finished out of the money only four times, and was as low as fifth only once. He finished with a career earnings total of $561,161.

The men who helped create Whirlaway always understood how big a role he'd played in their successes. Arcaro remains the only jockey to twice win the Triple Crown, and before he retired in 1962 after suffering a terrible case of bursitis in his arm, he'd won the Kentucky Derby three times, the Preakness six times, and the Belmont Stakes six times. He won 4,779 races and is still considered one of the two or three greatest riders of all time. He died on November 4, 1997. Ben Jones, meanwhile, would literally become the face of racing after his two Triple Crown triumphs, making it to the cover of the May 29, 1949, edition of *Time* magazine. He wound up training six Kentucky Derby winners, more than any trainer who ever lived, and earned a spot in the National Museum of Racing and Hall of Fame in Saratoga; he died June 13, 1961, at age seventy-eight, after a career in which he'd helped make Warren Wright's craziest dreams come true.

"All I ever wanted," Wright said before his own death at seventy-five on December 28, 1950, "was exactly what I wound up getting. What a blessed man am I."

Whirlaway never did get to race at Santa Anita, the track that had helped make Seabiscuit famous. Whatever hope existed that the racing ban might be lifted dissolved on February 23, 1942, when a lone Japanese submarine surfaced one mile off the coast of Santa Barbara, California, and fired at an oil refinery. The war had officially reached American shores. On February 19, Roosevelt had signed Executive Order 9066, authorizing the secretary of war to prescribe certain "military areas" and to exile "any or all" persons from those locations. These were mere euphemisms. What Roosevelt had done was doom 112,000 Japanese Americans to relocation camps. And his people in California had the perfect location in mind to establish one of these internment centers.

Santa Anita Racetrack.

———————————●———————————

Hank Greenberg and Bob Feller may have been the two major leaguers whose careers suffered the most due to World War II. By the time Green-

---

berg left the army he was thirty-four years old and had already lost his prime baseball years. He was discharged on June 14, 1945, thirty-seven days after V-E Day, two months and a day before V-J Day, and he returned to the Tigers lineup on July 1, in front of fifty-five thousand grateful Tigers fans. Just as he did during his last game for Detroit exactly four years, one month, and twenty-four days earlier, Greenberg announced his presence the best way he knew how: by clubbing a home run in the eighth inning. Amazingly, Greenberg was just as dangerous a hitter in 1945, even after all the time away. In 78 games he would hit 13 home runs, drive in 60 runs, and hit .311. And, most remarkably, on the season's final day, with the Tigers needing a victory over the Browns in St. Louis to clinch the American League pennant, Greenberg connected on a screwball from Nelson Potter and hit a ninth-inning grand slam that turned a 4-3 Browns lead into a 7-4 Tigers win. Capping his improbable comeback, Greenberg had two homers and seven RBIs in the World Series, as the Tigers outlasted the Chicago Cubs in seven games.

Still, even if his performance said otherwise, Greenberg knew he wasn't near the same player that he'd been. "The years had taken their toll," he would write. "The old legs didn't function. The game became drudgery." Yet he hit 44 home runs at age thirty-five in 1946. Greenberg would end his career with 331 lifetime homers, a staggeringly misleading statistic that hardly reflects his stature as the most feared slugger of the 1930s, placing him eighty-sixth on the all-time list at the close of the 2006 baseball season. If you take into account that he hit 41 homers in his last full year of 1940, and 44 in his first full year back in 1946, and grant him a conservative average of 42 per season for the years in between, that lifetime total would hover around 526 or so, vaulting him to a far more agreeable fifteenth place on the all-time list (just above where Ted Williams sits, without *his* war-adjusted numbers).

Greenberg finished out his career with the Pittsburgh Pirates in 1947, which allowed him one final shining moment on a ballfield, even in a season when his skills were clearly in repose. Early in the year, while the Pirates were playing the Dodgers, Jackie Robinson singled and was standing on first base. There were a lot of white players who made it their business to make Robinson feel as uncomfortable as possible in that difficult first year of baseball integration. Greenberg was not one of them. He'd absorbed his own share of ugliness through the years; once, a teammate named Jo-Jo White, raised in Georgia, had told him, with a straight face, "I thought all you Jews had horns on your heads." So Greenberg wanted Jackie to know that he understood what he was going through.

"Jackie," Greenberg said, "don't pay any attention to these Southern jockeys. They aren't worth anything as far as you're concerned." Then Greenberg asked: "Would you like to go to dinner?"

Robinson said he'd love to, but couldn't because of the stir it would cause. But he never forgot Greenberg's simple act of kindness.

Within a few years Greenberg became one of the few great players who ever made the transition to successful front-office man, when he took over the Cleveland Indians (becoming baseball's first Jewish GM) and assembled the parts that would yield a pennant-winning, 111-win season in 1954. On that team was an aging thirty-five-year-old former phenom named Bob Feller, who would pitch in only nineteen games that year.

Feller's war experiences would shape him the rest of his life. On the one hand, he was the most outspoken of the great players whose careers had been hijacked by war, often showing up at autograph sessions with cards that bore both his actual lifetime statistics and his projected numbers, too. In 1941 he was 22 years old and had won 25 games. In 1946 he was 27 and won 26 games. At minimum the laws of baseball probability say he would have won an extra 100 games if he'd been able to pitch in the interim, giving him 366 lifetime victories, which would place him fifth on the all-time list, only seven away from Grover Cleveland Alexander and Christy Mathewson, tied at third with 373.

Still, Feller is fiercely proud of his service in the navy, and it turned out to be "real time," too, exactly the kind of duty he'd asked for when he joined up—exactly what his overly exacting fans expected from him. He spent thirty-four months among 2,900 men on the USS *Alabama,* serving as chief of an antiaircraft gun crew, earning five campaign ribbons and eight battle stars. His service was interrupted only by an emergency leave granted in January 1943 when his father, Bill, lost a long battle with cancer.

"During a war like World War II, when we had all those men lose their lives, sports was very insignificant to me," says Feller, who in the summer of 2006 at age eighty-seven was still making regular appearances at ballparks, still as outspoken as ever. "I have no regrets. The only win I wanted was to win World War II. This country is what it is today because of our victory in that war."

———————●———————

There would be other times of hardship, times of war, times of tragedy, and times of madness when sport would provide an automatic buffer zone from the gathering storms of real life, of the real world. Sometimes, in fact, people were almost *too* quick to seek solace in the comfortable, familiar arms of the games people play. On November 24, 1963, two days after President John F. Kennedy was assassinated in Dallas, National Football League Commissioner Pete Rozelle ordered that his league play its full slate of games after consulting with Pierre Salinger, Kennedy's press secretary, Rozelle's college classmate at UCLA. "Pierre said that under the circumstances he really thought we should play the games," Rozelle would recall some twenty-five years later. "He was very close to Kennedy and after talking to Pierre, I decided we *should* play. It was a difficult decision because of the emotional nature of a terrible tragedy. In retrospect, I wish I hadn't made that decision." Nine years later, Avery Brundage, the despotic head of the International Olympic Committee, argued weakly and woefully that sports and politics should never be intertwined in making the dubious decision that the Games of the Twentieth Olympiad in Munich be resumed after a delay of but twenty-four hours following the slaughter of eleven Israeli athletes.

Mostly, though, sport would follow the blueprint laid out by World War II, and by that seminal year that preceded it in America, when striking the proper balance between the real and the surreal, real life and the diversions that make it truly livable, became of paramount importance. In 1989, the San Francisco earthquake interrupted for ten days the World Series between the neighboring San Francisco Giants and Oakland Athletics. Yet when play resumed, less than two miles from where the Bay Bridge had nearly fallen into the water, baseball provided a necessary salve to help ease the healing process in that broken city. In September 2001, when a terrorist strike leveled both towers of the World Trade Center, when it occurred to many in New York City and beyond that sports could never truly matter again in a way they had before September 11, sports instead became a way for citizens to recall what normalcy was supposed to feel like, and the extraordinary seven-game World Series between the Yankees and the Arizona Diamondbacks that was played out less than two months later served as a life raft for so many people who wanted to reach out for that old version of their lives without letting go of the grief they felt for their fellow citizens. Four years later, when Hurricane Katrina nearly wiped New Orleans clean from the map, when so much pain and suffering manifested itself on so many faces, much of that grief was channeled the very next week into watching the Louisiana State University Tigers make a stirring comeback on the football field against Arizona State University. And just over twelve months later, it was a sporting event—a Monday Night Football showcase between the hometown Saints and the Atlanta Falcons—played inside the Superdome, the symbol of Katrina's vast cruelties, that announced to the world that New Orleans was indeed still standing, still viable, still vibrant.

Sports didn't solve any of these crises, much as sports didn't make any of the mounting calamities of 1941 any less real, or any less toxic. They simply provided the best possible escape hatch for a couple hours at a time, to watch some of the most extraordinary athletes of the century perform some of its most extraordinary feats and string together what was, and what remains, the greatest year sports has ever seen.

ACKNOWLEDGMENTS

The seeds of this book were planted slowly, deliberately, and unwittingly over a couple of wonderful decades. My father, Mickey, was the one who sparked my interest in sports, an awareness that grew into a curiosity, and then a fascination, and then an obsession, and then, quite miraculously, into a profession. He was never a guy who would rail about how much better things were in the old days; instead, he'd start telling stories about watching DiMaggio when he was a kid, or heckling Ted Williams, or waiting outside Yankee Stadium for autographs from Bob Feller and Hank Greenberg, and that tended to make the same point in a far more entertaining way. Writing this book has been a chance to take those old stories, and a thousand of our past conversations, and bring them—and him—back to life, if only for a few stolen hours at a time.

I was writing this book long before I knew I was writing this book, thanks to all the times I'd been lucky enough to interview Phil Rizzuto through the years, and Dominic DiMaggio, and Johnny Pesky, and Tommy Henrich, and even Joe DiMaggio one long-ago Old-Timer's Day, a too-brief encounter that made my old man smile for two days when I told him about it. In 2001, when I was working for the *Newark Star-Ledger,* I wanted to write a different kind of column about the day DiMaggio's streak had ended, and thanks to the help of a couple of wonderful baseball writers, Dan Castellano and Moss Klein, I wound up talking to Lou Boudreau, the man in whose glove the streak died that night, since it was Boudreau who started the 6-4-3 double play that ended DiMaggio's final turn at bat. He couldn't have been nicer, and more generous with his time, and he filled an entire reporter's notebook, on the front of which I marked the date in black magic marker: July 14, 2001. This became especially poignant less than a month later, on August 10, when word came that Boudreau had passed away at age eighty-four.

Unfortunately, because I didn't start putting this book together until nearly sixty-five years after all of the events described in it took place, many of the people I've written about have also died. But thanks to a rich network of friends and family members, I've tried to faithfully reconstruct what it was like to have lived in 1941, to have been a sports fan in 1941, to have been an American in 1941, which wasn't only the greatest year in sports, but one of the most remarkable years, period.

The most helpful resources that I used in the research for this book were newspapers, and if you'll allow me a moment's indulgence, it was an especially important time for me to have lost myself in so many dark rooms, slumped over so many rickety microfilm machines, peering at so many acres of blurry film that just thinking about it makes my eyes itch. I've been lucky enough to earn a living at newspapers for eighteen years and counting, newspapers have given me everything, allowed me to see things and talk to people I never otherwise could have. It hasn't been an easy time to be a member of the media the past few years, it's a business that's become an easy target and has absorbed shot after shot after shot, not all of them undeserved. Specifically, though, it's been even more disquieting to work in newspapers, the foundation upon which all media is built, but a segment of the culture that we hear is growing more irrelevant by the hour. I've heard the same doomsday predictions for years, from the first time I wrote stories for which I was paid, at the *Glen Cove Guardian* and the *Floral Park Dispatch*. Newspapers are dying, we've been told. They're already dead, we've been warned. Allegedly, we keep getting lapped by other media: radio, television, Internet.

Yet newspapers have prevailed, and working on this project has done nothing but reinforce how invaluable they really are, and always have been. The following paragraph contains a list of the newspapers that I used as primary source materials; the one after that is an alphabetical listing of the reporters and columnists whose work helped guide me through the year 1941, and after all this time made me feel like I was reading about ball games, prizefights, and horse races that had taken place just the night before. I owe these men (and, yes, in 1941 it was strictly a boys' club) a debt of gratitude; my wish is that I may return the favor in days or years to come, if a writer sometime ever stumbles across my work in the *New York Post,* the *Newark Star-Ledger,* the *Kansas City Star,* the *Middletown Times Herald-Record,* the *Northwest Arkansas Times,* the *Olean Times Herald,* the *Bona Venture,* the *Glen Cove Guardian,* the *Floral Park Dispatch,* the *Nassau Illustrated News,* or *Tarmac.* And I hope he or she will find that I got it right at least as often as these gentlemen did.

Newspapers: *New York Times, New York Post, New York Daily News, New York Journal-American, New York Sun, New York World-Telegram, New York Daily Mirror, New York Herald-Tribune, Pittsburgh Press, Pittsburgh Post-Gazette, Detroit Free Press, Detroit News, Chicago Tribune, Chicago Defender, Boston Globe, Boston Post, Boston Record, Boston Herald, Boston Traveler, Philadelphia Inquirer, Wilmington News-Journal, Cleveland Plain Dealer, Cleveland Press, Cleveland News, Newark Star-Ledger, Newark Evening News.* Also: *Life, Time, Newsweek, The Saturday Evening Post, The Sporting News, Ring, The Blood-Horse, The Daily Racing Form.* Also: www.baseball-reference.com.

The writers: Al Abrams, Fred Barry, Eddie Beachler, Meyer Berger, Havey Boyle, Lester Bromberg, Al Buck, George Burt, Lewis Burton, Gordon Cobbledick, Bob Considine, Tim Cohane, Robert Cooke, Bill Corum, Jack Cuddy, Ed Curley, Arthur Daley, John Drebinger, Bob Dunbar, David Eisenberg, Herb Finnegan, Stanley Frank, Frank Gibbons, Frank Graham, Sam Greene, Milton Gross, Hy Hurwitz, Hype Igoe, Jimmy Jones, Victor O. Jones, Harold Kaese, James Kahn, John Kiernan, Joe King, George Krehibie, Franklin Lewis, Michael Lewis, Jack Malaney, Ann Marsters, Whitney Martin, Dick McCann, Tom Meany, Sid Mercer, Jack Miley, Gerry Moore, Everett B. Morris, Edward T. Murphy, James O'Leary, Frederick Olmsted, Dan Parker, Arthur Patterson, Cy Peterman, James Pooler, Shirley Povitch, Jimmy Powers, Arnold Prince, Rud Rennie, Lester Rice, Art Rosenbaum, Damon Runyon, John N. Sabo, H. G. Salsinger, Arthur Sampson, Charles Segar, Jack Singer, Chester L. Smith, Jack Smith, Dale Stafford, Len Tracy, Joe Trimble, Edward Van Every, Richards Vidmer, Charles P. Ward, Buck Weaver, Melville Webb, Regis M. Welsh, Burt Whitman, Eugene Whitney, Walter Winchell, Frank Woodford, Bob Yonkers, and James Zerilli.

This was a project that needed a lot of believers to help shepherd it from idea to concept to book, and I can't possibly thank them enough. Working with Jason Kaufman at Doubleday, I can understand a little better what Joe

DiMaggio meant when he described playing for Joe McCarthy: "When I'm around him, I feel like a smarter ballplayer." Jenny Choi has always provided a kind word and a helpful hand; in return I can only offer her my sincerest gratitude. I would also be remiss if I didn't thank Sean Mills, in the Doubleday copyediting department, and Dean Curtis, whose gentle, exacting eye cleaned and tightened the manuscript; whatever errors remain are mine alone to answer for. And without Greg Dinkin and Frank Scatoni at Venture Literary, who are wonderful agents and even better friends, I might still be dreaming about writing a book someday instead of completing my second one. This is as much a testament to their faith as to mine.

My pop was able to live long enough to see me get a chance to write a column at the *New York Post*, the paper he'd bring home from work every day when I was a kid, and I don't know that he ever got a bigger kick out of anything than that. For that, I am forever grateful to Greg Gallo and Dick Klayman, who run the best sports section in New York, and to Col Allan, who oversees the product that reminds everyone in New York City that even in a digital age, a feisty newspaper can still kick a little ass every morning.

Many years ago, in my younger and more tempestuous days, I woke up one morning and found myself fired from a small paper in Arkansas; my friend Adrian Wojnarowski called me that morning and ordered me to stop feeling sorry for myself and get busy making something out of my career, and he may never know just how important that call was. Marc Berman, Les Carpenter, Jack Curry, Ian O'Connor, Joe Posnanski, and Joel Sherman are old confidants whose wisdom and support I find myself leaning on more and more as the years go by, and I'm amazed at how lucky I am to count among my closest friends a journalistic support system that would make anyone look smarter than they really are. For that, I must thank Dominic Amore, Harvey Araton, Don Burke, Dave Buscema, Pete Caldera, Rich Chere, Brian Costello, Chris D'Amico, Mike Fannin, Chris Faytok, Kevin Gleason, Dan Graziano, Mark Hale, Pat Hannigan, Jon Heyman, Kim Jones, George King, Bob Klapisch, Kevin Manahan, Dinn Mann, Tom Missel, Steve Politi, Chuck Pollock, Ed Price, T. J. Quinn, Lenn Robbins, Mike Rodman, Tara Sullivan, Wright Thompson, Chuck Ward, Charlie Wenzelberg, Dan Wetzel, and Steve Wright. I owe an especially large debt of gratitude to two newspaper gentlemen whose collective careers span more than a century and whose collective wisdom humbles me whenever I'm fortunate enough to draw upon it: Jerry Izenberg and Dave Anderson. And it isn't just newspaper folks who help a guy out with a project like this, so I must also recognize Charlie Albanese, Amy Carr, Nick Cusano, John Egan, Esq., Dr. George Evans, Bill Going, John Hammersley, Bro. Robert Lahey, John Lovisolo, Scott Mackenzie, Mike MacDonald, Tim McMahon, Melanie Rolli, Paul Sabini, and Dr. Richard Simpson. My thanks to Marty Appel, and also to Marc Bona, who lent an extraordinarily generous helping hand with an important segment of research. And given the events of the past twelve months, I'd be remiss if I didn't also mention the extraordinary talents of Dr. Wayne Huang, Dr. Marc Cohen, and Dr. Marcus Williams, all of whom figured out a way to keep my heart working long enough to get to the final word of this book. Pithy commentary aside, I owe, quite literally, my life to them.

I'd mention my beautiful bride here, but since she got the dedication this time around you can check out how much I dig her there. And, lastly, thank you to my mother, Ann McMahon Vaccaro, who always sees sunshine where others see shadows, who always sees the good in people when all anyone else can see is the bad, and who makes it impossible to be cynical when you're anywhere within the same area code. That's a rare, and entirely extraordinary, gift.

Mike Vaccaro
Hillsdale, New Jersey
January 2007

INDEX

© Charles Wenzelberg

MIKE VACCARO is a lead sports columnist for the *New York Post*. He has won more than fifty major journalism awards and has been cited for distinguished writing by the Associated Press Sports Editors, the New York State Publishers Association, and the Poynter Institute. He lives in Hillsdale, New Jersey.

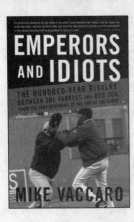